Sparrows' Nest of Letters

HILLSBOROUGH, N. C.
Military Academy,

Edited by Joy W. Sparrow

The
Scuppernong Press
Wake Forest, NC

Sparrows' Nest of Letters

©2011 Joy W. Sparrow

First Printing

The Scuppernong Press
PO Box 1724
Wake Forest, NC 27588
www.scuppernongpress.com

Cover and book design by Frank B. Powell, III

International Standard Book Number ISBN 978-0-9845529-4-8

Library of Congress Control Number: 2011929780

Dedicated to:

My Late Husband
Thomas Glenn Sparrow

Sons
Thomas Daniel Sparrow
Steven Glenn Sparrow

Grandchildren
Justin Thomas Sparrow
Sawyer Cline Sparrow
Emily Ruth Sparrow
Steven George Sparrow

My Late Mother and Father
Laurice Westbrook and Daniel Fulton Whisonant

Joy W. Sparrow

Table of Contents

Introduction

George Attmore Sparrow's life and that of his family is told throughout this book of letters written between the years 1856 and 1922 and other writings. Providence surely played a role in the safe-keeping of the George Attmore Sparrow letters as they survived two house fires which burned to the ground, one in 1931 and one in 1961. George's father, Thomas Sparrow III, kept a diary and was a prolific letter writer.

When my husband Thomas Glenn Sparrow was setting up an insurance business in 1968 and cleaning out an old desk given him by his father, he tossed a bundle of old papers into the trash. My mother Laurice Whisonant asked, "What are you throwing away?" He replied, "It's just a bunch of old papers." Mother pulled the bundle from the trash and discovered the George A. Sparrow letters!

Included in *Sparrows' Nest of Letters* are the George A. Sparrow letters; some of Thomas Sparrow's letters; excerpts from Thomas Sparrow's diary while he was a prisoner of war; Major Sparrow's Address to Negroes made on July 4th, 1867; and a report given by Thomas Sparrow of the State Judiciary Committee at the impeachment of North Carolina Governor William W. Holden.

In addition to the Sparrow letters, diary, and speeches are Civil War recollections of two of George's sisters — Annie Blackwell Sparrow (Mrs. R. H. Lewis) and Elizabeth Sparrow McCord; excerpts from Rev. Sparrow's *Book of Illustrations*; brief histories and pictures of some of the churches Rev. Sparrow was associated with; interesting happenings taken from Mrs. George A. Sparrow's *Ideal Scrap Book*; and family pictures and places.

Spelling and punctuation are left as originally written unless required for ease of reading.

I was grateful to get the Thomas Sparrow material from the East Carolina Manuscript Collection, J. Y. Joyner Library, East Carolina University, Greenville North Carolina and the Thomas Sparrow Papers in the Southern Historical Collection at the University of North Carolina, Chapel Hill, North Carolina.

Woven through the pages of these letters are the inmost thoughts of a Southern boy who was born into one of the worst periods of American history. By having an astute father and loving family and by the grace of God, he was able to overcome hardships and trials, especially a problem of serious drinking. Following the war, his years were spent as a farmer and lawyer followed by his call into the ministry which began the most productive and rewarding years of his life.

My family has been very patient and understanding during this time. I have missed many of my grandchildren's wrestling matches, baseball games, tennis matches and track and cross country meets! They have looked forward to the finished product.

I have enjoyed very much working on this book. The letters have made me appreciate more what our forefathers went through to establish freedom for everyone! Hopefully, all who read *Sparrows' Nest of Letters* will enjoy and treasure it for years to come.

Joy W. Sparrow

Acknowledgments

Many people have assisted me in putting this book together. First and foremost, Janice Currence, my secretary and typist, was a God-send! Not only did she do the typing but also did footnotes, e-mails, phone calls and much, much more. She has been a real work horse! Also her husband Bob Currence listened to letter readings and explained some of the words.

The late Dr. Keats Sparrow, Dean Emeritus of the Thomas Harriot College of Arts and Sciences at East Carolina University, read the George Attmore Sparrow letters and encouraged me to have them published.

Sally Thompson Kendrick McGinnis volunteered to help in any way she could and went to several libraries gathering important material. My cousin Betty Logan was the first person to help me read and transcribe some of the difficult words in the letters. She kept reminding me that "now" is the time to complete the book. Jimmy and Alice Thompson let me go through their box of Sparrow records and make copies of anything needed.

Bernice Blackwell answered my letter to the Arcola newspaper and sent the Blackwell family history. This was a tremendous help in identifying some of the people in the letters. The late Annie (Nancy) Jarvis welcomed me and my family to Washington, North Carolina, took us on a tour of the town, and gave us a copy of the Sparrow family history.

Others who helped greatly were:
- The late Sister Mary John Madden of Sacred Heart College of Belmont, North Carolina.
- Ursula Loy, Co-editor of *Washington and the Pamlico*.
- Victor Jones, historian of the Kellenburger Room, New Bern Craven Public Library, New Bern, North Carolina.

- Carol Newman of the George H. and Laura Brown Library, Washington, North Carolina.
- Jantha Rollins, Historian from Arcola, Illinois helped greatly with the book by identifying some of the people and describing some of the events that took place in Okaw/Arcola, Illinois.
- Elizabeth Read, Historian, The Alliance for Historic Hillsborough, Hillsborough, North Carolina.
- Jessica Voorhees, Secretary, and Lamar Howe, Historian, Olney Presbyterian Church, Gastonia, North Carolina.
- Betty Cochran, Historian, St. Peter's Episcopal Church, Washington, North Carolina.
- Sharon Byrd, Special Collections Outreach Librarian, E. H. Little Library, Davidson College Archives, Davidson, North Carolina.
- Helen Grant, Church Historian, and husband Cary, Bethel Presbyterian Church, Clover, South Carolina.
- Jim Geary, Historian, First Presbyterian Church, Franklin, North Carolina.
- Staff, First Presbyterian Church, Concord North Carolina.
- Rev. Paul Mulner, Pastor, Sandy Plains Presbyterian Church, Tryon, North Carolina.
- Joan Wall, Historian, Rutherfordton Presbyterian Church, Rutherfordton, North Carolina.
- Jane Yates, The Citadel Archives and Museum, Charleston, South Carolina.
- Mark Turner, First Presbyterian Church, Raleigh, North Carolina.
- Sherri Smith, Secretary, First Presbyterian Church, Belmont, North Carolina.

- Chris Meekins, North Carolina Department of Archives and History, Raleigh North Carolina.
- Eric Blevins, North Carolina Museum of History, Raleigh, North Carolina.
- Janice Short, Secretary, Union Presbyterian Church, Gastonia, North Carolina.
- Kathy Kytle, Session Representative, Union Presbyterian Church, Gastonia, North Carolina.
- John Andrews, World War II Historian, Gastonia, North Carolina.
- Kim Cumber, North Carolina State Department of Archives and History, Raleigh, North Carolina.
- Burke County Library, North Carolina Room, Gail Benefield, Curator, Morganton, North Carolina.
- Matthew Turi, Manuscripts Research Librarian, Research & Instructional Services Department, Louis Round Wilson Special Collections Library, The University of North Carolina at Chapel Hill, Chapel Hill North Carolina.
- Dale Sauter, Manuscript Curator, Special Collections Department, Maurice C. York, Assistant Director for Special Collections, East Carolina Manuscript Collection, J. Y. Joyner Library, East Carolina University, Greenville, North Carolina.
- Rev. Dr. Jerry Bron, Senior Pastor, Southminster Presbyterian Church, Gastonia, North Carolina and former Pastor First Presbyterian Church, Washington, North Carolina.
- Kelly Digh, Gastonia, North Carolina for artwork and photo retouching.
- Gaston-Lincoln Regional Library, Reference Department Staff, Anne Gometz Supervisor, Gastonia, North Carolina.
- Charlotte-Mecklenburg Library, Carolina Room Staff, Charlotte, North Carolina.

- Sue Diehl, Montreat College Library, Montreat, North Carolina.
- Mary Laura Kludy, VMI Archives and Records Management Assistant, Virginia Military Institute, Lexington, Virginia.
- Judith Berdy, Roosevelt Island Historical Society, Roosevelt Island, New York.
- Keith Longiotti, Photographic Archives Technical Assistant, University of North Carolina Collections, Chapel Hill, North Carolina.
- Diane Jensen, Librarian, and Paul King, Finch Library, Peace College, Raleigh, North Carolina.
- Carolyn Burke, Reference Librarian, Beaufort-Hyde-Martin Regional Library, Washington, North Carolina.
- Donna Kelly, Editor in Chief, the *North Carolina Historical Review*, Raleigh, North Carolina, for review of the book and her helpful suggestions.
- Bonner McAllestor, Great Granddaughter of George A. Sparrow.
- Mary Alice and Jere Thomas, special cousins, for opening up their home for me (and cousin Betty Logan) on our trips to Washington, North Carolina and New Bern, North Carolina.
- Allen Millican, Museum and Photo Restoration, Belmont, North Carolina.
- Anita Fletcher, Chairman, Octagon House Restoration, Inc., Hyde County, North Carolina.

Illustrations

George Attmore Sparrow

Geeorge Attmore Sparrow, oldest son of Thomas Sparrow III and Annie Mariah Blackwell, was born in Beaufort, North Carolina on July 14, 1845. His father Thomas III was a distinguished lawyer having graduated from Princeton College as valedictorian of his class in 1842. George's mother, Annie Mariah Blackwell, was the oldest daughter of John Blackwell and Nancy Ann Selby, prominent citizens of New Bern who later moved to Arcola, Illinois. The Blackwells were from New York and Annie was a granddaughter of Col. Jacob Blackwell who assisted in establishing American independence while serving in the Provincial Congress 1775-1777.

George's grandfather, Thomas Sparrow II born at Smith's Creek, Craven County, North Carolina was the son of Thomas I (1751-1822) and Rhesa Delamar Sparrow. As an adult Thomas II lived in New Bern where he was a prosperous shipbuilder and shipyard owner. The three-story house which he built at 220 East Front Street still stands today, overlooking the Neuse and Trent rivers. Thomas Sparrow II married Jane Jennett Sparrow (born October 3, 1788 at Mattamuskeet, died May 24, 1856 at New Bern) daughter of Paul and Ann Jennett Sparrow.

Thomas Sparrow House
New Bern, North Carolina

The five sisters and one brother of George A. Sparrow were: Annie (Nan) Blackwell who first married William Foreman and second marriage to Dr. R. H. Lewis; Jane Jennett (Jennie) married Oliver Jarvis; Margaret Justice (Maggie) married C. M. Payne; Elizabeth (Lizzie) married H. A. McCord; Caroline (Caddie) married Frank Dalton; and John Blackwell married Fannie Payne.

In 1859 the Sparrows moved to Arcola, Illinois to join the Blackwells who had settled there some years before. Thomas Sparrow III was settling up his business in North Carolina when trouble broke out between the North and South.

He brought his family home at the first opportunity and enrolled George at Hillsborough Military Academy where he stayed for a short time before running away and joining the Confederate Army. His father Thomas III was captain of the Washington Grays. Both George and his father served with the Confederate forces until the end of the war.

After the war ended, George farmed and studied law under his father. He practiced law for sixteen years serving as a Solicitor for eight years. In 1874 he married Susan Selby Brown, daughter of Sylvester T. and Elizabeth Bonner Brown. Elizabeth's paternal ancestors played an important role in the Revolution among them being Captain George Hubbard and General Thomas Holiday. Her maternal grandfather was James Bonner, the founder of the town of Washington, North Carolina, and her maternal great grandfather was Richard Bonner, prominent citizen of Beaufort County, North Carolina.

George A. and Susan Brown Sparrow had eleven children. Born in Washington, North Carolina were Thomas Sparrow, August 31, 1875; Sylvester Brown, September 23, 1877; George Brown, October 23, 1878; Annie Mariah, November 10, 1880; Annie Foreman, January 19, 1882; Elizabeth Bonner born about 1883 and Minnie Shepherd, November 6, 1887. George Attmore, Jr. and Hubert McCord, twin sons, were born at Franklin, N. C. on February 7, 1891. Born in the manse of Union Presbyterian Church, Gastonia, North Carolina were Elizabeth Bonner, January 23, 1894 and Evans Crabtree, April 7, 1896.

The first George drowned in the Pamlico River at age eleven; the first Annie and first Elizabeth died in infancy in Washington, North Carolina, hence the use of those names for later children.

George A. Sparrow felt the call to become a minister in the late 1880s and was licensed by Albemarle Presbytery in 1890. With his wife and children, he left his comfortable home in Washington, North

Carolina and served in the mission fields of Franklin, Dillsboro, and Morrison, North Carolina where he stayed for approximately fourteen months. His next pastorate was at Sandy Plains Presbyterian, Tryon, North Carolina and Rutherfordton, North Carolina where he served from 1891-1893. In 1893 he was called to the pastorate of Olney Presbyterian and Union Presbyterian churches in Gastonia, North Carolina. He served as minister at Olney Presbyterian Church from 1893-1921 and at Union Presbyterian Church from 1893-1922.

Susan Brown Sparrow died April 19, 1908 and is buried in Union Presbyterian Church cemetery. Rev. Sparrow married Elizabeth Bryan Ewing of Washington, D. C. in 1910. Elizabeth was the daughter of Rev. Daniel B. Ewing, DD and Frances Todd Barbour. She was a well known landscape and nature artist and head of the Art Department at Flora MacDonald College, Red Springs, North Carolina for a number of years.

George A. Sparrow's sudden death occurred on July 24, 1922 within two weeks after his seventy-seventh birthday. He was spending a few days at Montreat, and passed away as he sat on the veranda at the Chapman home. He is buried in the Union Presbyterian Church cemetery.

Elizabeth Bryan Ewing Sparrow died on January 22, 1934 and is buried in the Union Presbyterian Church Cemetery.[1]

---

[1]Sparrow family records, Blackwell family records, Minutes of the Synod of North Carolina for 1922.

Joy W. Sparrow

Chapter 1

Early Days in Washington, North Carolina

George Attmore Sparrow's childhood days were spent at the family home in Washington, North Carolina and with his grandfathers Thomas Sparrow II and John Blackwell in New Bern, North Carolina. When George visited his grandfathers in New Bern he attended the First Presbyterian Church there.

The Presbyterian Church played a big role in the lives of the Sparrow family. Attending church was a regular habit with George as is revealed in his letters. The following record was taken from the Sparrow family Bible:

George Attmore Sparrow & Ann Blackwell Sparrow were baptized in the Presbyterian Church, Washington, N.C. on Sunday a. m. the 13th day of May 1849 by Rev. James Stratton. Both behaved well.

Also found in the family Bible is the obituary of Sarah, a faithful servant:

Died on Friday the 21st day of Dec. 1849 at 1 o'clock. Sarah a free colored girl aged about 24 years. She was a faithful, willing, industrious & obedient servant, ready at all times to do her whole duty. She was with us at the birth of Annie and Jane. Nursed all three of our children & was much attached to them. They called her "My Sarah." Her death was sudden and unexpected. She acted well her part in life and her virtues entitle her to this tribute of respect to her memory. We hope she is now in the service of her Master in heaven.[2]

---

[2]Thomas Sparrow Papers, Collection No. 1, East Carolina Manuscript Collection, J. Y. Joyner Library, East Carolina University, Greenville, N.C.

Market Street, Looking North, Washington, N.C.
Courtesy of Beaufort Hyde Martin Regional Library

The majority of George's letters are to his father Thomas Sparrow III while he was serving in the House of Commons, Raleigh, North Carolina. The letters give a glimpse of what a young boy's life was like in a small North Carolina coastal town in the late 1850s.

George's First Letter to Me

Washington, N.C.

December 11 1856

Dear Father

I went in town this morning and got 15 bushels of corn. I am staying home from school this morning because it was a raining. The wagon broke down Tuesday morning and has been there ever since. The axle tree is broke off short and ma could not get it home. Mr. Thomas put it on the side of the road. Ma had to borrow Mr. Burbank's cart this morning to bring out the corn. This morning when I came out with the corn, Bill got so tired he like to fell down. When he was coming up the red hill he slipped down. I have just written to Aunt Maggy.[3] I put it in this envelope with yours. You must answer my letter soon. We are all well. Maggy says she wants to see her pa. Annie and Jennie want to know when you are coming home. Good bye.

Your son,

George A. Sparrow

Give my love to all the folks.

Tell Aunt Lucy[4] Jennett sends her love to her

Margaret says give my love to Papa.

You must answer my letter soon. Please give this letter to Aunt Margaret. I want to hear soon.

---

[3]Aunt Maggy is Margaret Ann Blackwell, George's mother's sister. She married James Cicero Justice on June 29, 1843. Source: *Hyde County Historical and Genealogical Society,* Volume XIX, Spring, 1998, No. 1, Fairfield, N.C., p. 10.

[4]Aunt Lucy is Lucinda Sparrow, George's father's sister. She married Dr. John McDonald. Source: Sparrow Family History.

Washington, N.C.

Jan. 13th 1858

Dear Father

It has been now nearly two weeks scince I wrote to you last, and as Ma is writing to night, I thought it a good opportunity to write myself. It has been quite cold here for the last two or three days, and last Tuesday morning we had some skating and it was a great treat, I can tell you, because we don't have "ice" here often. A wedding took place in town last night and the streets have been full of ladies all day long. Dr. Tayloe gave a party at his shop this afternoon, and Monday Mrs. Geer gave one and Tuesday Mrs. Bryan. The other day I carried Mr. Sherwood two dollars and Grandma's address to send her the North Carolina Presbyterian.[5] Cousin William Spencer [6] dined here yesterday and took tea at Aunt Caddies'[7] last night and Ma ate supper there too.

Aunt Caddie Fowle

---

[5]*The North Carolina Presbyterian* was published weekly in Fayetteville, N.C. 1858 – 1898. Source: The Library of Congress, Chronicling America, About this Newspaper: North Carolina Presbyterian.
[6]William Spencer married Emma Matilda Blackwell in 1863, sister of Annie Blackwell Sparrow. Source: *Hyde County Historical and Genealogical Society,* Volume XIX, Spring 1998, Number 1, Fairfield, N.C., p. 11.
[7]Aunt Caddie is Caroline Louisa Blackwell, sister of Annie Blackwell Sparrow. Caddie married James Luther Fowle May 12, 1852. Source: *Hyde County Historical and Genealogical Society,* Volume XIX, Spring 1998, Number 1, Fairfield, N.C., p. 10.

Sunday night just as the bells were ringing for church Mr. Cowling was going along and smelt a smoke and went in and a free Negro[8] was standing in the middle of the floor in flames and on Monday she died. I go to church every Sunday night and to Prayer Meeting every Tuesday night with Ma. Ma altered those pants which you gave me and I bought a nice coat at Mr. B's and Ma's watch, and I am quite a "bean."

Your Obedient Son,
George A. Sparrow

——————

Washington, N.C.
Jan. 20 1858

Dear Father

I have been sick all this week and yesterday I was abed all day long with a hot fever. Ma has just been trying to make some cakes, but she made them too rich and they would not do. Ma has got a cornpopper she bought from Mrs. Pew, and we haven't got any pop corn and so we pop common corn and it pops nicely. We have been living on hog meat ever scince ma got her hogs and I will be glad when all the spare ribs and bones are gone. My head hurts me so I shall have to stop.

Your son,
George Sparrow

---

[8]Was unable to find the name of this free Negro or name of the church.

Dear Father

I have been up only two days and to day is the first time I have been out of my room. When I first got up out of the bed I was so weak I could scarcely walk across the room. Capt. Fowler came yesterday (Sunday) and brought oranges and other fruits and Ma gave John[9] some money and told him to buy some. She said that that was one piece of extravagance she was going to be guilty of anyhow, that we had been living so economical all the time and she wanted something good to eat. There is a man here "Wyman the Wizard"[10] the celebrated juggler and ventriloquist that performed in New York and around, I suppose you have heard of him. He will perform three nights only and I shall not be able to go and see him. While I was sick Ma promised me a "small party" when I got well but I told I would rather save the money to carry out "west." I wrote to Uncle "Sam"[11] yesterday and after I had written I did not know how to direct my letter but Ma said she would find out from Mr. Hanks to day.

---

[9] John was probably a servant.

[10] For 45 years Wyman with twin talents of ventriloquism and magic brought pleasure to those who visited his show along with gifts such as gold watches, family Bibles, table sets, canes, silverware and pen-knives to lucky ticket holders. He was completely reliable, an honest professor of legitimate deception, a talented entertainer. On four occasions President Lincoln had Wyman entertain his guests at the White House. Source: Todd Karr, Editor, Gary Hunt, Advisor Emeritus, *On-Line Journal of Magic History, 45 Years A Wizard by Milbourne Christopher, Magical Past-Times*, sponsored by The Miracle Factory, 2004.

[11] Samuel Blackwell, brother of Annie Blackwell Sparrow and uncle of George, was born in New York. He married Eleanor Elizabeth Spencer September 7, 1866, the daughter of Henry Selby and Emeline Ann Higson Spencer of Hyde County, North Carolina. Eleanor died April 25, 1912 and Samuel died May 2, 1920; both are buried in Arcola, Illinois. Source: *Hyde County Historical and Genealogical Society*, Volume XIX, Spring 1998, No. 1, Fairfield, N.C., p. 10.

Sally & Sam Blackwell, Georgia Osborne

Aunt Caddie found a very complimentary piece in the <u>North Carolina Presbyterian</u> about you and showed it to Ma. It said that you were the most "<u>polished</u>" and accomplished gentelman in the Legislature." Ma went over to Mrs. Fannie Bryan the other night and Dr. Bryan was praising you very highly for passing the fish bill,[12] and shortly afterwards Dr. Bryan sent Ma a very nice shad present and the first one we have had though I could not eat any of it. While I was sick Dr. Tayloe inquired very anxiously about that doctors bill[13] he was very anxious that it should pass. Pa you don't know how kind Ma was to me when I was sick, sometimes she sat up all night without taking off her clothes,

---

[12] Enacted by the General Assembly of the State of North Carolina to open the Pedee and Yadkin Rivers for the passage of fish and to be kept open from the 1st of March to the 15th of June in each and every year. Reference: Public Laws of the State of North Carolina, passed by the General Assembly at its Session of 1858-'59, Chapter 244, Raleigh: Holden and Wilson, Printers to the State, 1859.

[13] An act to incorporate the Medical Society of the State of North Carolina, and for the establishment of a Medical Board of Examiners. Reference: Private Laws of the State of North Carolina, passed by the General Assembly at its Session of 1858-'9 Chapter 258, Raleigh: Holden and Wilson, Printers to the State, 1859.

and watched me. Pa I want you to bring her a "nice present" for me when you come home. Ma says she don't know wether she will get anything from the vessel or not but she certainly will from Aunt Caddie for she has got a nice bunch of bananas the capt brought for him. He also had a bunch with three hundred on it for six dollars which was only two cents apiece.

Lizzie and Caddie are on the floor looking at picture papers. Lizzie says tell pa about her toe hurts her. Caddie has got so she can walk a few steps alone and say "yes." Ma bought some whale bone from Mr. Pannles which proved to be gutta-percha[14] and Ma took one piece "to stir up the children" and it has gone by the name of Willie Bogart[15] ever scince. Frank Hanks just been here and paid us a visit and he says the mill is going this morning. He used to come twice a day when I was sick and sit some time and it always made me feel better when he came. Aunt Mary's[16] folks are all well and Aunt Mary sent me a partridge and turkey for my dinner yesterday and Mr. Ware sent me a partridge the day before and so you see I have got some friends anyhow. I could not find any pens about the house to suit me and so I wrote with a led pencil. Ma got a letter or rather a short epistle as he calls it for a very short one it was, in which he said "Ma would not be able to swear to his signature for to his lengthy epistle he signed Samuel. He says that it

---

[14] A rubbery substance. *The American Heritage Dictionary of the English Language*, Fourth Edition, Houghton Mifflin Company, 2006.
[15] William (Willy) Bogart was a teacher at the Academy in Washington, N. C prior to the Civil War. Source: Ursula Loy and Pauline Worthy, *Washington and the Pamlico*, Washington-Beaufort County Bicentennial Commission, Edwards & Broughton Co., Raleigh, North Carolina, 1976, p. 251.
[16] Aunt Mary was Mary Field Blackwell, sister of Annie Blackwell Sparrow and aunt of George. She married Henry D. Jenkins March 16, 1866. Mary Field was the second daughter of John and Ann Selby Blackwell with that name. The first Mary Field was born August 17, 1837 and died June 30, 1841 in New Bern. Source: *Hyde County Historical and Genealogical Society*, Volume XIX, Spring 1998, Number 1, Fairfield, N.C. p. 11.

is very cold there and the thermometer is seventeen degrees below zero and that they were trotting races on the ice which made it look quite lively. The fire bell is ringing now but I don't know where the fire is and I can't go out. I will wait and tell you all about it when John comes. I see a great cloud of smoke. Mr. Hanks stables burnt down and a house next door. I don't know who lived in it but it was a considerable fire. I don't believe it is all out now as John has not come home to "<u>dinner</u>" yet and it is 1/2 past "<u>one</u>." Lizzie can sing every song she ever heard almost and Ma thinks she is going to have a good voice and ear for musick and if she does she will be the only one yet. Well, Pa I must stop for I am wound "clean up" as the children say and so good by. Give my love to Miss Rachel and her sister and to Mr. Leach. Write soon.

Your son

George A. Sparrow

Washington, N.C.
February 6th 1858

Dear Father

I received both of your letters and was very much pleased with both especially with the last to think that you were so much pleased with my letter and the "illustrations," scince I have been sick I have amused myself with drawing and writing the figure that you see in the corner is a specimen of my drawing. Not long ago I wrote a long letter to Grandma and one to John Harvey[17] and I told him I supposed from his not writing to any one of us that he had forgotten he had any cousins named Sparrow at all. The other morning Jane[18] came out of the room with a great piece of hair in her hand and on enquiring it proved to be Lizzies and she said she cut it off for Toby Blackwell[19] and was going to put it in one letter and send it to him! I sent a small piece of it to Grandma and the rest I sent to Cora.[20]

---

[17] John Harvey was the son of Eliza Paynter Blackwell (sister of Annie Blackwell Sparrow) and William H. Harvey. Source: James Riker, *History of the Blackwell Family, Annals of Newtown in Queen's County, New York*, pp. 117-180.

[18] Jane was the only slave left of the three the Sparrows owned. She was about Annie's age. Thomas Sparrow Papers, Collection No. 1, East Carolina Manuscript Collection, J. Y. Joyner Library, East Carolina University, Greenville, N.C.

[19] Toby Blackwell was probably a cousin.

[20] Cora Blackwell (June 2, 1846 – March 9, 1932) aunt of George, sister of Annie Blackwell Sparrow. Cora married John Luther Polk November 2, 1875. Source: *Hyde County Historical and Genealogical Society*, North Carolina, Volume XIX, Spring 1998, Number 1, Fairfield, N.C., p. 11.

Cora Blackwell Polk

Ma and the children have gone to the Methodist Church to hear Mr. Pell and I fixed up to go and after that Ma concluded that as it was so damp and I was so weak that it was best for me to stay at home with Cad and Liz and as I did not write yesterday when the others wrote I thought it a fine opportunity to write you a few lines in answer to your letter. Mr. Wiley[21] told Ma that he saw it in some paper (I forget the name) "that you <u>were very modest in the beginning</u> but in the end you were one of the most <u>creditable members</u>." You are growing very popular in the public esteem. I did not tell you about the "<u>pudding</u>" Ma had the other day, she was over to Mrs. Thomas and she was making a suet pudding and she wanted Ma to take some suet and try one and so next day Ma had the "<u>pudding</u>" for dinner

---

[21] Mr. Wiley was a teacher at the Academy, Washington, N. C prior to the Civil War. He was a nephew of Calvin H. Wiley, one of the great educational leaders of North Carolina. Source: Ursula Loy and Pauline Worthy, *Washington and the Pamlico*, Washington-Beaufort County Bicentennial Commission, Edwards & Broughton Co., Raleigh, North Carolina, 1976, p. 251.

and every body thought it was delightful but it made Ma sick and she lost all her dinner and the pudding too, it was to rich for her. Pa here I am writing with a pencil again and I know it is wrong for if I keep on I will get in the habit of it and that I dont want to do, but the pens around here are so mean that actually I cannot write with them and if you have got any good pens up there please sir send me one in your next letter and hereafter I will try and write with a pen. Pa please dont forget my "signatures" or whatever you call them, if it is no trouble for if it is the least trouble in the world I dont want to bother you. Aunt Mary and her family are all well and she and Mamie were down here the other afternoon. Uncle Jim[22] and Mr. Stanly[23] have both got one of those lamps that you were talking about and Mr. Stanly has got his suspended from the ceiling and it hangs down nearly to his table, it is in the office. Yesterday Ma bought a whole parcel of remnants (calico) at Mr. Telfairs [24] for a shilling a yard that he used to sell for "twelve-and-a-half cents," to make garments to carry out west.

---

[22] James Luther Fowle was the husband of Aunt Caddie (Caroline Louisa). Source: Sparrow Family Records.

[23] Edward Stanley, born in New Bern, N.C. on January 10, 1810 was a North Carolina politician and orator. He attended New Bern Academy and graduated from the American Literary, Scientific and Military Academy, Norwich University in 1829. He then studied law and was the first law partner of Thomas Sparrow, father of George Attmore Sparrow. From March 4, 1837 – March 3, 1843 he served in the 25th, 26th and 27th Congresses. Also he served as member of the House of Commons from 1844-1846 and again in 1848, 1849 and was Speaker of the State House 1844-1846. In 1862 Stanley was appointed Provisional Governor of eastern North Carolina by Abraham Lincoln with the rank of brigadier general. *Biographical Directory of the United States Congress: Edward Stanley*. Norman D. Brown, *Edward Stanly: Whiggery's Tarheel Conqueror*, University of Alabama Press, 1974.

[24] Thomas Telfair was one of the founders of the Presbyterian Church, Washington, North Carolina in 1823. Source: The History of the First Presbyterian Church 1823-1973, Washington, N.C p. 5.

Joy W. Sparrow

Lizzie and Maggie were <u>delighted</u> with your letters and Lizzie was so glad she laughed so I could hardly read it. Lizzie says tell Pa to come home and sing for her but I expect she will have to sing for you. Pa I wish you were here to see Liz play she is the funniest thing you ever saw, she genraly goes through about fifty transformations in a day, she is every body in town she can think of. When I was sick and Dr. Tayloe bled me Lizzie said she loved Dr. Ruffian but she did'nt love Dr. Tayloe and she was going to ask Dr. Ruffian to mind buddys arm. Well Pa I believe I have told you all the news I can think of at present but I will write again soon. Give my love to all. Good bye.

Your son

George A. Sparrow

Hon. Thomas Sparrow Esqr
of the House of Commons

––––––––––

Washington, N.C.

February 13th 1858

Dear Father

It snowed very hard yesterday and the examination was put off until Monday. I had a great deal of fun in the snow yesterday snowballing the men down town. Mr. Whitehurst and Dr. Cott wallowed me in the snow two or three times. The Trustees went up to the Academy to hear the boys speak their dialogues Thursday afternoon, and we boys went up there Friday morning but it snowed so hard that Mr. Wiley put it off until Monday night. I was very much disappointed because I could not go a gunning on account of the rain.

Your affectionate son

George Attmore Sparrow

Washington, N.C.
March 8th 1858

Dear Father

Annie, Jennie, and myself all went to church yesterday morning and Mr. Sherwood preached a very good sermon from the text "The rod has blossomed." Ma went to church last night but I was sick and could not go. It is raining very hard and we cannot go back to school to day and Ma told me to write to you for she said she was afraid you would scold her if she did. Ma says please ask Aunt Maggie where she got little Maggie's dress and get her one yard more. There was not any Sunday School yesterday evening and we all got a hymn. We have not heard any up town news to day and my letter is confined within the limits of our own affairs. Annie, Jennie, and Maggie are all sewing. Ma bought Maggie a new dress for she said the one she had on was too ragged to wear.

Your affectionate son,
Geo. Sparrow

My love to all.

————————

Washington, N.C.
April 4th A.D 1858

Dear Father

The children were very much disappointed at your not coming yesterday morning. Ma is quite sick and Lizzie and Maggie are both worse. Lizzie is broke out with the scarlet fever. Every body in town is afraid of us, and Mrs. Geer shut up all of this end of her house and Mrs. Latham asked Dr. Tayloe to please give her some bellodonna[25]

---

[25] The very toxic Belladonna is also known as the deadly Nightshade Plant. Belladonna first became known to homeopathy when it was noted for having the same symptoms of scarlet fever. It was then used in the treatment of

to put on her child to keep her from having it. Aunt Caddie has been down here every day until to day scince Fowle was sick last night and Martha has just been down here to see how we are. I forget to tell you that Jane was sick and Ma had to get up out of bed to wait on the children.

Your son

G.A.S.

––––––––––

Washington, N.C.

Nov. 18th 1858

Dear Father

I have not written to you scince you have been gone but the reason of it was that I have been waiting for a chance to write you a nice long letter and to day is Thanksgiving day and I thought it a first rate chance. You may think it strange that my letter is dated the eighteenth and you receive it the twenty eight, but I commenced to write it the other night and did not finish it. Cousin William Spencer[26] is in new bern and is coming over to see Ma in two or three days. I received the governors message you sent me and was very much obliged to you for

scarlet fever with some success. Web Source: Home/Health/Alternative & Natural Homeopathy. " Homeopathy Using the Deadly Nightshade Plant," Article by Manda Spring, Edited and Published by Maria Rippo on August 26, 2009.

[26] William Henry Spencer married Emma Matilda Blackwell, sister of Annie Blackwell Sparrow on September 28, 1863. He was the head of "Spencer's Rangers," a local militia group in Hyde County during the Civil War. The group was accepted into service February 7, 1863 after a skirmish near Fairfield. Spencer was captured along with twenty-seven other men. It is interesting to note that between these two events he and Emma were married. After the war the couple resided in Terre Haute, Indiana before moving to Arcola, Illinois where they both are buried. Source: *Hyde County Historical and Genealogical Society*, North Carolina, Volume XIX, Spring 1998, Number 1, Fairfield, N.C., p. 11.

it. We get the register regular and Ma is reading one now. I have just brought it from the office. I must tell you what I heard two gentlemen say today in the barber shop. One said that if you went to the Commons again the next time you would be ready for jail, and the other one said that they did less in that house than any other house in the union and that they only staid there an hour and 1/2 and most of the members were drunk then. John and myself went a hunting to day and I will tell you what we killed, one rabbit, three larks, one robin, one yellowhammer, and one snipe.

Your affectionate son

G. A. Sparrow

Washington, N.C.

December 4th 1858

Dear Father

I have been sick for two or three days with a very bad sore throat and to day it is worse than ever, and it is so very sore that I can hardly swallow. I received your letter and the document and was very glad to hear from you. Ma went to Mrs. Sherwoods the other day and while there Mrs. Sherwood told her all about Mrs. Dupree and her two daughters and what good cooks they were and so you dont live quite as hard as anyone would suppose with your jellies and pies. To day is Sunday and Ma and the girls have gone to church and I am here alone and I thought it a very good opportunity to write you a "nice long" letter, as the others have not been very good specimens of letter writing. I have to stop every minute or two to goggle my throat and spit, so my letter cannot possibly be very uniform. There is a piece in the North Carolina Presbyterian[27] I want you to read if you can get that paper (and I suppose you can or I would have sent you the piece.) It is called "Lotus letter to the children of the Presbyterian" describing New berne and the Synod and all about it. Ma is going to give us a mess of oysters to day for the first time this year and the girls are making great calculations on their dinner and as for me I cant make any for I cannot eat them. Aunt Caddie and the baby are both right smart and the baby is the nicest young baby you ever saw. Uncle James is very proud of it but indeed its something to be proud of. The doctor and every body says it is the prettiest young baby they ever saw any where. I have been wishing for a rifle a long time and I heard you say that you were going to buy a gun, and please you buy a rifle instead of a gun, mine is enough to shoot prarie chickens with. Ma has packed up the box of crockery and while she was packing, I saw her put the microscope in and asked her what use we would have for it. "She said to look at prarie chickens eyes with." John went a gunning the other day. Mr. Ware to and shot at eight wild turkeys, but did not have any thing but bird shot, but they killed two squirrels and a duck however. I believe I have told you all the news now and with that I close.

Your affectionate son
G. A. Sparrow

---

[27] *The North Carolina Presbyterian* was published weekly in Fayetteville, N.C. 1858 – 1898. Source: *The Library of Congress – Chronicling America.*

First Presbyterian Church,
Washington, North Carolina

The First Presbyterian Church of Washington, N.C. was organized in 1823. The first church building, four years in construction, was destined to survive only four decades. Federal troops took possession of the town in May 1862 and the church was burned when the Federals evacuated the town. As the Union army left Washington in April, 1864 they burned the church.

At a meeting held February 10, 1867, a Building Committee was appointed to take the necessary steps toward rebuilding the Church. Major Thomas Sparrow served on this committee. The present building was erected; the cornerstone was laid May 28th 1867, and the Church was dedicated on Feb. 24th 1871. Among the Sunday School superintendents of the early period were Major Sparrow and his son John B. Sparrow. Both served as faithful and consecrated Elders for many years. The Vanguard Class, the Men's Bible Class, was organized February 6th 1910 by John B. Sparrow who served as its teacher until his death in 1943. [28]

---

[28] Source: *The History of the First Presbyterian Church, Washington, North Carolina, 1823-1973*, pp. 5, 20.

Joy W. Sparrow

St. Peter's Episcopal Church
Washington, North Carolina

Rev. Edwin Geer
Rector 1851 – 1868

The first mention of any Episcopal activity in Washington is in 1819 in the form of a letter concerning the erection of a church building in Washington. The Convention encouraged the building of such a church. The cornerstone of St. Peter's Episcopal Church was laid on May 29, 1822 and consecrated on January 20, 1824.

In April, 1864 as the Union army departed Washington, North Carolina they sacked and burned the western half of the town. Because of a southeasterly wind, St. Peter's was spared but only for a few weeks. On May 9th, 1864 a fire broke out at the Lafayette Hotel and as the fire spread, it destroyed the entire west end of town burning the church as well. Late in 1867, rebuilding was begun and on September 14th, 1873 the first service was held in a new sanctuary.

Rev. Edwin Geer came to St. Peter's in 1851. He was married to Elizabeth Margaret Blount of Washington, North Carolina. He continued to serve the people of Washington through the difficult war times even though they had nothing with which to pay him. He died July 29th, 1880, and is buried in Oakdale Cemetery, Washington, N.C.[29]

---

[29] Betty Cochran and C. A. Mann, *St. Peter's Episcopal Church,* Washington, North Carolina, 1822-1997.

First Presbyterian Church, New Bern, N.C.

First Presbyterian Church, New Bern, N.C. was organized on January 7, 1817 at a meeting in the home of Mrs. Elizabeth Minor by the Rev. John Witherspoon, native of New Bern, grandson of a signer of the Declaration of Independence. Mural tablets in the sanctuary affirm that there were 13 original members.

During 1861 – 1865 the church building was the Federal Regimental Headquarters for worship until the epidemic of yellow fever when it was made into a Federal Emergency Hospital; the manse being used as surgeon's headquarters. At the end of the Civil War the building was recovered from the Union army and was renovated, repairing damage done by the troops.

George Attmore Sparrow's grandfather Thomas Sparrow II and Susan Brown Sparrow's grandfather Sylvester Brown were original pew owners of this Church.[30] Sylvester Brown was one of the first trustees and Thomas Sparrow II served as one of the early elders.[31]

---

[30] Smith, John Murphy, *The History of The First Presbyterian Church of New Bern*, Griffin & Tighman Printers, Inc., 1988, p 127.

[31] Rev. L. C. Vass, A.M. *History of the Presbyterian Church in New Bern, N.C.* Whittet and Shepperson, Printers Richmond, Virginia, 1886, pp. 127, 183.

Chapter 2

Settling in Okaw/Arcola, Illinois

George's grandparents, the Blackwells, and some of the Blackwell family moved to Illinois in 1857. They settled in a little settlement called "Okaw" where grandfather Blackwell started the first lumber yard and was the town's first magistrate![32] John Blackwell also supplied part of the lumber for the Presbyterian Church of Arcola[33].The Blackwells found a pleasant and prosperous life in Okaw and the Sparrows followed them in 1859. Thomas Sparrow III stayed in Washington for several months to settle up his affairs. George's letters from Okaw/Arcola give a good description of the daily activities of a teenage boy in this little prairie town in Illinois.

John Blackwell   Ann Selby Blackwell

---

[32] Angelique Cain and Brandi Hymer, *Murder & Mayhem in Old Arcola*, Warria, Lexington, KY, 2000, p. 20.
[33] *The History of the Arcola Presbyterian Church.*

1st September, 1859

Arcola

My Dear Sister,

I suppose that you have "entirely" forgotten that you had a brother at all, although I have written twice or three times to you, have never received any answer, and in all of Ma's letters you never mention my name. I will grow quite discouraged after a while. I am growing more and more reconciled to the place but still I cannot help from thinking of the nice times I have spent at Portsmouth and when I do I most always feel home sick. I went to Bourboun last night (a small town about six miles from here where the girls have some friends) with Aunt Fanny[34] and Emma[35] to see Mrs. Niles and Mrs. Sinclair and had a very nice time indeed.

Fanny Blackwell McCann

[34] Aunt Fanny was Frances Waters Blackwell, sister of Annie Blackwell Sparrow. She married John McCann November 12, 1860. Both are buried in Arcola, Illinois. Source: *Hyde County Historical and Genealogical Society,* Volume XIX, Spring 1998, Number 1, Fairfield, North Carolina, p. 10.
[35] Aunt Emma was Emma Matilda Blackwell, sister of Annie Blackwell Sparrow. She married William Henry Spencer September 28, 1863. Source: *Hyde County Historical and Genealogical Society,* Volume XIX, Spring 1998, Number 1, Fairfield, N.C., p. 11.

There was Cousin Billy[36] and Mr. McKan[37] and two or three other gentelman and myself and Aunt Fanny. Sally[38] and Emma they danced some and had a fine time. We did not get back until two o'clock. Sister I have wished a thousand times scince I heard that you were at Portsmouth that I was back there with you and Aunt Caddie. I would have fine times I know. The plums are just beginning to open and I wish you were here to go to the woods and get some but – never mind. I will save you a bag of Filberts any-how. Give my love to Livy Tayloe and ask her if I can have the "excuisite pleasure" of writing to her and if she will answer my letter. I did not get to bed until two last night as I said before and had to get up and come down to the office and I have been taking a good nap in the back room. Give my love to Aunt Caddie and tell her that I am going to write her a nice long letter and I hope she will prove the best writer of all. Ma received a letter from Pa at Beaufort and he expected to stop at Portsmouth and find you there. Tell Aunt Caddie that she must write to me and I will tell her all the latest news. Write as soon as you get my letter and tell all of my friends to write to.

Your affectionate Brother

P.S. Please show this to no one except Aunt Caddie and tell no one any thing in it.

---

[36] Cousin Billy was William Harvey, uncle of George, who married Eliza Paynter Blackwell on July 9, 1846. Source: Sparrow Family Records.

[37] Mr. McKan (also spelled McCan at various times) is John McCann, a family friend who married in 1860 Aunt Fanny (Frances Waters Blackwell), sister of Annie Blackwell Sparrow. Source: *Hyde County Historical and Genealogical Society*, Volume XIX, Spring 1998, Number 1, Fairfield, North Carolina. p. 10.

[38] Aunt Sallie was Sarah Jane Blackwell, sister to Ann Maria Blackwell, who married Robert S. Warne September 8, 1863 and lived in Auburn, New York. Source: *Hyde County Historical and Genealogical Society*, Volume XIX, Spring 1998, Number 1, Fairfield, N.C., p. 11.

Arcola, IL.

7 September 1859

My Dear Father

Ma received your letter yesterday afternoon and although it was a very short one it was very acceptable, for Ma had concluded that you had forgotten her. Mr. Scram has put on the window blinds and has nearly finished painting the house. He is painting it a very pretty colour. The Book Cases have been down some time but have not been put up yet. Grandpa has just gone up to see about putting up a stove. It is very cool here nights and mornings and Ma has been quilting for some time. She is going to move in the other room as soon as possible. Cousin Billy is here yet and is getting little Law cases all the time. He says that this can be made one of the best law points in the United States and if you were not going to settle here that he would. He says he has made over "seventy dollars" scince he has been here and could have made more. They had quite a Law suit here this morning a criminal case. Cousin Billy as counsel for the defendant, a Mr. Henry for the people. He was indicted for shooting a horse but they could not bring sufficient witnesses to prove it on him and so he was discharged. Mr. Berry has cut down all the weeds in our yard and it makes the house look quite different. I go to ride now very often with Aunt Fanny. I went to the woods with her yesterday afternoon and got some plums and grapes. They are very nice now indeed. Pa when you pack those things please don't forget to send my game bag and other implements. I believe I have told you all at present. Write soon.

Your obedient son,

George A. Sparrow

Joy W. Sparrow

OKaw Illinois

My Dear Father

It has been some time scince I have written to you now, but I have had so many things to do that I could not write. You dont know what a good carpenter I make. I built Ma a wood house and chicken coop, and the last week I have been working on a "<u>Corn Crib</u>" for Grandpa. We received those boxes and Uncle Sam says he has got a bill of laden for the others. Mr. Allison comes to see us now quite often he came Saturday. Mr. McKan has been to see us a good many times. He was here last night and staid until late. I am going hunting with him tomorrow. There are a great many chickens now but they are very wild. Uncle Sam and Mr. McKan advise me to get five sheep and keep them. They say if I will do that in a few years I will have a nice flock. Ma says she would like for me to have some and to ask you to send me fifteen dollars. Mr. McKan has got a flock of select sheep and he says he will let me have them cheap and that I may choose those that will have lambs before long and next spring my flock will be doubled. The sheep will come to ten dollars and I want a little to buy cover with. He says I can buy cover standing for $1.50 an acre. Mr. McKan says he will give me the materials for making a shelter. Uncle Sam is very anxious for me to have them. Send me the money and I will credit you with it on the note. I went out with my gun the other morning after breakfast and killed a duck and three quails in "two shots." They tell me about such cold weather in this country. I have not seen any of it yet and it is full time for it. I send you a due bill that came in the Presbyterian. Aunt Maggie is still here and enjoying herself. No more news at present. <u>Love to all</u>.

Your dutiful son
George A. Sparrow

OKaw Illinois

Oct. 21ˢᵗ 1859

My Dear Father

It has been some time scince I have written to you now, and this morning as I am staying at home, I think this is a fit opportunity to write to you. Ma has received letters from you very regular now for some time and in all of them you say you very seldom get a letter from her and she writes every week. Aunt Maggie is still here and thinks of going in a week. Uncle Cis[39] is all the time writing for her to come home.

Margaret Blackwell Justice

---

[39] James Cicero Justice (8/07/1821 – 5/11/1905). On June 29, 1843 he married Margaret Ann (Aunt Maggie), sister of Annie Blackwell Sparrow, George's mother. Source: *Hyde County Historical and Genealogical Society,* Volume XIX, Spring 1998, Number 1, Fairfield, N.C., p. 10.

She is making a very pleasant visit. Uncle Sam brought me, down from Chicago, a full Bred pointer. He is Black all over and a nice dog. Mr. McKan says he will take very little training to make him a nice hunting dog and I hope that by the time that you come he will be sufficiently trained to go hunting with. We had quite a little accident happened on the Rail-Road about three miles north of here. The early Passenger Train ran off the track and smashed the engine all to pieces and turned the tender[40] and the baggage car upside down on the track and all the trains for that day were stopped and it being so near our house we had quite a sight, and very fortunately no one was injured.[41] Every one around our house says that Caddie is more like Mary Burbank[42] than any two persons they ever saw. Grandpa and Grandma both have taken a great fancy to her. I have not been to the woods to gather nuts but once and then Aunt Maggie and all hands staid all day. We got a wagon load of walnuts and we could find no others, they had all been gathered. Ma bought two dozen chickens from Mrs. Flint, the first we have had scince we left home. Ma has turned tailor and is making me a pair of pants. Okaw is improving every day, somebody's building all the time.

Your affectionate son,

G. A. Sparrow

---

[40] Tender. A railroad car attached to the rear of a locomotive, designed to carry fuel and water. *The American Heritage College Dictionary*, Third Edition, Houghton Mifflin Company, Boston, New York, 1993.

[41] Train Wreck: " Sad Accident – On Friday morning last owing to the breaking of a track, passenger engine #10 ran off the track near Okaw on the I.C.R.R. (Illinois Central Rail Road) making a complete wreck, but seriously injuring no one." Jantha Rollins, Historian, Arcola, Illinois, *Central Illinois Gazette,* October 26, 1859.

[42] Mary E. Burbank (10/01/1827), sister of Thomas Sparrow, married W. R. S. Burbank. Source: *Sparrow Family Records.*

OKaw, Ilinois
October 21, 1859

Dear Father,

I have written the letter to Mrs. Miller that you wished me to, and I send it to you with brother's letter. If you think it is fit to be sent to Mrs. Miller I would be very much obliged to you if you will send it, if not you can do what you think best. I was all yesterday morning writing it and have been all the morning copying it, it is now a quarter past eleven. Dear Father you must forgive my writing you only these few lines, but as I am very tired, I will write you a long letter, telling you a hundred little matters in which a Father ought to be concerned. Give my love to all inquiring friends. And believe me as ever,

Your affectionate daughter
Annie B. Sparrow

––––––––––

OKaw Illinois
November 19, 1859

My Dear Father

I received your kind letter and, as I had been expecting one for some time it was very acceptable indeed. Grandpa was sitting near at the time I got it and I handed it over to him to read. Cousin Billy has got back from "Texas" and sleeps at our house. He is going to remain with us until you come out and then if you are willing is going into business with you. He seems to be doing very well. There is no "Lawyer" here now but himself. Mr. Henry has "absquatulated" (run away). Next week I am going to build a plank walk from our house to Grandmas. I am beginning to have a specimen of Illinois, I. E. the mud. Our little "town" is growing nicely, and I begin to feel more reconciled to the country. It has been quite lively here now for some time in consequence of the corn. They are shipping a great deal of corn from here now. I have counted twenty two cars of corn at one time on the switch ready to be shipped. There was a man got killed on the freight train night before last. We have been feasting some time now on fish and roe. It seems as if I cant get enough fish. Mr. Allison is going to leave us and is going to move to Indiana, but he says he will preach once in four weeks. They are all very sorry he is going to leave. Mr. Allison gave Grandpa some flowers, and I set them out. The children all write.

Your devoted son,
George A. Sparrow

––––––––––

Thomas Sparrow came to Okaw the last of November, 1859 and remained until the end of February, 1860. During this time son John was born on January 19, 1860.

––––––––––

Okaw Illinois
March 1st 1860

My Dear Father

It has been only two days scince you left and I shant have much news that you will feel interested in except that we are all well with the exception of Lizzie who has got a bad cold. It has been raining very hard all day and is muddyer than I have seen it since I have been in Illinois. I made Ma a nice little bed-stead for Caddie to sleep on yesterday. I cleaned out the pig pen and attended to all those things that you left for me to do except that I could not prevail on Mr. Smith to take any pay.

Your obedient son
G. A. Sparrow

OKaw Illinois

March 5th 1860

Dear Father

I have just cleaned out the hog pen and taken out the old straw and put new in. Aunt Sallie has left. Mary has taken her place. Liza[43] went to Bourbourn yesterday. We had all the work to do this morning. The carpenters have finished their work on the new house and now the masons are at work. We have had delightful weather and everything looks like spring. It has been very muddy until a few days back and it has dried up very nicely. Mr. McKan and Aunt Fanny were here to tea last night and had all to themselves the Parlor last night. Ma is just telling me to tell you what a splendid Boy John was, she says he grows every day and every night. They held a meeting at the school house to take in consideration the incorporation of our town. They will hold a meeting this Wednesday night to vote for it. Mr. McKan was at first strongly opposed to it on the ground that they would tax his land too much and make him build too many Plank walks but I believe they have coaxed him over. Last Thursday they held a church meeting at the school house, and some of the men got so excited they called one another liars and the meeting like to broke up in a Roar. Every morning now the fence and the yard is full of larks and I take my gun out with me mornings and shoot them. Cousin Billey and Mr. Campbelle[44] raised an objection to my distributing those Sunday school papers on the ground that they would

---

[43] Liza was Eliza Paynter Blackwell, sister of Annie Blackwell Sparrow. On July 9, 1846 she married William H. Harvey who served as postmaster in New Bern from 1849–1852. They later lived in Arcola and are buried there. Source: *Hyde County Historical and Genealogical Society*, Volume XIX, Spring 1998, Number 1, Fairfield, N.C., p. 10.

[44] David Campbell was a Constable in Okaw. Source: Jantha Rollins, Historian, Arcola, Illinois.

injure their subscription and I consulted with Mr. Hickock[45] about it and he said it was no objection in his mind at all, and if they make a fuss inside I will distribute them outside. We received the letter and the paper you sent from Memphis, and I took the paper up and commenced to read it and I thought it rather a strange Sunday Paper until cousin Billey threw some light on the subject by telling me it was in "<u>New Orleans</u>" on Sunday morning. I suppose it is a small specimen of the place. Mr. Bradberry[46] is putting up quite a large Bakery on the corner by Mr. Joslins store. I am very glad to see it for I think he will do well. There has been no flour in town for some time now in consequence of the mud and we are living on corn meal. Jennie has been sewing and Ma is very much pleased with her, and Ma has been in high spirits for the last two or three days and all are getting on Finely,

Your most obedient Son,
George A. Sparrow

Give my love to Ed Geer and Liv. Tayloe

---

[45] Dwight Hitchcock owned a general store in Arcola. Angelique Cain and Brandi Hymer, *Murder & Mayhem in Old Arcola,* Warria, Lexington, Kentucky, 2000, p. 11.

[46] Mr. Bradberry was an Englishman who built the first flour mill in Okaw. Source: Jantha Rollins, Historian, Arcola, Illinois.

OKaw Illinois
March 13th 1860

Dear Father

The wind is blowing very hard this morning from the North and it is quite cold but we have had splendid weather for two weeks past and it was just like summer. I have just returned from cleaning out the pig pen and I found it cold work. I went to church with Ma yesterday. Mr. Rork[47] preached and he preached the best sermon I ever heard from him. Ma staid at Grandmas to dinner yesterday, they had wild ducks for dinner. Mr. McKan went up in Mr. Flint's[48] corn field the other afternoon (late) and killed six fine ducks and sent Grandma four of them. Saturday afternoon I went up there myself and found beside Mr. Smith and McKan several other gentelman all of whom were hid in a corn shuck waiting for the ducks to come but there were so many there that they would shoot at the ducks before they came within gun-shot and consequently did not kill any themselves and kept others from killing any. I have been thinking about it and have consulted several other gentelman that it would be best to harrow up the front yard and sow it in timothy grass and clover and then bush it over with a bush if there isn't something done with it – it will all grow up in weeds. Weeds look very bad for a front yard. It will not take over a half bushel of timothy and two or three pounds of clover. The back lot I am going to plant most of that in corn and leave a space for a garden. Mr. McKan says it will raise a good crop of corn. Mr. McKan and Aunt Fanny came over last evening and staid to supper and until late last night. It looked quite funny to see Mr. McKan with

---

[47] Theophilus Rork was a major land owner west of Okaw and was a United Brethren minister and circuit rider. Source: Jantha Rollins, Historian, Arcola, Illinois.
[48] William Flint and his wife Mary were farmers in Okaw. Source: Jantha Rollins, Historian, Arcola, Illinois.

Joy W. Sparrow

Johny jumping him up and down, he says you asked him to come every Sunday afternoon and he is going to do it. Johny grows "bigger" and "fatter" and "better" "looking" every day and Caddie and Lizzie and the children nearly kiss him to death. He hasn't cried but three times since you left. I have just come from rocking Johny in the cradle. Ma and the girls are sewing. Caddie has just got all tangled up in Ma's yarn. Liza is washing. Maggie and Lizzie are playing and Johny is laying in the cradle looking around the room. Mr. Berry and myself Saturday afternoon built a manure pen and a plank walk to the pig pen. The manure pen is seven feet square and five feet high. I have finished Napoleon and his Marshals and have got pretty well advanced in the first volume of Irvings life of Washington. I find them very interesting both of them. Our town is incorporated now and trustees elected. Good Bye.

Your obedient son,
George A. Sparrow

——————————

OKaw Illinois
March 20ᵗʰ 1860

Dear Father

I have just returned from working in the garden. I am making some beds in the back yard by the division fence between you and Grandpa, to plant vegetables on. I am going to set out a half a dozen Pie Plants.[49] Mr. Berry is going to kill the hog tomorrow and I am going to get two little ones to raise. They had a Grand Time here when they elected Trustees. They had two sets of candidates, Whiskey, and No Whiskey. One party was for granting a liscense to sell Whiskey and

---

[49] A type of Rhubarb. *The American Heritage College Dictionary*, Third Edition, Houghton Mifflin Company, Boston, New York, 1993.

the other party was opposed to it. The No Whiskey one beat and they appointed Mr. Barnhart, Scouten, Hewit, Reeney, Taylore for Trustees and Dr. McAlister for Mayor, a Temperance set so we are likely to have a temperance town "after all." The day of the election Mr. Felthoune was quite busy all day canvasing for whiskey men. They had quite an exciting time at the election and Mr. Joslin said it was necessary to carry on the meeting "to have a Nigger driver among them attending to Grandpa" and Grandpa got up and said that it was necessary to have a Jack-ass among them. Last Friday the hog got out and I had a hard time to get him in. The first I knew of it Nan came running down to the office and said the hog was out and gone and I came home and took a rope and caught him. Cousin Billey is having the office lathed and plastered. Ma has got her table and in the parlor, it improves the looks of the parlor a great deal. We had quite a company here last night and it looked quite natural to see them all singing. Uncle Sam has not gone up yet.

Your obedient Son

George Attmore Sparrow

OKaw Illinois

March 29th 1860

Dear Father

In your last letter you said you had not heard from us scince you arrived at Washington. We have written 8 times scince you left and have heard from you five times scince you left. Mr. McKan and Aunt Fanny were last evening as usual on Sundays. They come over Sunday afternoon about five o'clock and stay until ten. We had two splendid wild ducks for dinner yesterday, more than we could eat. I killed one

Friday and one Saturday. Ma is going to have another B[50] Thursday and I am going to try and kill four wild ducks before that time. I go up in Mr. Ewings corn field about five o'clock and sit down until dark and the ducks come around thick. Next Sunday is the day to elect new officers for the Sunday School and I expect we will have a grand time. The opposition party is very diligent in trying to get Mr. Allen elected Superintendent. Mr. Campbelle is mad with Mr. Hickock and I think acts very foolishly about it. All of the Blackwells and our crowd will vote for Mr. Hickock and I think he will be elected. I have been working in my Garden for two weeks past and I have got from the steps half way down. The back lot made up in nice big beds. I have got some splendid Pie plants. They have only been set out about a week and they have got leaves on them now. Mr. Flint is going to plough the back lot this week and I am going to plant corn. Grandpa and myself made a bargain. I am to help Mike and Mr. Berry plant his and they are to help me plant mine. Good Bye. Write soon.

Most Sincerely,

Your Son George A. Sparrow

Aunt Fanny is over here spending the day and she sends her love to you.

OKaw Illinois

April 2nd, 1860

My Dear Father

We had an election at Sunday School and we had quite an exciting time. Mr. Hickock was elected Superintendent by twenty nine votes. Mr. Wright was the opposition he received Twenty votes and Mr. Hickock Forty-nine. I was elected Librarain. I received Twenty-Five votes and S. A. Wright (a son of the old gentelman) received Twenty

---

[50] Quilting Bee.

two. Cousin Billy has been up at Tuscola at Court all this week and he says it was a very busy week for him. That case of yours against John Webber was not reached this court. Mr. McKan and Aunt Fanny were here last night as usual. I believe I did not mention anything about my reading in my other. I have finished the first volume of "Irvings" Life of Washington and I am half through the Second. I like it better than any-thing I have ever read. I am coming on nice in my garden. I have got several things up already. Maggy is sitting down on a stool holding Johny. He is a great big boy now and he gets nocked around a great deal. Now he seldom ever cries at all. Ma takes him a visiting and all about. Ma says she is getting old. She has had the rheumatism in her shoulder for the last two or three days. Caddy is sitting down on the floor, she says she wants to send it to Pa and Henry Brown. We live on Game most of the time now. Tell Ed Geer and Camey Bryan that if they want to learn how to shoot they better come to Illinois. I am going out hunting this afternoon to kill some ducks for dinner to morrow. Ma has learned to eat ducks first rate.

Very Truly
Your Son,
George A. Sparrow

———————

OKaw Illinois,
April 5th 1860

My Dear Father

This is not my usual day for writing and something very "unusual" for me to be writing on any other day. I can assure you but as I have some things of interest to tell you I will make an effort to write you a short letter to day. Mr. McCan received a letter from you on last

Saturday, March the 31st dated March the 7th. You directed it to Coles County and it was sent to a man in Coles County by the name of John McClain and Saturday he brought it to Mr. McCan. So hereafter I think it would be safe to direct your letters to Douglas County. I have got the back lot ploughed and I am only waiting to get it harrowed up to begin my farming operations. I have got some of my garden laid off in beds and a good many of my seeds up. Ma is just preparing for a visit over to Grandma's for all day. Johnny Sparrow is nearly as big as Caddy and he laughs and clowns and tries very hard to talk but he can't come it yet. Yesterday afternoon about three o'clock the wood pile down at the Depot took fire from the passenger train and no one discovered until it was to late in flames and from that the tank standing by it took fire and it was the Grandest scene I ever witnessed. The flames would play nearly across the street and they had very hard work to save the stores. It was so intensely hot that the men could not remain on the roofs and they had to make fortification of boards and wagons between them and the fire and keep the stores wet all the time. It was so hot that some of the men's clothes took fire on them. Dr. Henry recovered all of his goods. And by almost Superhuman efforts they were saved. It seems almost a miracle. The town is up in arms against the Rail Road Company for pulling wood in the town and they say they are going to indite it for a nuisance and if they can't get clear of it one way they will another. Write soon.

Your obedient Son,
George A. Sparrow

OKaw Illinois
April 10th 1860

My Dear Father

I suppose you have heard of both of our fires by this time but not the full perticulars of the last one. Two nights after the wood pile burned down, the stables of the Arcola Hotel took fire, or as it is supposed were set on fire intentionaly. It was about three or four O clock and burned down to the ground in an hour. There were four horses, two cows, six or seven pigs, three or four dogs, one wagon, seventy five bushels of corn, twenty five bushels of turnips and a hay stack. I have just been setting out willows around that little house out in the back lot until I was compeled to come in by the rain. It rained quite hard for a few minutes and then it lightened up again. I was very glad to see it for it was so dry that everything needed it very badly. I received your very interesting and valuable letter dated March 29 and the money 28 dollars and the flowers for which I am very much obliged both to you and the young lady. I entered upon my career a Sunday School Librarian yesterday and I think I shall like it very much. Aunt Emma has just gone from here. She came over here last night and staid all night so as to help this morning. Liza was at Bourboun. She got up and made the coffee and I cleaned up the dining room. I am going to harrow my ground this afternoon or tomorrow morning. I borrowed a harrow from Mr. McKan and a horse from Cousin Billey. I have got Onions, Radishes, Cress, Parsnips, Tulips and Hyacinths all up and Pie Plants nearly large enough to eat. I was up the track one day last week and killed two ducks.

Most Sincerely,
Your Son
George A. Sparrow

T. Sparrow

Joy W. Sparrow

OKaw Illinois
April 1860

My Dear Father

I have just come from working in my Garden. I have been planting some green peas this morning, and as I did not have enough to
finish Mr. McKan is going to give me some. The children commenced
school this morning some to Miss Wright and some to Mr. Wright, no
relation to the former at all. He is a young man and I think will make
a very good teacher. Ma is waiting for me to finish my letter so that I
can take Johnny over to Grandma's. She is going over there to spend
the afternoon. Mr. McKan and Aunt Fanny were over here last night
as usual. Mr. McCan loaned me his harrow last week and I could not
get a horse long enough to harrow but a small piece of land and his was
very sorry. Last night when I told him of it and said he would have lent
me one. Mr. Hickock was taken very sick yesterday morning and had
to leave school and I being next to him in office, I had to act as Superintendent and Librarian to. I read a chapter in the Bible and gave out
a hym and closed the school. Beside all my other duties Grandpa sent
for me this morning to come and show Mike how to set strawberries.
I put them on a bed four feet wide three rows on a bed and eighteen
inches apart according to Buist.[51] Those that you ordered for me have
not arrived.

Your affectionate Son
George A. Sparrow

---

[51] Robert Buist, *The Family Kitchen Gardner*, Orange Judd & Company,
New York, published 1805 – 1880. Contained plain and accurate descrip-
tions of all the different species and varieties of specifically American culi-
nary vegetables, fruit, and herbs. It included the best mode of cultivating,
propagating, and managing them in the garden.

OKaw Illinois

April 23rd 1860

My Dear Father

This is Monday morning and I am very anxious to get to work in my garden but I must postpone every thing until your letter is written. In your last letter to me you spoke of some of my letters being written in haste and carelessness but you must charge all of that to my garden and not to myself. It was quite cold yesterday afternoon and last night and I was very much afraid that it would kill the things in my Garden but I was very happy to find on getting up this morning that it did not hurt them. Mr. McCan and Aunt Fanny[52] were over here last night as usual and Mr. Warne and Aunt Sally[53] over to Grandmas. Johny is laying on Ma's lap holering and she is dressing him. Grandpa thinks there never was such a Boy. When he comes over he takes John in his arms and nurses him all the time. As I am Ma's Butler and have to tend to all the money matters I will give you an account of the last Instalments. We paid Grandpa thirty-seven $ the Balance of Lizas money. I paid Mr. Hickock's Bill which was 17.92, Seven dollars and seventy four cents of which you got before you left and did not pay for. I paid Mr. Gibbs Bill which was $37.68, $22.04 of which you left unpaid which makes one Bill $15.64. Last Saturday I went to the woods the Boys and myself and we got a load of Currant Bushes and Rasberry vines. They were very nice and as good as I want. They say down here they are a very fine Rasberry. I am going again next Saturday and set them all

---

[52] John McCann and Aunt Fannie (Frances Waters Blackwell) were dating. They were married November 12, 1860. Source: *Hyde County Historical and Genealogical Society*, Volume XIX, Spring 1998, No. 1, Fairfield, N.C. p. 10.

[53] Mr. Robert Warne and Aunt Sally (Sarah Jane Blackwell) were dating. They were married September 8, 1863. Source: *Hyde County Historical and Genealogical Society*, Volume XIX, Spring 1998, No. 1, Fairfield, N.C., p. 11.

around the lot. I believe no one has ever told you of the flute Cousin Billey sent John Blackwell one morning to get it. The man had come for it that was going to give him forty dollars for it, but Ma would not part with and they were all opposed to it over at Gandmas.

Yours most truly
George Sparrow

OKaw Illinois
April 30th 1860
Monday 8 A. M.

My Dear Father

I received your letter of the 22nd and was very glad to hear something from you and the New Bern folks. It is raining and cloudy to day and I shall not be able to work on the garden and so I will try and make my letter more agreeable. The Strawberries you said you had orded have not arrived nor the Barrel of Potatoes that Gentelman was going to send so fast. Mr. Flint was to harrow the ground this morning but I think it very doubtful whether he does it or not. You must try to be out here by the fourth of July as I understand they are to have great doings here. Liza went to Bourboun yesterday and Ma spent the day over to Grandma's. There was no Preaching yesterday. It was Mr. Rorks Sunday and I understand Dr. Henry told him he ought not to Preach. It is very evident something was to say for he never missed a Sunday before. Ma is having one of her loving fits over Johny. He is the fatest and the best boy I ever saw. He will lay in the cradle by the hour and never cry. When you come out you must bring some flowers with you. Tell Aunt Caddie that Grandma is making great calculations on her visit this summer. She has got a room prepared for her and she is talking about it all the time. My Garden is a long way ahead of Grandmas. I have got most of my things up and she has not got any.

Your affectionate Son
George A. Sparrow

—————————

OKaw Illinois
May 7, 1860

Dear Father

We have had very warm weather now for some time, and no rain and everything is very dry. I was at work most of last week planting corn for Grandpa. I have been hard at work ever scince the first of March and I have got my Garden all finished and up, and my corn planted and my Irish Potatoes and this week I am going to work planting my watermelons and muskmelons. I intend to raise a Great many of them. The Barrel of sweet Potatoes never came but Grandpa is going to give me as many Plants as I want, he has some bedded. I have got every kind of vegetable in my Garden that I could procure. I sent down to Flat Branch for some vegetables, Egg Plant, Okra, Cabbage and two or three kinds of Tomatoes. I am in hopes by the time you come out I will be able to give you a nice dinner with Pie Plant, watermelon and Rasberries for your dessert. I have got to go up the track some time to day and get some willows to stick my peas with. Mr. McKan thinks that I can easily raise an hundred bushels of corn of what I have got Planted and this summer I am going to cut a stack of Prarie hay or hire some one to do it so you will have to buy nothing to feed your stock with next winter. Grandpa takes a great interest in my farming and he says he is willing to render me all the assistance in his Power. The front yard looks Beautiful, the trees are loaded with Green leaves and the wheat in the front yard has come up and it looks like a green velvet carpet. As soon as it get a little higher I am going to get Mr. Berry to mow it down and keep it mowed down so it will look like Grass. The Praries are full of Flowers and look very pretty and yesterday afternoon I walked up the track and found several birds nests a Partridges among the rest and I know where a ducks nest is and a prarie chickens but I would not touch them for the world.

Your affectionate Son
George A. Sparrow

This spring weather animates and puts new life in every thing as you can perceive by my letter being four <u>pages</u> long.

––––––––––

OKaw Illinois
May 14th 1860

Dear Father

I have just been studying my lessons Latin, Grammar and Arithmetic. I have not commenced Reading any thing yet as Cousin Billey thought it best that I should not until I got somewhat advanced in the Grammar. I received a letter from you last week dated the 3rd of May and three days after that the children received one of the same date. Theirs came by the Northern Route and mine via Baltimore. Hereafter I will direct all our letters that way. Uncle Blossom[54] and Uncle Sam go away to day. Uncle Sam looks quite thin. He has not succeded in get-

---

[54] Uncle Benjamin Blossom was married to Margaret Rapelyea Blackwell on September 20, 1820. He also married his first wife's sister Charity Field Blackwell in 1850. Margaret and Charity were daughters of Samuel Blackwell and Mary Whitehead Field, aunts of Annie Blackwell Sparrow, great aunts of George A. Sparrow. Source: James Riker, *History of the Blackwell Family, Annals of Newtown in Queens County, New York*, pp. 117-180.

ting a pass and he will not make his visits very often. Johny is lying in the cradle squaling. He is getting to be quite a large Boy and you would not know him. Grandpa and Smith and McKan are going pretty extensively. They are buying and shipping all the time. It is worth fifty one cents in Chicago. You will very likely have to bring a Bridal Present out for Aunt Fanny as it seems to be the prevailing opinion that it is alright between her and Mr. McCan. I was out to Mr. Hickocks one day last week and he was showing me around his lot. He has got a very nice place, trees and shrubs of all variety and he has some very rare and valuable ones. I hope we will have some to.

Yours,
George Sparrow

———————

OKaw Illinois
May 21st 1860

Dear Father

This is Monday morning and I have just finished getting my lessons. Jack Harvey and Tim and Myself all recite to Cousin Billey and Nan to Aunt Sallie and Jen to Aunt Mary and they learn more in one hour than they learned in one month at the School house. The teacher gave them from fifteen to a hundred pages and it was an utter impossibility for them to get them and so they have all turned Teachers. We have got a very nice Sabath School now larger than it has ever been before and the People generally seem to take more interest in it. Yesterday Dr. Henry moved that we take up a subscription. He thinks that we can get ten or twenty dollars easily and Mr. Hickock appointed Aunt Fanny, Mrs. Joslin, and Miss Richardson to take up the collection. If you wish to do any thing for the A.G.G. you can send some money by mail or you can send some Books as the money is to Buy an entire new set of Books which we very much need. Saturday the Boys and myself went to the woods in the wagon for the purpose of getting Pea sticks and Bean Poles. We staid all day and had a very nice time. We brought all the wagon would contain and I got half and Grandpa half and I stuck my Peas and Beans. I had a very nice lot of Cabbage Plants some two or three thousand and the Bugs ate all of them except two or three Hundred. You cannot raise Cabbage Plants in this country unless they are off of the Ground. It is a small Bug just like the flea. They call them the Cabbage flea. They get on them as soon as they come up and kill them right down. They cannot hurt them after they get any size.

Your Son,

George A. Sparrow

P.S. Ma says you must not dispose of that little watch as you gave it to me and I am going to Buy some land with it.

––––––––––

OKaw Illinois

May 27th 1860

Dear Father

This is Monday morning and we have just finished eating Breakfast. I have been up ever scince four O clock this morning working on sweet Potatoe rows. I want to set out a thousand or fifteen hundred Plants. Mr. Sylvester Promised to let me have them and when I went after them said he was not going to sell any more and now I am going over to Carmargo about sixteen miles from here and get Plants for myself, Grandpa, and Mr. McKan. I was going to Buy a Bushel of Potatoes and Bed them myself. But Grandpa said he would have enough for himself and me to and his did not turn out well and so I have got to get mine as I can. Your man did not keep his promise about the Barrel of Potatoes. I set out about a hundred Plants last week and not a "one" out of the whole died. Saturday and Friday Jack, Tim, and myself shelled Corn for Smith and McKan and Grandpa at two cents and a half a Bushel and we shelled 100 Bushels in two days, fifty a day. Friday morning Mr. Smith came to me and asked me if I did not want to go up to Tuscola with a man and Bring the Buggy Back. I told him yes and started from here at ten O clock went to Albany sixteen miles over and I had the nicest ride I ever had in my life passing that pond in the woods that we went to that day. We saw an old wild duck and her young Brood swimming after her. It looked very pretty. From Albany we went to Tuscola and there I left my Passenger and came to OKaw alone. We had a very nice rain last week and it made every thing Grow nicely. Our lot begins to look like some thing with the Picket Fence and Green Trees and Potatoes and vegetables. There are plenty of ripe strawberrys on the Praries now and the children are strawberry crazy. Yesterday afternoon the Boys went to walk out on the Prarie and came running back and said they had seen a Rattle snake eight yards long and I went myself and did not take anything to kill it with thinking it was a fish tale and going out met Mrs. Joslin and when we came to the strawberry patch she liked to slipped on him and he threw himself up and rattled and so we had to let him go but to day I am going down and shoot him. I was just telling Ma that I could write all day but will be compeled to stop and go to work.

Your Son
George Sparrow

Tell Aunt Caddie to write to me.

Arcola, Illinois

June 4th 1860, Monday 8 A. M.

My Dear Father

Annie and Jennie received letters from you last week dated the 24th of May both of which were very welcome. I was at work all of last week weeding and hoeing in my Garden. I generaly got up at day light and then worked until Breakfast time, then get my lessons and go down to Cousin Billey and recite them. I do not study any thing but Latin, Grammar and Arithmetic now. This week I will have to get to work Ploughing and hoeing my corn and Irish Potatoes. My Corn looks very nicely and is growing "<u>fine</u>." We have had several nice rains lately which started everything to growing nice. It Poured down yesterday (Sunday) and wet the Ground twelve inches deep and this morning every thing looks as bright as a New Penny. I succeded in getting my Sweet Potatoe Plants last Wednesday. Jim Harvey and my self went over to Albany and got two thousand Plants, 1000 for my self and one for Grandpa. We got back about five O clock and when I came home Ma and all the children were at work making holes and bringing water and we all turned out and set them out before night. Grandpa was spending the day here that day and he said I did not have enough ridges made up and he sent Mike and Mr. Berry over here and they helped me. Planting Corn is the only help I have had this "Spring." We have had the nicest Spring I ever saw in my life and so everybody saw rain just where we wanted it. Grandpa is going to let us have a Pig this morning.

Your affectionate Son

George A. Sparrow

P.S. Tell Aunt Caddie that I say if she will stay here some when she comes out that I will feed her on good things all the time, give my love to Sue and Uncle Jim and Anna and "Bill."

OKaw Illinois

June 11th 1860, 7 A. M.

Dear Father

I received a letter from you last week dated the 31st of May and I was very much pleased to hear from you. You said something about not coming until late in July. You must try by all means to be here by the "fourth." We are going to have a nice time. Jack, Jim and myself are shelling corn in preparation for that event. We are going to buy the materials and Grandma's folks and our folks are going to make a big Flag four or five yards long with "Bell and Everett" on it and if you should chance to be here by the fourth you will see at the "dawns early Breaking," the "stars" and "stripes" of the "Union Flag waving Proudly in the Breeze." Our Sunday School contemplates having a "Pic-Nic" on the fourth and in preparation for that event we meet every Sunday morning at half past eight and sing. Some time ago we sent off and got a hundred singing Books and every scholar has got one and they know several Hymns now and it sounds very well to hear them all sing small and large. Yesterday (Sunday) Liza was to Bourboun and we had all the work to do in the afternoon. The girls and myself were away and Mr. McKan made a fire in the kitchen stove and then nursed John while Aunt Fanny and Ma sat the Tea Table. I think if you don't get out here by the Fourth the little children won't know you for Cad and John and Liz love him as good as any body in the house and whenever he comes here he has something for one of them. Yesterday he gave Cad an orange. Aunt Fanny is all the time at him about loving them better than he does Mat.

Your affectionate son

George Sparrow

Presidential Candidate John Bell and
Vice Presidential Candidate Edward Everett
Courtesy of the Library of Congress LC-USZ62-92282

As the time approached for the 1860 presidential election differences developed in the Democratic Party that could not be resolved. The extremists (seceders) withdrew and formed a "Constitutional Convention" and placed in nomination John C. Breckinridge of Kentucky for President and Joseph Lane of Oregon for Vice-President. The Convention nominated Stephen A. Douglas of Illinois for President, and Herschel V. Johnson of Georgia for Vice-President. Previous to this (May 9, 1860), the National Constitutional Party had nominated John Bell of Tennessee for President and Edward Everett of Massachusetts for Vice-President. On May 16th the Republican Convention met in the "Wigwam" in Chicago and nominated Abraham Lincoln of Illinois for President, and Hannibal Hamlin of Maine for Vice-President. The four distinct tickets in the field were:

1. The Northern Democrats (the Douglas and Johnson party), who thought that the people of each territory should settle the question of slavery in that territory, but they pledged themselves to abide by the decision of the Supreme Court.
2. The Southern Democrats (represented by Breckinridge and Lane), who declared that it was the right and duty of Congress to protect slavery in the territories.
3. The Republicans (whose nominees were Lincoln and Hamlin), who asserted that it was the right and duty of Congress to forbid slavery in the territories.
4. The American Party (represented by Bell and Everett), who pledged themselves to support the "Constitution, the Union, and the enforcement of the laws."

The results of the election in November were as follows:

	States	Popular Vote	Electoral Vote
Lincoln	17	1,866,352	180
Breckinridge	11	845,703	72
Bell	3	589,581	39
Douglas	2	1,375,157	12

The election of Lincoln set the stage for the Civil War, and South Carolina issued an address to the other slave states inviting them to join her in the formation of a Southern Confederacy.[55]

---

[55] Edward S. Ellis, A.M., *Library of American History*, Volume 3, The Jones Brothers Publishing Company, Cincinnati, Ohio, 1919, pp. 299-301.

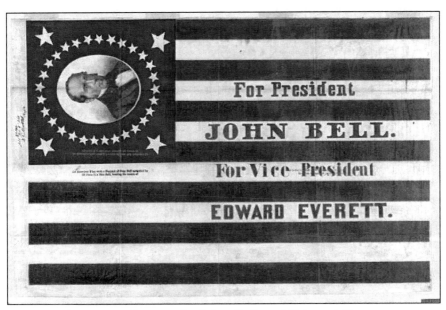

Campaign Banner for John Bell and Edward Everett
Courtesy of the Library of Congress LC-DIG-pga-01638

Okaw Illinois

June 19th 1860

9 A. M.

My Dear Father

Annie, Jennie, and Ma received letters from you yesterday all of which were very welcome both to us and to Grandma's folks also as they contained news from Aunt Caddie. Every afternoon when the Southern Mail comes over and Ma makes me go to the mail and she waits here until I come back. Ma came to me a little while ago and asked me if I would go down to the Garden with her. She goes down every morning and looks at the "Green Peas." I have got a bed loaded with Peas. They are so full they can hardly stand up. We thought we would have some for dinner tomorrow but they are not quiet full enough. Every Wensday Grandma comes over to spend the day. Uncle Sam came down last Friday and Saturday night. They had Ice Cream over there and Mr. McKan and Mr. Warne were there, and last night Ma had Ice Cream and all the folks were over here. They were in the Parlor singing and now and then you would hear some one say Oh! How I wish Mr. Sparrow were here! They always miss you when they "sing." I think by the time you come out I shall be able to sing several tunes. I wish you were here to help us along. We meet every Sunday morning an hour before the time and practice singing. We have got a small singing book with thirteen of the sweetest Tunes I ever heard and with Mr. Hickock to "lead" we are progressing fast making preparations for the "Fourth." The boys and myself are shelling corn for Grandpa and Mr. Smith and we only get two cents a half a Bushel for shelling and fanning. The last time we shelled we got 0.2½ for shelling alone. We only work afternoons as we have to recite to Cousin Billey in the morning. Ma has just gone over to Grandma's to spend the day. They are having a "B" over there today for Cousin Billey's benefit. He has had his office all plastered and fixed up and he is going down there to stay. They are making his carpet. They are working on the roads down town now and Felthoune is supervisor and they couldn't find one man in a thousand that would do as well as he. "Good Bye."

Your Affectionate Son,
George Sparrow

OKaw Illinois
June 22nd 1860
8 A. M.

My Dear Father

This is Friday morning and not my usual day for writing but as Ma does not feel well I shall have to take her place. You will not find my letter quite as agreeable as usual this morning as I relate mostly to Business. Ma received a letter from you Wenesday dated the Twelth inclosing a "check" for Twenty-five dollars Fifteen of which she owed Grandpa Ten for paying the Taxes on this House and five borrowed money which left her Ten Dollars. After the Groceries that we got in Chicago gave out we were compeled to buy them here and pay 10 cts for common Brown Sugar which you can get in Chicago for seven and 30 cts for candles which you can get for "eleven" there and 10 cts a Bar for soap which you can get there for "Four" so you see it makes quite a difference so Ma sent to Chicago for them by Uncle Sam. You said in your letter to Ma that you would have to go where the man lived that had to sign the Land Warrant and Ma says that as soon as you can send it. Ma had left me Johny to take care of so I must close. One more word before I quit. You said you had not heard from Ma in two weeks. She has written regular and she answered your letter as soon as she received the check for Fifty Dollars.

Your affectionate son
George Sparrow

Librarian of the A.S.S.N .and
Secretary of the Homilies

OKaw, Illinois
July 3, 1860
10 A. M.

Dear Father

We thought we should not write any more letters to you but some things have happened which make it necessary that I should write this one any how. Mr. H. C. Piridell arrived here yesterday on a visit to you. He came up here after dinner and staid all the afternoon and took tea at Grandma's. He seemed very sorry indeed that you were not at home. He said that he did not know you were here until the day before he left. I told him that you thought something of coming out by the way of Louisville and he seemed very glad to see you once more. He says he will expect you. This is one reason why I write another and a more important one. Ma was taken down about three hours ago with an attack of Colic. She is better now. She has been very unhappy ever since you wrote her you were going back again. She does not sleep any and looks badly.

Your affectionate son,

G. A. Sparrow

P.S. Do not let this worry you at all. She is better.

OKaw Illinois

July 21ˢᵗ 1860

Dear Father

Ma received a letter from you yesterday saying you would not be here until the fifteenth of August. The day before that we got one from you saying you would be here today (Friday). The children felt quite disapointed and every Train of cars Caddie saw Caddie would say there comes my Pa. Ma and the children all went to ride yesterday down to the woods and enjoyed it very much indeed. Aunt Caddie is having a nice time with all the folks and as they have no girl she sees a sample of Western life. I suppose you have before this heard of Dora's[56] death. She was taken sick while at Grandmas not much sick with a little fever and as it was very warm over there she came over here and from here she moved to Bourboun, staid there about two weeks and died. Ma received a check for fifty dollars yesterday and the day before $2.50 Gold Piece. You will find enclosed in this two letters from New York. We would have sent them before but you wrote us not to write after the first of July.

Your Affectionate Son
George A. Sparrow

———————

OKaw Illinois
Monday, July 30th 1860, 8 A. M.

Dear Father

This is the last time you will hear from me and after this week you will not hear from any of us any more. I was in hopes that you would get here before my Garden got to yielding much but we have been living off of it some time now. I don't know what we would do without it. All we get to eat now-a-day is what we get from the Garden. I have got such a variety we never get tired of it. I got the first mess of Corn this morning and we have got suckertash and okra for dinner. I suppose you know what I mean by suckertash Corn and Beans (Lima). I wish you had been here yesterday to help us eat Rheubarb Pie. It was the nicest desert I have eat since I have been here. The Plants have been ready to cut for a month but I have been saving them all along think-

---

[56] Dora was probably a servant.

ing you were coming in July and when you wrote us word that you were not coming until August I had to cut them. We will have a great many things when you come out. There will not be but a few things gone. I have got the nicest watermelon patch of any of my neighbors. It is just loaded with them and I expect some of them will be ripe some time this week. Ma says that there is not a day passes but what I must go and look at them. I asked Mike how much he thought my "Farm" was worth, Corn, Potatoes, and everything. He said if it were his he would not take less than a $100 dollars for it though I don't suppose it is worth that much. Grandpa gave Ma a little Pig soon as you left of his fine Breed, a sow. He only had six and gave Ma one. Ma gave it to me and it is now nearly twice as large as its Brothers and Sisters. I am going to save her for a Breeder. Pa I wish you would send me two or three dollars if you can spare it. Ma would give it to me if she could do without it but she cannot at present.

Your Affectionate Son
Geo. A. Sparrow

P.S. Write to me once before you come out.

Okaw Illinois

August 30th 1860, 9 A.M.

Dear Father

Uncle Henry[57] arrived here day before yesterday (Monday) and it was a very great surprise to all of them and he says that you are having such a glorious time up the country with the Girls that you are in no hurry to get home. Mr. McCan's Brother arrived here with three Gentelman from Cincinati on a Hunting frolick. The chickens are very scarce this year and that together with the prospect of his coming matrimonial alliance has kept him from Hunting. We are all having a Glorious time now. I am just reaping the benefits of my labors. We are "rolling" in fruit of all description and we have all the watermelons, muskmelons, sweet potatoes, etc. that we can consume besides supplying my less fortunate neighbors. And we keep the nicest Hogs you ever saw on vegetables alone and we have to throw away quantities. There is at the back door now a "Bushel" of the nice great big tomatoes that I shall have to throw in the manure pen. I did not tell you either that I had the Honor of raising the largest watermelon within ten miles of OKaw and I have beaten Grandpa so badly in some things that he is getting ashamed of it, for instance sweet potatoes. Grandpas and mine were set out the same evening and both came out of the same lot. He had his ground all broken up nicely and mine was full of lumps and straw. He had Mike and Mr. Berry to make the Ridges. I had no one but myself and now when mine are as big as your fist his are no bigger than your finger and when Aunt Caddie wants one for Mattie she has to send to me, and it is the same way with the watermelons. While we

---

[57] Uncle Henry (Henry Spencer Blackwell, 10/25/1834 – 1863) brother of Annie Blackwell Sparrow first married Martha Clark in 1858. After her death he married Annie Mitchell in 1861. They lived in Graham, N.C. during the Civil War Period. Source: *Hyde County Historical and Genealogical Society*, Volume XIX, Spring 1998, Number 1, Fairfield, N.C., p. 10.

are rolling in them they have not got any, only what I send them. I dug a vine of sweet potatoes the other day that had sixteen potatoes on it and I defy any man south to beat it. This is a glorious country to live in. Everybody is so independent. We are all bound to go the whole hog or none. It is hard times in this county for water. Our well gave out and we had it dug deeper and did not get water and now we are having another one dug. Ma says to tell you that you may bring all the silks and finery in N. Carolina that you can't bring anything to compare with our Present.

Your Son
G. A. Sparrow

—————————

OKaw Illinois
December 10th 1860

My Dear Father

This is not my usual time for writing to you but Ma and myself swapped and she took Monday and I Wedensday so hereafter you will always hear from her first and me next. We have had sleighings almost every scince you left and we have very fine sleighing now the weather has been quite cold. Ma and Mrs. McCan are still at Grandma's. They will likely get in their house next week. He has got very handsome furniture and carpets. Johny has been quite sick for two or three days past but is much better today.

I wish you could be here on the fifteenth of this month. John Henry is going to sell some horses, cows, hogs, and other things at Auction. He has been to me several times about that piece of land to know wether you had written anything about it or not. He says he has had several offers but waits to hear from you. You had better drop him a line as soon as possible and let him know. Mr. Flint hauled me a load of straw and I fixed the Pigs pen so that not a bit of cold could get in them at all. Scince you left I have taken to studying. I saw wood and do all I have to do in the morning and study in the afternoon. I have not been at it only about a week and I am getting along very well. If you should come across a set of Books (Ledger day Book) for sale cheap I wish you would buy them and send them in the Box. It would improve my writing and learn me to keep Books at the same time. I think when you come west again you will find the best thing you can do is to set up a store. I wish you would. Corn is selling at twelve and a half cents a Bushel. All well.

Your obedient son,
George Sparrow

––––––––––

OKaw Illinois
Dec. 15 –A.D. 1860
At Home 9 P.M.

My Dear Father

This is Saturday morning and quite late in the week for me to write but as Annie and Jennie are very busy and have not time to write I will take their place. They both send their "Love." We have had very cold weather ever scince you left. I think it is moderating some to day. I received two papers from you this week the New York Herald and the Raleigh Register. I read them both with interest especially the Herald as regards the congress and affairs at Washington City. Grandpa is at last fully convinced that we are to have war and that nothing but Providence can prevent it and all the family Grandma especially feel very bad about it scince it has become certain that we are to have trouble. He has turned a regular Northern man and all the family are "full Blooded Southerners" and every night when he comes home he catches it and whenever I go over there he always gets to talking secession. They are (the secessionists[58]) making a clean sweep down in New Orleans. I bought a paper on the Train the other day a Republican paper to and it says that when it was published, there was not a single Southern man in the city. They just swept them out fore and aft. They then had a meeting at one of the Hotels and as usual got to discussing the Abolitionist[59] when they got quite excited and one man said to be the wealthiest man in the City pulled out his purse and told them there was $5,000 dollars he would give for the assassination of Lincoln and Hamlin. Who would swelt the Pile? And in less than an hour they had collected $40,000 for the purpose of assassinating Lincoln and Hamlin.

Election Poster of the Abraham Lincoln
and Hannibal Hamlin Campaign of 1860
Courtesy of the Library of Congress LC-USZ62-5884

---

[58] The Secessionists were people who wanted their region to become separate from their country to which they belonged; in particular, the withdrawal by 11 Southern states from the Union in 1860-1861, precipitating the Civil War. Source: dictionary.reverso.net/english-cobuild/secessionist and thefreedictionary.com/secession.

[59] Abolitionists were people in the US who sought to abolish, or end, slavery in the 1800's. Whether or not to abolish slavery was a key issue that led to the US Civil War. Source: Answers.com: Who Were Abolitionists?

I saw in the same Paper where a man was traveling on one of the Rail Roads in Missippi and he saw two men hanging by the gallo and asking what for and why they were allowed to hang and rot in the sun, he was told that they would not "pollute their State by burying the Abolitionists in their soil." You must excuse my saying so much about Politics but as it is the all absorbing theme of the day I cannot help wandering off to it. All well. Write soon.

Your affectionate son

George A. Sparrow

OKaw Illinois

December 20th 1860

My Dear Father

It is getting very near "<u>Christmas</u>" now and consequently the children are all in a fever and cannot think of any-thing else but Santa Claus and Sugar Plums. I have just been down town and purchased a parcel of candies, nuts and the like so that they will not be disapointed. Any how, this is all we can afford to give them this time, but this will please the smaller ones as well as if they had something that cost a great deal. Mr. Harveys and Aunt Maggies boxes have arrived safe. They are both very nice boxes but Mr. Harveys in particular is a splendid one. It must have cost immensely. I think there is a Christmas Present in Aunt Mag's box for all of our children. Mr. and Mrs. McCan moved in thier new house yesterday and he has been running around town bying wash-tubs, tin pans, and the like domestic articles ever scince. They have got their house furnished very nicely and seem to be "<u>Perfectly</u>" happy and contented and so do all the rest of them feel on the subject. I suppose by the time this reaches you (if not already) we shall be living in a Northern Confederacy and although I like the country and the Place I shall dislike "very" much to be living in a country at enmity with the country that I was born and Raised in. I feel sometimes when I hear men talking of and abusing the South, who ought to be as dear to them as a brother or sister and who is bound to them by all the sacred ties of "Union" and all the "Hallowed" remembrances of our Forefathers they have disregarded the last "warning" of one of the Greatest men that ever lived when he told them to guard against sectionalism in all its forms. They can elect a sectional man to take the highest seat of the Nation and then stand up and say that the South is to blame seems to me inconsistent and when I think of all these things I think the South has a great case for the step which she is now taking. Grandpa last night paid Mr. Gibbs fifty dollars on our Bill out of the check that you sent. Exchange is worth to day ten cents and we shall get what ever the exchange comes to in Chicago. Well, the threating aspect of South Carolina and the other Cotton States has done one thing any-how if it never does another. So far it has placed a terrible damper on the financial affairs that are transpiring in OKaw. This is probaly the last time that I shall write OKaw in my letters as we have sent a Petition up to the Rail Road Company to change the name of the Station from OKaw to Arcola.[60] Wether they have been successful or not I do not know. I hope they have. Please give my "love" to all the folks at Home.

Yours most Truly

Geo. A. Sparrow

---

[60] When it became necessary to have a post office, Okaw had to be renamed because a town with the same name already existed in Illinois. On May 7, 1860 Okaw became Arcola, Illinois. Source: *History of Douglas County, Illinois, Arcola Township*, F. A. Battery & Co., Publisher, 1884.

OKaw Illinois
January, 1861

My Dear Father

Happy Christmas and new years. This is the first day of A. D. 1861 and Ma is out spending the day at Grandma's and for some reason I cant tell why I feel sad. What a vast difference between this day and this day one year ago. It then dawned on your Union as bright as the morning sun the foul hand of sectionalism had not entered our land but Alas! This time it no longer dawned on the U.S.A. but on two nations at war with each other with all the feelings of hatred and animosity gnawing in their bosoms. This union the glory and pride of the civilized world is about to be blasted at a blow and this blow is the election of Lincoln. We are all well at home. Ma has just finished a letter to you and I don't think it necessary for me to write any more.

Yours truly,
Geo. A. Sparrow

President Abraham Lincoln
By Alexander Helser, 1860

This particular letter was torn badly.
It was the last written from OKaw before returning home.

OKaw Illinois
January 17, 1861
Thursday, 9 PM

My Dear Father,

I have not written you a letter lately. I suppose I ought to wait as I suppose I shall not have many more to write as we expect Mr. Waters on the Train to day and if he comes "Prepared" we shall all go back with him and if not we shall start as soon as possible ourselves, the sooner the better and we are all anxious to get off. OKaw I think is improving very fast, the society is getting "Better." Last night I attended a "Party" at Miss Seviles and I cant think I could have enjoyed myself any better "South." At the party we had a Fiddler. As soon as you are able you should return to this country. I would like very much to stay. In a few years it could be quite a "City" and then I have an idea by my Friends and Relations and in good society think this country agrees with this. The last month I have gained almost "20 Pounds." I weigh now about _____. There is nothing that I would like better than to go into some "store" here if Mr. Waters moves out here. I suppose he would let me move in with him. I do not much like the idea of living on my father's coat tails and I am old enough to work for myself and so many girls in the Family too and then I have got a "good" character here which is worth ten thousand other things. I think Mr. Waters could do a fine business here now. Every store in the town is doing a smashing business now and making money fast. If he comes, you may expect us soon.

Yours affectionately
George A. Sparrow

Thomas Sparrow was settling up his business in North Carolina when trouble broke out between the North and South. He wrote his wife Annie that there would probably be war between the north and south and that he could not leave the south at such a time. Although opposed to secession, if it could be honorably avoided, he should, in case of trouble cast in his lot with his home and people. That she could come south if she wished in which case she might suffer many trials and privations, or she could remain with her family in the west where she would at least have care and comfort. Annie answered that she preferred to come south at the first opportunity, which she accordingly did – reaching North Carolina in April, 1861.

Annie (Nan) wrote that her father was deeply grieved at the turn of affairs and during the excitement of the time made a speech at a public meeting in the courthouse counseling his people to moderation and peace.[61]

Beaufort County Courthouse, Washington, N.C
Courtesy of Beaufort Hyde Martin Regional Library

[61] Annie Blackwell Sparrow (Mrs. R. H. Lewis), *Recollections of the Civil War,* Thomas Sparrow Papers, Collection No. 1, East Carolina Manuscript Collection, J. Y. Joyner Library, East Carolina University, Greenville, N.C.

Chapter 3

The Washington Grays

Captain Thomas Sparrow

Before President Lincoln's call for volunteers to suppress the secessionists, Beaufort County was predominantly pro-Union. When called upon to furnish troops to fight their neighbors of the South, North Carolina and Beaufort County refused and became bulwarks of the Confederacy. When Governor Ellis called for 20,000 volunteers, Beaufort County provided eleven companies between April 1861 and January 1862. Five of these companies were artillery units. They included the Washington Grays, Kennedy's Artillery, The McMillan Artillery, Rodman's Battery and Whitehurst's Battery. Five others were Infantry: the Jeff Davis Rifles, Southern Guards" , Pamlico Rifles, Confederate Guards and Beaufort Ploughboys. One company the Star Boys was a Cavalry unit.

The Washington Grays was organized in April, 1861. Thomas Sparrow who had returned from Illinois was appointed Captain by Governor Ellis. William Shaw, Jr., J. J. Whitehurst and A. J. Thomas were appointed lieutenants. Initially the Grays were assigned as Company A, 7th North Carolina Regiment (Artillery). This regiment was commanded by Colonel W. T. Martin and was given the duty of defending the hastily constructed forts along the outer banks.

When a Union fleet under Commodore Stringham and Union Army forces under Major General Benjamin F. Butler attacked Fort Hatteras, Colonel Martin ordered the Grays to the relief of Hatteras. They landed under heavy fire from the Union fleet after sunset on August 28, 1861.[62]

---

[62] C. Wingate Reed, *Beaufort County, Two Centuries of Its History*, Edwards and Broughton Co., Raleigh, N.C. 1962, pp. 175-176.

Gov. John Willis Ellis
Courtesy of the North Carolina Office of Archives and History
Raleigh, North Carolina

LETTERS TO GOVERNOR JOHN W. ELLIS
FROM THOMAS SPARROW

May 2nd 1861

Washington, N.C.

I made a tender of the services of my company in writing through W. B. Rodman, Esq. (William B. Rodman, Sr.) on the 25th ultimo. In a few days we shall be fully equipped and uniformed, tho' not armed. We drill three times each day. We await orders.

I desire information on one or two points.

First – Tender of service having been made, have I, or the officers, or the Company, the power on good cause shown, to release a volunteer from duty in the Company? There is at least one case in which I think it should be done.

Secondly. Since the tender was made, my company has increased, until it now numbers ninety. Will the additional volunteers on tender of services, be received as Members of the original Co.?

Washington, N.C.

May 8th 1861

Your esteemed favour of the 6th inst; is at hand.

I have notified my company to be in readiness to sail for Ocracoke on Monday next.

Will your Excellency please inform me where we are to receive arms. We have drilled as a rifle company.[63]

––––––––––

John Willis Ellis (11/23/1820 – 7/7/1861) was Governor of North Carolina at the beginning of the Civil War but died before the end of the conflict, serving 1859 - 1861. He was a native of Rowan County, a student at Randolph Macon and graduate of the University. He studied law under Judge Richmond M. Pearson. Ellis married Mary White, daughter of Philo White, August 25th, 1844 and later married Mary McKinley Daves, daughter of John Pugh Daves. When Governor Ellis realized that with the secession of some southern states coercion would probably follow, he recommended a conference of states and preparation for "any war."[64]

––––––––––

[63] *The Papers of John Willis Ellis*, Edited by Noble J. Tolbert, Volume Two 1860-1861. Raleigh State Department of Archives and History, 1964.
[64] Beth G. Crabtree, *North Carolina Governors 1585-1975*, North Carolina Division of Archives and History, 1974, p. 92.

Governor Henry Toole Clark
Courtesy of the North Carolina Office of Archives and History
Raleigh, North Carolina

Henry T. Clark succeeded Ellis as governor. Born in Tarboro in 1808, he received an A.B. degree from the University and was awarded an M.A. degree several years later. He was elected to the State Senate for a number of sessions. On June 27, 1861, the state convention informed Clark, as speaker of the Senate, of the governor's illness and Clark began his duties as chief executive. Clark was regarded as a man of high character and personal worth and commanded the respect of all parties.[65]

---

[65] Beth G. Crabtree, *North Carolina Governors 1585-1975,* North Carolina Division of Archives and History, 1974, p. 93.

Joy W. Sparrow

Washington Grays
Orders for Thursday, May 23rd 1861

No. 1. Lieut Thomas officer for the day.

No. 2. The Revile will sound at day break, and the men will form on the front lawn fifteen minutes thereafter to answer to roll call.

No. 3. Breakfast at 7 A. M. The chiefs of Squads will call their mess rolls at every meal, & report absentees to the Orderly Sergeant, who will report to the Officer for the day.

No. 4. Morning drill at 9 A. M. for two hours.

No. 5. Dinner at 1 P. M.

No. 6. Afternoon drill at 4 O'clock.

No. 7. Retreat will sound at sunset for the purpose of warning the officers & men for duty, & reading the orders of the day. Roll call at Retreat.

No. 8. Supper immediately after retreat.

No. 9. The Tattoo[66] will sound at 10 O'clock P. M. after which no soldier is to be out of his quarters, unless by special leave.

No. 10. No non-commissioned officer or soldier is to quit camp without a pass signed by the Officer of the day or Captain.

No. 11. No officer or private is on any account to sleep out of camp without permission.

No. 12. No officer or private is to visit Beacon Island without a special permit in writing signed by the Captain.

---

[66] A signal sounded on a drum or bugle to summon soldiers or sailors to their quarters at night. *The American Heritage College Dictionary,* Third Edition, Houghton Mifflin Company, Boston, New York, 1993.

No. 13. Immediately after Revile roll call, the quarters & space around them will be put into complete order by the men, superintended by the chiefs of the Squads. Also the Guard House by the Guard.

No. 14. The officer of the day will in person inspect the mess rooms at 8 A. M. and at 8 P. M. and will report all uncleanliness or disorder to the Captain.

No. 15. The Company Surgeon will inspect the provisions prepared by the Company Cooks as often as convenient, and see that it is thoroughly cooked, & well prepared.

No. 16. The Priveys in the enclosure must be kept in cleanly order, and any man detected in a violation of this order will be put under arrest two hours for each offence.[67]

---

[67] Thomas Sparrow Papers, Collection No. 1, East Carolina Manuscript Collection, J. Y. Joyner Library, East Carolina University, Greenville, N.C.

Joy W. Sparrow

Camp Washington
June 23rd, 1861
Sunday 4 P.M.

My dear Annie

I wrote you a hasty note yesterday just as Mr. Hancock and Robert Shaw were about to leave, and sent a basket with dirty clothes, and birds' eggs – the latter spoiled I fear. I took Mr. Jones and his daughter (a very sweet girl) and niece, with several others, to Fort Ocrocoke in the little steamer and then nearly to the Inlet. The sail was a pleasant one. Nan's friend Miss Jones saw her namesake "Annie Sparrow" at the Fort. The boys had a merry time in christening her, Lieut. Brantley, Col. Morris, and Capt. Agnew all being present. The latter is painting the name on the gun, across piece, and has one coat on. The Columbiad[68] next to this is to be named "Col. Morris."

Ten-inch Confederate Columbiad
Courtesy Civil War Harper's Weekly, February 16, 1861

They are the largest and most important pieces in the fort. An amusing story is told of Col. Brantley. He is very particular with these

[68] Columbiad: a large diameter smoothbore cannon capable of projecting solid shot and shells, with heavy charges of powder, at high angles of elevation. They were suited to the defense of naval batteries along the coastal waterways and navigable rivers. Jack W. Melton, Jr., *Civil War Artillery*, Artillery Glossary, www.jackmelton.com., 2011.

guns, and when the boys are christening her, (having first asked his leave) he stepped up to interfere. Charles Gallagher tendered him a drink of the rum he was pouring upon the gun from his canteen and the Lieut. at once became agreeable. He is very fond of this Ardent, and drinks a great deal, tho he is a man of some merit, and of an excellent family.

I am doing all the duties of the commander of the forces here, in addition to my other duties as Captain of the Company, and the burden is a heavy one. I have to draw on the Quarter Master and Commissary Departments for subsistence, water, fuel and other necessaries for all the Companies, give receipts, take receipts, and make daily reports to Gen. Gwynn of the conditions of the forces. Colonel Morris sometimes makes requisitions upon me for extra services of men several times a day. I am often worn out. I am high in favor with the Col. who always treats me with great kindness and consideration.

W^m J HARDEE

Gen. William Joseph Hardee
Courtesy of the North Carolina Office of Archives and History
Raleigh, North Carolina

Joy W. Sparrow

He yesterday presented me with a copy of Hardee's Tactics[69] just ordered from Memphis and wrote his respects on a fly leaf. I prize them very highly, and therefore have sent them to George. I desire him to keep them with care for my sake and the Colonels, and to study them carefully. He must especially master the first volume, as this will make him a good drill officer. Mr. Macon Bonner tells me that George had resigned. This should make no difference. In these times every one should make himself familiar with the Military Act. I would prefer that George should not lend these volumes to anyone, but keep them at home, and study them at night. He can borrow one to look over when at leisure in the store.

Mr. Oliver Jarvis has been appointed Commissary for this post – a fortunate circumstance for my company, as he will always look out for us. I shall have to supply his place as company commissary. I shall likely appoint <u>Charles Gallagher</u>, one of the best men in the Company. I last night received orders from Raleigh, to appoint an "Ordnance Officer" for the post, from among the officers of the companies. I shall likely appoint one out of my own, as we have had no "Commissary" from our ranks.

I have received various letters congratulating me on my appointment to be Colonel of the 7th Regiment. This is a mistake. I am acting

---

[69] William Joseph Hardee born in Camden County, Georgia was a graduate of United States Military Academy at West Point and was a career U.S. Army officer. In 1855 at the behest of Secretary of War Jefferson Davis, Hardee published *Rifle and Light Infantry Tactics for the Exercise and Maneuvers of Troops When Acting as Light Infantry or Riflemen* popularly known as Hardee's Tactics which became the best-known drill manual of the Civil War. Sources John H. Eicher and David J. Eicher, *Civil War High Commands,* Stanford, CA, Stanford University Press, 2009, p. 279; Trevor N. Dupuy, Curt Johnson and David L. Bongard, *The Harper Encyclopedia of Military Biography,* New York, Harper Collins, 1992, p. 315.

as Colonel by right of seniority and appointment by Gen'l. Gwynn[70] until one shall be regularly elected. I am for a <u>Military</u> man, and think that man will be Colonel Morris. He wishes me to have the office, but that is impossible. The elections are made by the Commissioned officers of the ten companies composing the regiment, and there are four of the companies at Hatteras, who do not know me. I could get the vote of several companies here. I am in high favour with the "Hertford Light Infantry," the largest on the Island, and next to my own, the best. I learn also that Capt. Martin's Company of Eliz. City will vote for me.

8 P.M.

I went to church this morning to hear Mr. Jones and wished to go tonight, but Sunday has got to be like any other day to me. Monday being mail day my correspondence has been crowded into Sunday. I sat down this afternoon to write about twenty letters, but presently in came Lieut. Humphrey of the Navy – then Lt. Fearing of the Eliz. City Company and two others, who all remained to tea. Then came Capt. Gilliam to get orders about picket guard on the beach, and so I am brought into the night, with Macon Bonner, and others talking to me all the while. There is hardly an hour in the day or night that calls of some sort are not made upon my time and patience. A Mr. Best, a Baptist preacher, has been sent here as Chaplain to this Regiment. He hung on to me for two or three days, and I yesterday sent him off on a furlough of two weeks to see the state authorities and learn something of his position and duties. He says he shall obey my orders in all re-

---

[70] General Walter Gwynn (February 22, 1802 – February 6, 1882) was an 1822 graduate from the United States Military Academy at West Point and was a civil engineer. Gwynn served as a brigadier general in the Virginia Provisional Army and then brigadier general in the North Carolina Militia, commanding the Northern Coast Defenses of North Carolina. Source: John Gilchrist Barrett, *The Civil War in North Carolina*, Chapel Hill, N.C., The University of North Carolina Press, pp. 32-33.

spects, but I think him rather a slow learner. He has a <u>wife</u> and <u>seven</u> children. I told him he must get quarters at Dr. Dudleys as I could not accommodate him at the hospital.

My men – rather my boys are beginning to annoy me to nauseation with applications to go to town. Their parents write for them – their aunts have come – or their mothers are sick. They are worse than school boys ten years old. I want you to tell Miss Martha Fowle, Clara Hoyt, and others of the young ladies, that I wish the Sewing Society to make up petticoats to be put on every one of <u>my company </u>caught in town after this date. I have sent Wm. Stevenson in charge of twenty men, ten from my company and ten from Capt. Sharp's, to Beaufort with a Barge loaded with guns. We have landed at the point across the creek beyond the Hospital nine gun carriages, and will land the guns there tomorrow. I am to have a Battery up there, by the forces on the Island. We are likely to have plenty to do.

We had stirring times last night. A steamer came just at dark along our beach and up to the bar. We thought she was coming in. She had sent a boat to scout the Inlet the day before, and we were so remiss as to let her get off. We had nothing to take her. I had the forces at all the camps to bear arms, and formed them in front of the Hospital. Here they were supplied with 12 rounds of ball cartridges, caps, canteens of water, and every necessity for a march or a fight. Macon Bonner organized a Company of Islanders and I armed them to act as scouts on the beach. Capt. Johnston hurried over to the Fort, had the lights extinguished and prepared to blow up the old house in front of the fort. He describes the panic among the Negroes as terrible. They poured out of the windows three and four at a time. There was a scene at Dr. Dudleys between Gilliam and his wife, and H. Ellison and his wife. The latter (H. E.) was sick but I made him fall in. One of my men – Stallings – refused to leave his room, when the drum beat to arms. Lieut. Thomas (one of my best officers) threatened to break his neck down stairs if he did not go. He came down in double quick time. We remained under arms all night. Mrs. Jones, Mrs. Ellison, Mrs. Gilliam, and many others came here and sat. The men sung songs, and had a merry time of it. About 1 o'clock I ordered Capt. Gilliam and Leith with their Companies to the beach, while Capt. Sharp, part of Capt. Johnston's and my own remained here. At 3 o'clock I took all of my Company to Beacon Island fearing that the fort might be attacked at daylight. The men quartered in an old warehouse, until sun rise, after which we returned. Most of the men were in the little steamer and on a flat boat. As we passed slowly across the water, a hundred bayonets in the air, it reminded me of pictures of the "Crossing of the Delaware" in 1776. We had had no alarm today. The Steamer must have stove off in the night. She was very near the beach. I am cultivating a mustache to avoid shaving. It is not very becoming. I am sadly disappointed that the girls did not come. I could have paid their passage. I want to see you, my own dear wife, very much, when you can come conveniently. Mr. Hanks is to run the *Oregon*. Billy has gone to Beaufort. I will write Nan and George shortly. Love to all, and to Fanny Grist. Kiss Johnny, Liz and Cad for me.

Sincerely,

Your husband, T. Sparrow[71]

---

[71] Thomas Sparrow Papers, #1878, Southern Historical Collection, The Wilson Library, University of North Carolina, Chapel Hill, North Carolina.

Joy W. Sparrow

Camp Washington
Portsmouth July 26th 1861
Friday

Dear Annie,

It is near dinner hour, and for the first time in several days is quite warm. Mr. Shaw and Warren have been off fishing and are now near my elbow. We are all to go to the fort after dinner.

I shall be at Hatteras tomorrow & may not be back in time for the boat on Monday, and therefore write now. I will get some one to conduct Nan & Jane to Dr. Dudleys tomorrow on their arrival. I shall try to get back from Hatteras tomorrow afternoon, but winds are uncertain. Johnston, Gilliam & others went down today on a steamer.

Major Robinson Inspector General of the Troops, & Mr. Lewis, Paymaster, were here yesterday. The former reviewed and inspected the troops at 9 O'clock, and the latter paid the men $10 each bounty money,[72] leaving in the five camps about five thousand dollars. The officers were paid <u>nothing</u> & the men only the <u>bounty</u>. If we join the State troops or go in for the war, we are to be paid off in full, & receive $15 bounty. Had we signed a muster roll for the war we would have been paid here. Otherwise we shall be paid in Newbern. I send you a little money for present necessities. When I get all, you shall have all & it will be a considerable pile.

Yesterday the Privateer Steamer Acarissee, Capt. Berry, captured off the bar, a splendid schooner from Cuba, bound to N. York, <u>loaded</u> with bananas & coaconuts. The Captains mate & crew were brought on shore, & put in my custody. They are all from Harwick, Massachu-

---

[72] Bounty System, in U.S. history, program of cash bonuses paid to entice enlistees into the army; the system was much abused, particularly during the Civil War, and was outlawed in the Selective Service Act of 1917. Civil War bounties were in cash only. "Bounty System." *Encyclopedia Britannica Online. Encyclopedia Britannica,* 2011. Web. 24 Feb. 2011.

setts. The captain was kept in my room. He is a good hearted clever man, & loses his all in the capture of his vessel. Tears often came to his eyes. He never voted for a President in his life, knows nothing of politics, & has no hard feelings for any one. I was greatly touched by his statements & impressed in his favour. I sent them all to Newbern this morning in the Minot, in custody of Wm. Stevenson & four men, with a note to Gen'l. Gwynn. I mentioned them favorly to the General & all others in authority & wrote a note to Cicero Justice, Wm. H. Oliver & others in his behalf.

I visited the Fruit Prize yesterday, & never before beheld such a sight. She is loaded with bunches of bananas, properly suspended & packed, from the keel to her deck, & then on deck above her railing. All the vacant spaces are filled with coaconuts. One bunch of bananas, the finest in her vessel, was labeled to "Neal Gilmartin, Esq. New York," the owner of the vessel. They are the large red kind, & would sell for $10 in N. York. Capt. Berry (of the Privateer) gave me this bunch & it is now hanging in my office. They are ripe & have to be eaten very fast. When Nan & Jane come, I will give them the ripest, & try to send you the residue by the boat on Monday. They are the finest you will ever see. Besides this, Capt. Berry promised to select a fine bunch, & send it to you by Oliver Jarvis on the Minot. She left this morning, & the bunch is no doubt safely on board. If not, I will send one on Monday by the "Col. Hill" in care of some of the boys. Jas. Mullium promises to take any I may send to you in person, on a wheelbarrow. The bunch I have, are as much as two men can carry on a stick. I ate so many bananas on the schooner yesterday that they vomited me last night, & purged me today. You must be careful not to allow the children to eat too many, & to eat only such as are fully ripe. I will send you some coaconuts also. I am very much afraid you will get none of the large ones I have spoken of, but I will try. <u>None</u> are plantains, but all bananas. I like the yellow ones best. The captured Captain's name is Daniel Doane. He has a wife & two children in Mass. He is quite anxious as to his future and delivered a message to Mr. Mooring who is to try to get to N. York.

The election for field officers of this regiment takes place tomorrow. I am no candidate, have electioneered with no one, expect nothing, and desire nothing.

9 O'clock P. M.

I have two nice bunches of bananas for you, besides the big ones, & 7 cocoanuts. Thought these enough. Sam Schenk is to put them up & send them to you. Don't eat them till thoroughly ripe. Be patient & they will get ripe. I sent you by last boat 6 doz. Mullets, also a barrel flour. The enclosed letter paper was found in the prize schooner taken yesterday. My orders for Newbern & Va. are revoked by the Governor. Order rec'vd. to night.

Your Husband
T. Sparrow

It is now 10 at night. A steamer is off the bar blowing her whistle, & guns have fired. One of our privateers I fear chased in. We saw the chase today.[73]

---

[73] Thomas Sparrow Papers, #1878, Southern Historical Collection, The Wilson Library, University of North Carolina, Chapel Hill, North Carolina.

Washington

August 20th 1861

My Dear Husband

Your letter written by the steamer which I ought to have got yesterday afternoon I never got until this morning. Thomas Hardenburgh went out in the country to see Mr. Selby as soon as he arrived and carried my letter with him. You can imagine what a fever I was in all night. This morning Sarah told me she saw him last night on main street with Jennett McDonald. I made George start by times this morning and told him not to stop until he found him. He succeeded in finding him and sent me up the letter just now by Truman Hanks but no dirty clothes. We received the two dozen mullets and return our sincere thanks. They were a treat we all enjoy very much. Don't neglect to write to Warren about your business with John Stanley, if you do you will never get one dollar out of him. I shall write to Annie and Jennie and tell them as soon as you leave Newbern I want them home. I am very lonely without them. I am glad your men are coming back particularly Ed Shaw. Be sure and write again when the steamer comes back. You may be able to tell me more about your future movements. Johnnie missed his farther very much. He went all about the house calling <u>Pappa</u>, it almost killed me to hear him it made me feel so sad. This war has been a terrible thing for all of us both north and south. Caddie was around yesterday. She spoke very affectionally of you and seemed to feel very badly about your going away. God help you my own dear husband watch over protect and take care of you will be the constant prayer of the loved ones left behind.

Your friend,

Annie Sparrow[74]

---

[74] Thomas Sparrow Papers, Collection No. 1, East Carolina Manuscript Collection, J. Y. Joyner Library, East Carolina University, Greenville, N.C.

Portsmouth, N.C.

Sunday, Aug. 25th 1861

Dear Annie,

Marching orders have not yet been received, and I am still here. Confidently expecting them last week, I wrote to Newbern to have arrangements made for my reception there. It will be a disappointment to Nan & Jane & to others. It requires a long time for orders to reach me here from Raleigh. My men are getting very impatient. We are here in an independent position & are not under Johnston & Gilliam.

I received no letter from you yesterday. I suppose there is some good reason for this. You can write me by Wednesday's boat as I shall be still here. I sent some word by the last boat, & also some by the Minot, & a bag of clothes by the latter. I sent a bundle of clothes by the Steamer with this, which you can have washed, & then await further directions. I send you 2 doz. Nice mullets. If they shall have kept well, send Mrs. Small a bunch with your (or my) respects. They were caught on Friday. It rarely happens that I can get them just on the eve of the departure of the boat. You may send the carpet bag here instead of to Newbern. I have made all my arrangements, & am in readiness to depart, but cannot say when my orders will come to hand. I shall await them with patience. I have felt quite unwell during the week, but feel today much better. Have told Mr. Hanks that I shall dine with him or Col. Hill. I am tired of Camp fare, tho we have been having mullets, birds, & soft crabs. We have as yet got no negro to go as cook for us, but will be able to get one no doubt. William does not wish to go.

Levindells Company are at the Fort, and seem quite happy to get here. Poor fellows, they have had a hard time of it, & been cuffed about without mercy. The fault must lie with the Commander. He has not stood up for his rights as he should have done.

We have a new Hospital Surgeon here, a Dr. West, of the Confederate States, covered all over with gold lace. He called to see me last night & became very intimate on short acquaintance, calling me "Sparrow" quite familiarly. He seems to be a clever man. Dr. Warren left, shortly after his Hatteras electioneering tour, and has not since returned. Col. Bradford, of the Ordnance & Artillery dept. is here – a very clever officer & gentleman. He it was who surrendered the Fayetteville Arsenal to a large force of N.C. State troops.

We have quite a Naval fleet here now – four in number, but the privateers have not lately been in.

My love to Sally Ann & Fanny Grist, Caddie & all friends. Kiss the little ones for me, & tell Johnny his pa wants to see him very badly. Love to George. He must write to me often. God bless you my dear Annie & all our children & watch over you.

Your Husband

T. Sparrow[75]

---

[75] Thomas Sparrow Papers, #1878, Southern Historical Collection, The Wilson Library, University of North Carolina, Chapel Hill, North Carolina.

INTRODUCTION
"The Fall of Hatteras"

Captain Sparrow of the Washington Grays kept a diary detailing all of the action in the battle of Fort Hatteras; the ocean voyage on the *Minnesota*; his imprisonment at Fort Columbus, Governor's Island, New York; and his imprisonment at Fort Warren, Boston, Massachusetts. Chosen excerpts are taken from Captain Sparrow's diary which show his devotion to the men in his Company, his unyielding optimism, and his hope and trust in God.

The fleet opening fire in capturing the forts at Hatteras Inlet, August 28, 1861. Sketch by A. Waud. *Pictorial War Record*, January 21, 1882.

THE FALL OF HATTERAS

Diary of Captain Thomas Sparrow
Company K, Tenth Regiment, 1 Artillery
North Carolina Troops
Portsmouth, North Carolina, Ocracoke Inlet
August 1861

August 27, Tuesday. The privateer steamer Gordon ran into the inlet some time in the afternoon, and put David Ireland and two others of the crew on the shore. They reported in camp, the appearance of a fleet of United States steamers, seen off Hatteras, after they left that inlet. This news corresponded with a letter previously received by Capt. Muse of the navy, giving notice of the expedition.

Capt. Lamb and Clements were at Portsmouth from Hatteras attending a court martial. These gentlemen expressed their desire to return to their commands at Hatteras at night. I detailed Privates Wm. H. Hanks and Woodley to take the steamer M. E. Downing, & carry them. They left in the steamer about 10 o clock.

During the afternoon I went to Fort Ocracoke with officers Johnston, Gilliam, Luke, Lamb and Clements, and took with me Sergeant William H. Von Eberstein to assist in defence of the fort, and to act as Ordnance officer. He went immediately to work preparing cartridges and putting things in order.

AUGUST 28, WEDNESDAY

I rose and dressed at reveille and went on drill with the co. on the parade ground near the church. Drilled two hours.

On return from drill Major Gilliam called me to the front fence and stated that Col. Martin had sent a dispatch, ordering all the forces at Ocracoke to Hatteras, and requesting <u>me</u> to go. (I had been released from service in the 7th Regiment, and was expecting orders to join Col. Tew's in Virginia.)

I at once gave orders for the men to get breakfast, prepare two days' provisions, pack their knapsacks, take their tent flys,[76] (for they had no tents) and prepare to embark.

I appointed T. Hardenbergh a lance Sergeant, and left him in charge of the camp, giving him written orders. Among these was one, that he should request Mr. B. J. Hanks to take certain of my command expected from Washington, on the steamer Col. Hill to Hatteras in the afternoon. Another was on the approach of an enemy, to take all the valuable baggage and the remaining men in camp to Fort Ocracoke, and if defeated in an attempt to do this, then to make the best of his way up the sound to Washington.

The Washington Grays, 49 in number, exclusive of commissioned officers were in line, uniformed and equipped at 10 o clock. I marched them to the wharf, and embarked them for Hatteras, on the Schooner Pantheon.

The Morris Guards, Tar River Boys, and Hertford Light Infantry, embarked in other vessels.

The Morris Guards took a vessel at Beacon Island, and so had several hours advantage. The others were towed by the Steamer Ellis. Capt. Muse embarked on her. So they had an advantage.

Wind and tide being against us, we took a longer route round Royal Shoal, and so were the last to arrive at Hatteras. The Ellis, with her tow, was only half a mile or so ahead of us when we arrived.

When within eight or ten miles from the inlet, we began to see the fleet off the fort, first from the rigging, then from the deck. As we drew nearer we began to count them – one, two, four – ten – thirteen!

---

[76] A fly refers to a tent without sides (walls), is usually strung up with rope and is generally used as a shield from rain or sun. Source: Wikipedia. Categories: Camping equipment, Survival skills. 27 May 2010.

There is a large fellow – there three others – there the small ones! Occasionally a gun was heard – then another – then three or four in quick succession.

The breeze freshened and favored us, and we began to make the fort and all about it very plainly. The decks and gunwales & every available point became crowded with the men eager to catch a glimpse of the bombardment, insomuch that the helmsman, a negro, could hardly see to steer the vessel. I had to order them constantly to trim the vessel.

We soon had the fleet and both forts in full view. The Tar River Boys were just ahead of us, towed in by the steamer Ellis. The Morris Guards were in a schooner at anchor near the Swash. We followed hard after the Ellis.

We had an uninterrupted view of the fight. It was beyond description. There lay the formidable fleet of large and small vessels off Forts Clark and Hatteras, and seemingly in the inlet was a steamer of moderate dimensions, afterwards known to be the Monticello.

Part of the fleet were firing upon Fort Clark, and part on Fort Hatteras, but the principal engagement seemed to be between Fort Hatteras and the Monticello. We could trace every shot fired at the latter, and see every gun fired by her. Some shots from the fort struck the water beyond her, some to the right of her, but a number we could see went into her. Eight struck her hull, and several penetrated through and through. We thought from our position that both forts returned the fire. This we learned afterwards to be a mistake. Fort Clark did not reply, being at that time in possession of the enemy. It was hard to distinguish sometimes, between the bursting of a bomb in a fort, and a gun fired from the fort. Almost every shot was remarked by the eager men on board. "There goes the big fort – there goes the little fort – that shot was too high – that too far to the right – there, that one plumped her in the side, good for that boys. There goes a broadside from the big steamer! How the shells burst over the fort! What beautiful white clouds of smoke they make!" Such were some of the oft repeated remarks made by the men around me.

I had never before seen a shell explode. It was sometime before I got to understand the thing. I saw from time to time beautiful little puffs of white silvery smoke hanging over the fort, without at first being able to account for them. I soon learned to know that it was where a shell had burst in the air, leaving the smoke or gas behind it, while the fragments had descended on their mission of destruction. As remarked before, there was such a continual roar of artillery, that we could not at our distance of one, two and three miles, distinguish the bursting of a shell from the firing of a gun.

At three quarters of a mile from shore the Ellis grounded. The schooner in tow of her, containing the Tar River Boys was then detached and came to an anchor. The schooner with Capt. Gilliam's Company, was at anchor outside of all of us. We had passed her. This, as well as I could judge, was near 5 o clock. My pilot did not know the way through the channel to the fort. About this time the firing had almost ceased on both sides and the Monticello had hauled off the inlet.

ON THE BEACH AT HATTERAS

What was to be done! I came to anchor, had the boat lowered, and went off to the Ellis. Capt. Muse informed me (by hail) that Fort Clark had surrendered, and that two men had been killed. He offered me a pilot, Mr. Mayo, and put him in my boat. I returned immediately to the Pantheon, ordering the anchor to be weighed, before I boarded.

Just then two boats, with Capt. Muse, Lieut.-Col. Johnston, and others pulled from the Ellis towards the shore. I was off in a few moments, beating up the channel, towards Fort Hatteras. When this was discovered by the enemy, they began to fire rifle shot and shell at us. The shells fell short, but the rifle shot flew by us in quick succession. I had to make great exertions to keep my men below decks, out of the way of the shots. I remained on deck, near the galley.

Soon we discovered crowds of men sitting on the outside of the fort. We knew not what to make of it. No flag was flying in the fort, and I began to think that all was over.

I ordered two hands in the boat, and pulled for the shore. The shot continued to fly over and beyond us, but none took effect.

Landing, I gave orders that the vessel should go close to the shore, and disembark the men as soon as possible. I then hastened to the fort, and entered through the sally port.[77]

The soldiers sitting on the outside of the parapet,[78] and on each side of the sally port, looked fatigued and care worn, but their faces lighted up as I saluted them, gave them a word of encouragement and passed into the fort. I found the men standing about in various directions, some with arms, others with muskets stacked, and all looking glad that the day's fight was over, and that reinforcements had arrived. They openly expressed their joy at this latter occurrence. Capt. Lamb greeted me shortly after I entered. He was cheerful as usual and told me that he had defended Fort Clark during the morning until he had shot away every pound of powder.

On the front of the fort facing the ocean, leaning against a traverse, I found Col. Martin, Capts. Johnson and Clements. The Col. seemed feeble and worn out. All expressed the opinion that we should be attacked at night by the enemy's forces in possession of Fort Clark. Estimated to be about <u>eight</u> hundred.

[77] Sally port. A gateway permitting the passage of a large number of troops at a time. Source: Dictionary.com.
[78] A parapet is a low, protective wall to protect soldiers from enemy fire. *The American Heritage College Dictionary*, Third Edition, Houghton Mifflin Company, Boston, New York, 1993.

Joy W. Sparrow

The Pantheon, containing the Washington Grays, sailed close into the shore and soon landed the men. I ordered Jesse Liverman, one of our cooks, to be sent up to assist in preparing coffee and food for the soldiers. A Yankee cook, from one of the prize schooners (the Samuel Chase) I ordered to be kept on board, fearing that he might desert, and communicate with the enemy. I also ordered E. Harvey and A. Buckstarf to be left on board to guard the vessel, and prevent the hands from running her off. I did not allow the knapsacks of the men to be landed, fearing that they might fall into the hands of the enemy. For a similar reason, I did not allow the Tent Flys to be landed.

I anticipated the result before leaving Portsmouth, and wrote a letter to my wife, to prepare her for the worse. I knew the enemy could shell us from the ocean, and that the armament of the fort was not sufficient to make a successful resistance. I told the Adjutant General this in Raleigh, the last time I was in that city.

All the men in the fort were in want of nourishment, my own men, and self included. We got a little bread and coffee, but this was not general.

The Winslow, C. S. Steamer, arrived after dark, bringing Commodore Barron,[79] Lieuts. Murdaugh and Wise of the Navy. Major Andrews, Capt. Muse and several of his sailors and midshipmen also came into the port.

Col. Martyn and Major Andrews, both voluntarily surrendered the command to Com. Baron, who thereupon assumed it.

---

[79] Commodore Samuel Barron (November 28, 1809 – February 26, 1888) born in Hampton, Virginia was the son of a U. S. Navy Commodore who died in 1810. As a tribute to his father, Samuel was appointed midshipman on January 1, 1812 at the age of two. He entered active service in the Navy in 1820 and by 1855 was a captain. By 1860 he served as chief of the Bureau of Detail and was one of the most powerful men in the Navy. Source: *Civil War Interactive, A Civil War Biography*, Samuel Barron, www.civilwarinteractive.com/biosmain.

Lieut. Col. Johnston had entered the fort a little in advance of myself. Major Gilliam arrived after dark.

The night was somewhat advanced before the Morris Guards and Hertford Lt. Infantry got into the fort.

It became difficult after dark to find an officer, until by common consent, the tent of Capt. Cahoon in the south angle of the fort, towards

Fort Clark. This became head quarters for the balance of the time, until the surrender.

ORDERS FOR THE NIGHT

A sort of consultation was held on the steps near the Navy gun, by Com. Baron and the superior officers at which I chanced to be present.

Lieut. Col. Johnston remarked to me that he intended to take "that concern" meaning Fort Clark, during the night.

This project was discussed, and inquiry made as to the number of the enemy on the beach. The impression which I derived from the answers of Capt. Clements, Lamb and others, was that they numbered from 700 to 800. They had landed howitzers and rifle guns, and had possession of two field pieces abandoned by our forces that morning.

The forces in the fort were worn down with fasting and fatigue. Part only of the forces from Ocracoke had been landed, and it was well in the night before all were on shore.

We were short of powder, shell and shot, provisions and water. All these had to be got into the fort. We had to send off for underline candles underline, as not one was to be had in the fort. These were needed by the Ordnance Officer to make up cartridges for the morrow's use.

CONCLUSION

It was concluded that we might hold the fort another day, and that on the night following we should take Fort Clark.

It was also resolved that we should waste no ammunition, and should fire only when we could so do with effect.

ORDERS

I was ordered to detail an officer to take charge of a picket guard of 100 men, and to select 30 men from my own company for this duty. I named Lieut. James J. Whitehurst to take charge of the guard, and ordered him to select from our company 30 men, which he did.

I was also ordered by Major Andrews to select a force from the various companies, and to get a 10-inch Columbiad from the sound side into the fort, and to put it in position during the night. I detailed ten men from my own company, ten from Capt. Sharp's, and five each from four other companies for this duty. I gave charge of the whole to Private William B. Willis, who was a ship carpenter and had handled heavy guns successfully at Ocracoke.

WANTING

There was no block and tackle, nor anything of the sort, and no shears that could be used in moving or handling the gun. We succeeded in getting a line, and some pieces of scantling for slides.

I was engaged at the shore in a seemingly vain effort to move the Columbiad, with our imperfect means, when I was ordered to desist by Major Andrews, he alleging as a reason for the order that "there were neither 10-inch shot nor shell in the fort, and therefore the gun would be useless if mounted."

THE NIGHT

Besides such of my men as were on picket duty, and other duty, several of them with Lieut. Shaw, were occupied in landing men, water and ammunition a good part of the night. This left but few in the fort not on duty. These I left with Sergt. Robbins behind the second traverse from the sally port, facing the inlet, where they remained during the night. They leaned with their muskets against the traverse, or slept upon the gun platform as best they could, without blankets or covering of any sort.

There came up a little scud of rain in the night, and to protect their muskets, the men generally turned them butt upwards, with the bayonets in the sand.

The soldiers, were some in the bomb-proof, some against the bomb-proof on the outside, some behind the traverses, some on the platforms, and some in the tents.

I slept but little – not half an hour in all. I sat in Capt. Cahoon's tent with Col. Martin at times, tried to sleep in my chair a little, and would go thence to where my few men were. I always found Sergt. Robbins awake.

FORCES IN THE FORT

Washington Grays, Capt. Sparrow 47 men, 4 officers
Independent Grays, Capt. Cahoon 69 men, 3 officers
Roanoke Guards, Capt. Lamb 98 men, 3 officers
Morris Guards, Capt. Gilliam 64 men, 4 officers
Hamilton Guards, Capt. Clement.
Tar River Boys, Capt. Johnston.
Hertford Light Infantry, Capt. Sharp   64 men, 3 officers
Jonesboro Guards, Capt. Duke 66 men, 4 officers
North Carolina Defenders, Capt. Luke   47 men, 3 officers
Lenoir Braves, Capt. Sutton   __ men, 3 officers

RETURN OF THE PICKETS

Just before day, while it was yet dark, a body of men were seen to approach the fort from the direction of the inlet. In the dusk of the morning it looked like a large force. I at once took it to be the returning pickets, but others insisted that it looked too large. Quite a stir was made in the fort. All the men were called to arms. The guns bearing on the inlet and on the sally port were shotted with grape, and the men stood ready to fire. I could not understand how so large a force could have passed the pickets without creating an alarm, but then they might have landed in the inlet. It was well enough to be cautious. A man was sent out to challenge the force, but no answer was heard. The excitement became quite intense. Soon I recognized the voice of Lieut. Whitehurst and called out that it was the picket guard. This did not at first give satisfaction. Finally all became assured, and the guard came into the fort and reported.

They had advanced to within a few yards of Fort Clark and had seen no signs of an enemy. We learned afterwards that only a small force was left there, and they got drunk on the whiskey found there, and went to sleep. This is told by one of the free negroes who remained there. The fort might have been taken had the fact been known.

AUGUST 29, WEDNESDAY
PREPARATIONS

The cooks had been kept busy all night providing food and coffee for the men. Some time after daylight all got a little, but not much. Fasting, want of sleep and anxiety had quite exhausted me. A cup of coffee, and a little whiskey and sugar given me by Capt. Clements quite revived me.

The companies that had come from Ocracoke were to man the guns, while those who had been on duty the day before were to be relieved.

I was ordered to form 4 detachments from my company, of eight men each and a gunner. They were to have charge of two of the guns bearing on the inlet, one a 32 and one an 8-inch Howitzer. The detachments were to be in charge of one of my Lieutenants, and I was ordered to visit them in person during the fight. I appointed the following gunners. Sergt. John R. Potts, Private W. W. Willis, Ensign W. B. Cornell and C. K. Gallagher (a volunteer).

Gallagher came into the port from the brig H. C. Brooks, on which he was bound to Liverpool. He was fond of gunnery, had been drilled at Beacon Island, and I gave him a gun first assigned to W. W. Cordon. He was not called upon to fire it.

I gave the charge of the two first detachments to Lieut. W. Shaw, and the second to Lieut. A. J. Thomas, who was to relieve the first two every hour.

The Tar River Boys had charge of two 32 pounders on the same face of the fort as my two, facing the inlet, and to the left of mine.

My first two detachments and the Tar River Boys practiced at the drill of their guns, and received special instructions from Major Andrews as to the elevation of the guns.

The Morris Guards were assigned to two guns that bore on the enemy, to wit: The 8 inch Howitzer in the pancoup (or angle) bearing on the Inlet and Ocean (southeast), and the Basket 32 near this. A traverse was between them.

The 32 to the left of this was mounted on a ship carriage, on an elevated platform and was very slightly protected by the parapet. This gun was in charge of Lieut. Murdaugh, and a force from the Naval Steamer Ellis.

Stewart Johnson had charge of the Howitzer in the angle. Lieut. Grimes the 32 left of the traverse.

These three guns were the only ones fired during the engagement.

The Hertford Lt. Infantry had charge of a 32 on the face of the fort looking towards Hatteras woods, and Fort Clark. During the night part of a traverse had been taken down, so as to bring this gun to bear on the rear of Fort Clark. Capt. Sharp commanded here in person.

DISPOSITIONS

It was determined that only those on duty should remain in the fort. The detachments to man the guns were to remain near them, and the reliefs were to stay in the Bomb Proof, until called for.

All the men not on duty were ordered outside of the parapet facing the sound for their protection. I was ordered not to fire a gun until the enemy should come within full range of our guns.

Just to the right of my guns was a traverse already spoken of as the one where my men slept during the night. Just behind this I posted my men, so as to be in readiness to man and fire their guns when called on. Here I remained for some time before and in the early part of the bombardment. Here not a man was wounded.

MINNIE BALLS

Before the action began I was standing on the parapet near the pancoup facing the inlet and ocean, with Commodore Baron, Colonel Bradford, and others, when bang, bang, went some rifles at Fort Clark, and at the same instant the balls came whistling over our heads. The Germans there seeing us on the walls, took us as a target for their pieces. We got out of the way of course. They continued to fly over the fort for some time without doing harm.

UNPROTECTED

When guns were assigned to me, the first thought that occurred to me was that owing to the position the enemy's ships had taken, there was no protection for my men, as they would be subjected to a raking fire from them.

Looking from my guns seaward, I could see the broadside of the Minnesota between the rear of the two traverses at that angle of the fort. It was obvious that they would be unprotected at their guns.

I immediately took Commodore Barron, Major Andrews, and Col. Martin to the parapet, and pointed out to them this defect. Orders were immediately issued to Mr. Allen, the engineer, to take down a traverse in rear of the fort, and extend one in the angle named (at right angles to the face fronting the inlet), so as to protect the guns manned by my men. It was only half completed when the firing commenced, and so the guns were unprotected. In the engagement <u>both</u> were disabled by shells from the Minnesota.

THE ENEMY

The large vessels had steamed off some distance from the shore at night, and the smaller ones took shelter in a bight[80] under the cape near the shore.

At early dawn their heavy outlines could be descried off the bar to seaward, in all their formidable array. As the morning wore away at about 7 o clock, a signal gun was fired by the Flag Ship Minnesota, and soon the fleet were in motion for the shore. They moved in, took their position with apparent deliberation and came to anchor. The bombarding fleet consisted of the following vessels:

Minnesota Flag Ship	74 guns
Susquehannah	74 guns
Cumberland	75 guns
Wabash	74 guns
Harriet Lane	7 guns.

The Cumberland came into the action after the rest had begun to fire. The Harriet Lane joined them but did not confine herself to one position.

---

[80] A bight is a bend or curve, especially in a shoreline. *The American Heritage College Dictionary,* Third Edition, Houghton Mifflin Company, Boston, New York, 1993.

The *Minnesota*
Courtesy The Mariners' Museum, Newport News, Virginia

THE ACTION

This lasted three hours and twenty minutes. Such a bombardment is not on record in the annals of war. Not less than three thousand shells were fired by the enemy during the three hours. As many as twenty eight in one minute were known to fall within and about the fort. It was like a hailstorm, and how so many escaped is known only to Providence who sheltered us and preserved us. On this whole subject see the official reports of Commodore Barron,[81] Major Andrews and Col. Martin, which with the report of Commodore Stringham[82] I have preserved.

Union Commodore Silas H. Stringham

---

[81] On July 20, 1861 Commodore Samuel Barron was given command of the coastal defenses of Virginia and North Carolina and chose to administer his duties from Fort Hatteras. He arrived at the fort on August 28, 1861, the day after the bombardment by Union forces and was forced to surrender the following day. He was held prisoner of war until exchanged eleven months later. Source: Civil War Interactive, *A Civil War Biography: Samuel Barron*, www.civilwarinteractive.com/biosmain.

[82] Silas H. Stringham was Flag Officer commanding the *Minnesota* and the Atlantic Blockading Squadron. Source: John G. Barrett, *The Civil War in North Carolina*, The University of North Carolina Press, Chapel Hill, N.C. 1963, p. 37.

Joy W. Sparrow

How shall I describe the bombardment – how give an idea of what was going on in various parts of the fort – how express my ideas and my impressions on such a subject! It would be a hopeless task.

I was standing with my men behind the traverse spoken of, near the inlet, when the first shot was fired. This was according to our time at twenty minutes before 8 o clock. According to Commodore Stringham's account it was 8 o clock. We were all ready and were expecting it. As the report reached us, some one called out, "There they go, look out!" and all instinctively leaned closely against the traverse. The next moment the sharp shrill whistle of the shell was heard. It came from the direction of the Susquehannah and passed right over us. It was followed in rapid succession by others, which fell in all sorts of directions, many of them falling short.[83]

The flag was planted on the traverse next to the sally port just beyond us, under my directions. It was found to afford a mark for the enemy, and in about an hour was taken down. I sent John Blount to do it, but he called on W. B. Willis, who mounted the parapet, flaunted it at the enemy, and then brought it down. It was in the hottest of the fire.

The place where I was standing became very much crowded and I concluded to seek shelter elsewhere in a position convenient to my guns. I was told not to fire without orders, & unless an attempt was made to force the inlet. I therefore sought the entrance to the magazine, a few feet distant, and directly opposite my guns. Col. Carraway was in the magazine passing out the powder as it was called for. In the entrance with me were Lieut. Norman, Col. Martin, and part of

---

[83] "Captain Stringham, instead of anchoring, so as to allow the enemy to gain the right range, kept his four steamers (the *Minnesota*, the *Wabash*, the *Cumberland*, and the *Susquehanna*) circling about at varying distances. The plan was very successful." Source: Ellis, Edward S., *Library of American History*, Volume 4, The Jones Brothers Publishing Company, Cincinnati, Ohio, 1918, p. 49.

the time Lieuts. Whitehurst, Thomas, Shaw and others. It was a very dangerous place, but officers and men were continually coming and going. It was close and intolerably hot. We had to keep our hats going as fans to keep up a circulation of air.

The Naval gun commanded by Lieut. Murdaugh, and the guns commanded by Lieuts. Johnson and Grimes returned the fire of the enemy, but it was soon discovered that with the greatest elevation we could get, our guns did not reach the enemy. It was therefore a one sided business. It became a question of endurance on our part. Could we hold out during the day, we would take the enemy in Fort Clark at night.

While in the magazine, I could readily distinguish between the enemys guns, the explosion of their shells, and our own guns. When we fired, the concussion shook the entire bomb proof. We could tell where every shell was falling. Many of the fragments fell at the door. Had a shell fallen there, we would all have all been killed. We could hear them fall and explode all about and around us. Some fell so near that I became alarmed for the safety of the magazine. The door beyond us had to be kept open to give air to Col. Caraway, and to enable him to pass out the powder when it was called for.

While here, news of the killing of one and the wounding of another would be brought in by the men. Here I heard of Lieutenant Murdaugh's misfortune, and that Commodore Barron was killed. This proved to be a mistake. When a ball or a shell would strike the bombproof or a traverse, it would be with a very peculiar thud, and then all would listen for the explosion. In this we would sometimes be disappointed. It was because some of the shells did not explode when they fell.

LEAVE THE MAGAZINE

During all this part of the engagement, W. Willis had stuck to his gun, and could not be induced to leave it. Col. Martin once ordered him to leave. He stood upon the carriage and gave notice to the men whenever a shell was coming, fearless as to himself.

My men and Col. Johnston's were all ordered to leave their guns and take care of themselves as best they could. They all remained behind the traverses. One of Johnston's men was killed, and one of mine knocked down behind one of these.

On leaving the magazine (having been there near an hour), I went to where Grimes was firing his gun, on the front of the work. The shells were flying rapidly. I took shelter beneath the parapet. In a few seconds I was covered with sand and earth. A shell struck the parapet just over me and covered me. I got up, retreated to the end of an adjoining traverse, where were Lieut. Moore and others, held my head down, and brushed the dirt from my neck and head.

I went next to the end of a traverse near the southeast angle of the fort (towards Fort Clark), and back of Capt. Cahoon's tent already spoken of.

Here were Commodore Baron, Major Andrews, Col Martin and others. The tents were all on this (east) side of the fort, and the enemy made a mark of them as we afterwards learned. The shells now fell with fearful effect in all parts of the fort, and on the bomb proof, but more especially on this side. The tents and wood kitchens were literally torn all in pieces.

I remained at this traverse during the rest of the bombardment, sometimes in front of it, sometimes lying down on the East side of it, and once between it and the parapet. It was while I was there damaged by three shells, and the top of it was torn all in pieces.

While here, there came over me a feeling of perfect security, not to say indifference. I could tell every shell that was to pass by, and every one that was to fall. The one had a sharp, rapid, shrill sound, and the other a dull hoarse sound, as if almost exhausted. We would hear them strike with a <u>thud,</u> and in a second listen and look for the explosion.

Looking up, I would see many of them fly rapidly over, seemingly on an <u>eager</u> mission of destruction, fall just beyond the parapet, where the men were huddled together, explode and send into the air a column of sand and water. I saw many pass in this way. The only uneasiness I felt was on account of the men, several hundreds of whom were on the outside unprotected, where most of the shells were falling and exploding. Almost every minute some one was brought in from there wounded, and taken to the bomb proof where the surgeon was dressing wounds. More persons were wounded here than anywhere else.

NARROW ESCAPES

I was standing at one time at the corner of the traverse, and stooped down to say a word to Major Andrews. At that instant a rifle shot from Fort Clark passed through the corner of the traverse where my head had been but a second before. It made a beautiful, clean round hole. It was while here, that a shell exploded on the traverse above me, and a fragment tore my coat from my left shoulder and penetrated the tail, tearing it badly. While lying on one side of this traverse, leaning on my elbow, very much at ease, a large fragment of shell, fell from the air on the platform at my side, when there had not been for some seconds an explosion. It came like an aerolite, seemingly without cause and very much surprised me. While here another shell struck a gun near by, glanced off, bounded over the parapet, exploded, and sent up an awful column of sand and water. While I was at one time in conversation with the officers in command, at the end of this traverse a bomb fell with tremendous noise and force near our feet and exploded. I fell round the end of the traverse and all the rest crouched in a huddle together. No one was harassed.

BOMBARDMENT AWFUL

For the last hour, the enemy seemed to have got our range exactly, and almost every shot and shell fired from their ships fell into and about the fort. We had long since ceased to fire, as we could not reach the enemy, and to man the guns was a useless exposure of the men. It became apparent that in an hour or two longer, every man must be either killed or wounded.

The Circle of Fire – Bombardment of Fort Hatteras[84]
From the Original Painting by Warren Sheppard

A COUNCIL

It was now near 11 o clock, and matters were growing momentarily worse. Commodore Baron called a council of all the staff officers and Captains, at the end of the parapet, I have so long been speaking about. He said "You see how it is. We cannot do the enemy any harm.

---

[84] Edward S. Ellis, A. M., *Library of American History,* Volume 4, The Jones Brothers Publishing Company, Cincinnati, Ohio, 1918, p. 44.

Our guns do not reach them. Our men are all exposed, and we cannot protect them. What shall be done?" We discussed the propriety of a retreat. All favored this, if it were practicable, in preference to a surrender. There was serious doubt of this. All the vessels were a mile or more from the shore, and we had no boats. They would be exposed to the enemys shells, if they should come in, and the men would suffer dreadfully in getting to them. Col. Martin and Com. Baron were both extremely reluctant to surrender.

In deference to their wishes, it was at first resolved to try to effect a retreat, and to spike the guns. Lieut. Johnson was ordered to make a signal from the top of the bomb-proof to the vessels and steamers in the sound to come in. He performed this duty, and reported that the signal had been answered by Capt. Muse. Lieut. Johnson was then ordered with such means as were at hand to spike the guns. He went to a gun on the east face of the fort (towards the woods) and began his work, and was then ordered to desist.

AN ALARM

Just at this stage of affairs, it was reported that the magazine was on fire. The men came pouring out of the bomb proof panic stricken. It was said that they had run over the wounded in getting out. I saw just here Wm. H. Harvey, one of my men picked up, dead as I supposed. It turned out otherwise as his left hip was only dislocated.

It was in this stage of affairs that the council resolved that it would be best to surrender. All were unanimous in this final, but reluctant conclusion.

Accordingly a white flag was ordered to be raised upon the parapet. Lieut. Johnson I think it was, got a piece of white canvas or sheet – a sort of streamer, and waved it on the parapet fronting the ocean. No notice was taken of it by the enemy.

The interior of Fort Hatteras after the bombardment, August 29, 1861. Drawn by H. Sartorious. *Pictorial War Record*, February 4, 1882.

THE WHITE FLAG

Some one then got a large Confederate flag, tore all but the white bar from it, attached this to a pole, and planted it on the bomb proof. Two shots only from the enemy were fired after this. Both fell I think into the fort. The firing ceased.

THE SURRENDER

The bomb-proof was not on fire, but a shell had penetrated through one of the ventilators and exploded, falling among the men below. The smoke caused them to suppose it was on fire. It fell between two of my men. None were injured.

A feeling of sadness prevailed every countenance after the firing had ceased. Col. Carraway (Corporal), Ordnance Officer of Martin County, raved like a mad man. He swore he wanted to die right there, and never surrender. Two of my men, Schenck and Hall, both Northerners, wept like children. Many would have run for the shore to escape, but I forbade them. E. B. Shaw and W. J. Pedrich did so.

As soon as the firing ceased, the land forces at Fort Clark, under Colonels Max Weber and Hawkins, both Germans, came over the beach with the "Star Spangled Banner," towards Fort Hatteras. They planted their two flags in the sand and formed about them, at the distance from the fort of several hundred yards.

General Butler in the steamer Fanny, carrying two rifle guns, ran into the inlet, and fired a gun at the Winslow. <u>This</u> <u>was</u> <u>an</u> <u>outrage</u>, <u>as it was taking an undue</u> advantage of a flag of truce. Had the negotiation failed, he could never have got out again.

THE SOUND FLEET

During the morning, the Colonel Hill had come down from Portsmouth before the firing began, but not in time I suppose to land more of my men, who were no doubt on board. After the surrender, she, with the Winslow and all the other steamers and vessels, made the best of their way up the sound. They were spectators of the entire bombardment, and a grand spectacle it must have been to them.

Col. Martin and Major Andrews, went out of the fort to the nearest flag of the enemy, to bear Commodore Baron's terms to them. It was a long time before an answer was received, as they had to be sent off to the flag ship to General Butler and Com. Stringham.

INTERRYNUM

In the meanwhile, the enemy sauntered about the beach, in some <u>order</u>, and our officers and men strolled about the fort, looking at the damage done in various quarters. A cut of this in one of the pictorials of New York is tolerably correct.

During this interval the Chaplain from Fort Monroe, C. W. Denison by name, was going all about the fort, notebook in hand, examining everything, asking questions of officers and men, picking up and begging relics, and talking very patriotically. There was a wounded man in one of the tents thought to be dying, (as he was) and for him this Chaplain offered up a prayer, a crowd around him. He told me that he was the special correspondent of the *New York Tribune*. The articles in that paper are no doubt from his pen. Like every man connected with the press North, he deals in falsehoods, knowing them to be such.

ANSWER

Finally Col Max. Weber, a tall, sharp featured, sallow Dutchman that could hardly talk English, came into the fort, went into the officers tent, and carried Genl. B. F. Butlers answer. It was a refusal to grant our terms.

Commodore Baron called a council of officers and submitted the matter. He drew a final proposal and submitted it. We discussed it. There was no alternative but to surrender unconditionally, <u>except</u> that we were to be treated as prisoners of war. The terms were to be arranged on the flag ship.

Commodore Baron, Col. Martin and Major Andrews were taken by one of the small steamers off to the Minnesota to arrange the particulars. They then surrendered their swords to Commodore Stringham and did not return to the shore.

GENERAL B. F. BUTLER

This worthy, with his blue coat and brass buttons – his lop-eyelids – and swaggering, fussy, waddling mien, came to receive the surrender of the fort, and to embark the prisoners.

The Adelaide and another large passenger steamer came into the inlet for this purpose, besides several of the tug boats.

I was introduced to General Butler at the door of the officers' tent. Forgetting myself, and indulging my usual politeness, I said, when shaking his hand "I am glad to see you sir." He said in a familiar manner – "That is not true, you are <u>not</u> glad to see me." Oh! No said I, slapping him on the shoulder, I forgot myself. I am not glad to see you. I beg your pardon.

MARCH OUT

Major Andrews (who had returned) ordered all the Captains to form their companies for the Generals inspection, and to stack arms. We formed on the parapet facing the inlet near the sally port. Formed in two ranks, and stacked arms. Companies formed in different parts of the fort. The enemy landed near a thousand of their forces, and formed from the sound side up to the sally port, on one side of the causeway.

The General (Butler) inspected my men, as also the rest. I offered him my sword. He refused to receive it, and told me to hang it on the muskets which I did. The other officers did the same.

Some one asked him if he were not going to march his men in before we marched out. His reply was "No. I will never take possession until the men who have made so gallant a defence have marched out." The only honorable sentiment I have heard attributed to him. I heard the remark.

My company was about the second that left the fort. We also formed in two ranks in the causeway from the sally port to the sound. The Fanny (gun boat) was at the landing to receive us on board and take us to the Adelaide anchored in the roadstead. Genl. B. superintended the embarkation himself – stood at the landing – fussing and giving orders like a Boatsman's Mate or Boss workman – totally destitute of all dignity or propriety.

EMBARKATION

It was an hour before we were all on board. While standing in line, I gave C. K. Gallagher my torn coat to carry home, and wrote a hasty note to my wife. He had been released by Genl. Butler, and they promised to set him across the Inlet. This they never did, but took him prisoner to Fortress Monroe.

As we embarked on the Fanny the German mercenaries marched in. They raised the Stars and Stripes in several places on the bomb-proof, and formed on the parapet from sally port to sally port, one dense mass. Cheer after cheer rent the air, and they fired a salute of thirteen guns, some of them as they had been shotted by ourselves.

I saw the <u>grape</u> scatter across the water from one on that face of the fort.

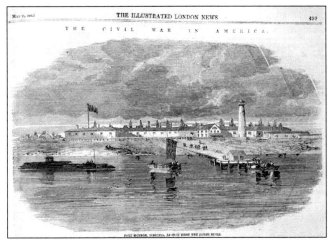

Fortress Monroe, Virginia as seen from the James River
The Illustrated London News, Vol. 38, No. 1090, May 25, 1861

THE ADELAIDE

This is one of the Norfolk and Baltimore Bay Streamers, a fine boat, and the one on which I traveled with my family on the way to Illinois. She was anchored about half a mile from the shore. The forces were taken on the gun-boat Fanny and taken off to her. I went in the first boat. The <u>men</u> were confined to the lower deck, and the officers and the wounded were assigned to the upper or berth saloon.

FOOD

Officers and men had been without food since early morning, and were very hungry, an unfortunate circumstance as no arrangements had been made to feed us on the Adelaide. Even <u>water </u>was scarce, and this we were greatly in need of. Servants were scarce, there being one <u>man</u> servant for the whole force. After an hour or two we had a tolerable supper, rather <u>scant</u>, and the men had to be content with a little hard bread. They were glad to get this.

GEN. B. F. BUTLER

This worthy busied himself chuckling and talking familiarly with the officers in the after saloon. His aim seemed to be to make himself free and easy with everybody, and to appear to be very clever.

THE WOUNDED

These were brought to the after part of the upper saloon, and arranged on beds as conveniently as possible with passage ways between them. There were fourteen or fifteen, some of them very badly wounded. Only one made much ado, most of them lying perfectly quiet. They were heroes.

SLEEPING

The state rooms were assigned to the officers, but it was a late hour before many of them could get to bed, the <u>one</u> servant having more than he could do. When I got hold of him there was not a room to be had. The servant however told me to follow him. I did so, through various apartments of the ship, and finally found myself in the <u>ladies</u> sleeping saloon, where the berths and sheets were very nice. An old Negro woman was there in her night clothes, and seemed quite astonished at our advent. She rubbed her eyes and shifted her quarters. Lt. Allen, Ordnance Officer, was with me. We were soon asleep, and had a good nights rest.

THOMAS SPARROW
Hatteras, N.C.
29 August, 1861[85]

---

[85] Thomas Sparrow Papers, #1878, Southern Historical Collection, The Wilson Library, University of North Carolina, Chapel Hill, North Carolina.

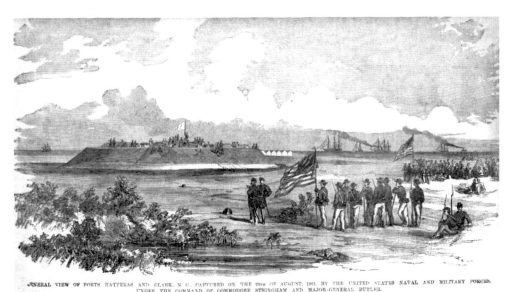

GENERAL VIEW OF FORTS HATTERAS AND CLARK, N. C., CAPTURED ON THE 29TH OF AUGUST, 1861, BY THE UNITED STATES NAVAL AND MILITARY FORCES, UNDER THE COMMAND OF COMMODORE STRINGHAM AND MAJOR-GENERAL BUTLER.

Surrender of Hatteras and Clark
Courtesy North Carolina Civil War Image Portfolio

Flag of the Washington Grays
Courtesy of North Carolina Museum of History

This flag was presented to the "Washington Grays" by Miss Clara B. Hoyt on behalf of the ladies of Washington before an estimated crowd of 2,500 enthusiastic citizens on May 20, 1861. Captain Thomas Sparrow received the flag and responded in his usually happy manner, and with all in a style which showed at once the Gentleman, the Christian, and one who will prove himself the able and efficient commander. The program was concluded with a prayer by the Rev. Edwin Geer.

After the capture of Hatteras on August 29, 1861, Major Sparrow returned this flag to his wife.[86]

---

[86] Glenn Dedmondt, *The Flags of Civil War North Carolina*, Pelican Publishing Company, Inc., Gretna, Louisiana, 2003, pp. 73,74,85.

U. States Flag Ship Minnesota[87]
Sunday
Sept. 1st 1861

My dear Annie,

Commodore Stringham has kindly notified us that he will forward from N. York via Norfolk any letters that may be written to our friends to be delivered unsealed. One of the officers of the ship, the first Engineer Loring, has also kindly conducted me to his state room & furnished me with materials for writing. And here let me say that we have received from the officer of this ship (one of the finest in the Navy) nothing but civility and kindness, since the hour that we came on board.

From the letter which I left for you at Ocracoke, which I hope you have received, you have been prepared for this result. I am sorry that the fortunes of war have kept you many days in suspense as to my fate. Say to our friends in Washington & the country, that not one of my Company has been killed nor seriously wounded. Seven received slight wounds, but no one of the seven is in the hands of the surgeon. All are well and in good spirits.

We are bound to New York, & are now only some sixty miles distant. I cannot now inform you where we will be confined, nor what will be our treatment. We are prisoners of war and will no doubt be humanly treated. I have no fears on this score, and wish you to feel no uneasiness. It is possible that I may be permitted to communicate with

---

[87] USS *Minnesota*, a sailing/steam frigate, was launched in 1855 at the Washington Navy Yard and commissioned eighteen months later. She was decommissioned some five years later, but at the outbreak of the Civil War, returned to service as the flagship of the North Atlantic Blockading Squadron. *Dictionary of American Naval Fighting Ships*, www.history.navy.mil/danfs/abbreviations.htm

our numerous relatives & friends in & about the city, sufficiently at all events to get an outfit. I brought but two shirts with me & only the clothes that I had on. I have however my overcoat & blanket, and these have been already a great comfort to me.

In the engagement at the fort, I met with some narrow escapes, (as my sack coat will testify), though I did not expose myself. The two guns assigned to me, could not be brought to bear on the fleet, & were not fired. <u>Both of them</u> were disabled, and had my men been required to remain at them, many of them must have been killed.

You must keep a stout heart, & a cheerful disposition, and look forward through these clouds of darkness to brighter days. George will be a dutiful son, & a father to the little ones. Nan and Jane will return home no doubt from New Bern and be a great comfort to you. Tell them that none of them shall ever have cause to be ashamed of their father.

We had service on board ship this morning, & the familiar old tunes & hymns, carried me home to our Circle of eight, and to the church where we worship. God bless you all & take care of you.

Your Husband & Friend,

T. Sparrow [88]

---

[88] Thomas Sparrow Papers, #1878, Southern Historical Collection, The Wilson Library, University of North Carolina, Chapel Hill, North Carolina.

U. S. Flag Ship Minnesota
Wednesday, Sept. 4, 1861

Dear Annie,

I wrote you a short note from Hatteras by C. K. Gallagher, who had been discharged, & sent some little mementoes. He has been taken a prisoner to Fortress Monroe & therefore you will not receive them.

We are to go this morning to Bedloe's Island, a pretty spot in this harbour, which you have seen a thousand times. I understand that our quarters there will be very comfortable. I have written to N. York this morning for an outfit, and shall in a short time be comfortable in that respect. I have seen none of your numerous relatives, & do not care to see them. Have seen & heard from other friends.

Be of good courage. Love to George & the girls & a kiss to little Johnny.

Your Friend,
T. Sparrow

Mrs. T. Sparrow
Washington, N.C.

Our treatment on this ship has been very kind & we feel that we are about to leave our friends.[89]

---

[89] Thomas Sparrow Papers, #1878, Southern Historical Collection, The Wilson Library, University of North Carolina, Chapel Hill, North Carolina.

Bedloe's Island
Courtesy of New York Public Library

Perhaps the best-known piece of sculpture in America, Bartholdi's huge female figure of Liberty Enlightening the World, commands the Upper Bay from the east end of the twelve-acre, egg-shaped Bedloe's Island. The statue is a gift of the French people to commemorate "the alliance of the two nations in achieving the independence of the United States of America, and attests their abiding friendship."[90]

---

[90] Lou Gody, Editor-in-Chief; Chester D. Harvey and James Reed, Editors; *New York City Guide*, Federal Writers' Project, Random House, New York, 1939, pp. 411-412.

New York

September 10th 1861

Thomas Sparrow

Dear Sir,

I learn you are a prisoner at Governor's Island. I have been trying to get a permit to visit you, but find I cannot succeed, we can have no communications with any of the prisoners except by letter. I congratulate you that you are in so safe a place. You are now free from all danger. If it were possible I want to write to your wife assuring her of your safe return to her. As far as the dangers of the war is concerned, how are you – do you want any help – if you do to a very moderate amount, these hard times I will assist you. Write to me. I have just sent some things to J R Potts & some to the Son of Jno. G. Williams which they have written for & which we charge to their Fathers. My wife & daughters all send their best respects to you. My wife says she would like to see you, to hear from you & know how much fun you think there is in war. I am pleased to think you are so well & so very safe.

Your Friend,

R. M. Blackwell[91]

No. 144 Front Street [92]

---

[91] R. M. Blackwell, son of Samuel Blackwell and Mary W. Field, brother of John Blackwell, married Eliza Paynter May 26, 1823. He was Annie Blackwell Sparrow's uncle and father of five daughters. Source: James Riker, *History of the Blackwell Family*, Annals of Newtown in Queens County, New York, pp. 117-160.

[92] Thomas Sparrow Papers, Collection No. 1, East Carolina Manuscript Collection, J. Y. Joyner Library, East Carolina University, Greenville, N.C.

Governors Island, Fort Columbus, New York
Courtesy of Governor's Island Community Profile

Governors Island, originally called Nutten Island, was ignored by the Dutch until Wouter van Twiller, second governor of New Netherland, purchased it in 1637 from two Indians for one or two ax heads, a few nails, and other trifles. In 1698 the New York Assembly set the land aside "for the benefit and accommodation of His Majesty's governors." This gave rise to its present name.[93]

---

[93] Lou Gody, Editor-in-Chief; Chester D. Harvey and James Reed, Editors; *New York City Guide,* Federal Writers' Project, Random House, New York, 1939, pp.414-415.

Fort Columbus

Sept. 11th 1861

Dear Sir

I am in receipt of your favour of the 10th. I came from Hatteras without a change of clothing but my wants have been supplied by the voluntary kindness of friends in your city. My family, whom I left well and cheerful four weeks since, are provided for in any emergency, & have no doubt before this time heard of my "safety." I wrote to them by Commodore Stringham who kindly offered to send our letters under a flag of truce from old Point Beaufort to Norfolk.

The sentiment which prompts your congratulations upon my personal <u>safety</u> can meet with no response in my bosom. My <u>wife & children</u> would scout such an idea. <u>Safe</u> as I am, they would prefer to see me where I would prefer to be, in another "Fort <u>Hatteras</u>" with guns that would reach, or on the tented battle field. I can make allowances for your rejoicing at my captivity, living as you do under the shadow of <u>Fort Lafayette</u>![94]

My very best regards to Mrs. Blackwell and the young ladies. She would like to know of me, how much fuss "there is in war." I would like to have permission to gratify her curiosity. We whose homes are invaded and desolated do not regard it as a very amusing matter. But I must forbear.

---

[94] Fort Lafayette in the harbor of New York is a quadrangular work, detached, standing on a shoal about an acre from the shore of Long Island, having guns on every face, a row in barbette, and three rows in casemate. With regard to the treatment of prisoners now in Fort Lafayette, in all respects the prisoners are well treated They are comfortably lodged as is consistent with safe keeping. They are fed by the Government at its own expense and with the best material that the market can afford. Source: *Harper's Weekly*, September 7, 1861.

Fort Lafayette in New York Harbor
Courtesy of Wikimedia Commons

Please say to Charles Blossum that the Wm. H. Harvey, whose name he saw in the papers, is a private in my Company from the Country near Washington, and not the man he thought it was.

Very Respectfully Yours,

T. Sparrow

Mr. R. M. Blackwell, 144 Front St., N. York[95]

New York

Sept. 16, 1861

Mr. Thomas Sparrow

Dear Sir

I have just returned with my family from the western part of this state, and learn that you are here a prisoner. It would be insincere for me to express sorrow for it, but I do feel great regret that we cannot have our usual agreeable personal intercourse.

[95] Thomas Sparrow Papers, Collection No. 1, East Carolina Manuscript Collection, J. Y. Joyner Library, East Carolina University, Greenville, N.C.

Joy W. Sparrow

Any service that I can be to you, any alleviation of the discomfort of your position, consistent with my obligations to my country (which I hold superior to the claims of friendship or kindred) would be a source of pleasure to me – will you please command me.

Yours truly,

James M. Blackwell [96], [97]

––––––––––

(Annie Sparrow's letter written to her husband)

September 21, 1861

My dear Husband,

We have received two letters from you. They were an unexpected pleasure and a great comfort, not only to us, but to the whole town and surrounding country. Annie and Jennie came home on Friday after Hatteras surrendered. On Saturday I took all the children and went out to Ben Tripps where we staid two weeks. It was much more quiet and I suffered much less than I would have done in town. We are all home again and all well. The children never enjoyed better health in their lives. Make yourself perfectly easy my dear husband on our account. God has raised up many kind friends for us. Our wants are all abundantly supplied. John McDonald has been home for a few days. He was well and in good spirits. Put your trust in your Heavenly Father my dear and whatever your fate may be he will never forsake you. Your numerous friends and relatives are all well and hopeful. As for me, God's precious promises are my comfort and consolation. Not

[96] James M Blackwell was the son of Samuel Blackwell and Mary W. Field and was the brother of John Blackwell. James married Jeannette D. Engs on February 18, 1844. He was Annie Blackwell Sparrow's uncle and the father of five children. Source: James Riker, *History of the Blackwell Family, Annals of Newtown in Queens County, New York*, pp. 117-180.

[97] Thomas Sparrow Papers, Collection No. 1, East Carolina Manuscript Collection, J. Y. Joyner Library, East Carolina University, Greenville, N.C.

only to those who love him and put their trust in him, but to their seed after them. God bless you.

Your Friend,

Annie Sparrow

P.S. I am well and in good spirits and so are all the friends. I am still staying at Mr. Telfair's store. Mr. Warren has got charge of your affairs. They could not be in better hands.

Your Obt. Son,

G. A. Sparrow

Give my love to all the Grays and tell Sam Schenk that I have got charge of his things. Tell him to write me.

I had dreamed for several nights of home, and of the friends in Illinois. On the morning of Saturday, I laid on my bed before rising, disturbed for the first and only time about the condition of my wife and children. This letter came as a kind messenger to dispel all fears, and remove all doubts.[98]

––––––––––

Fort Columbus

Governors Island

Sept. 25th, 1861

My dear Annie

I have written <u>two</u> short notes to you since my arrival at this place, but despairing of securing the conveyance of either, have suffered them to remain in my trunk. I find that Flags of Truce pass occasionally between Old Point & Norfolk, & that certain of the officers with me here receive answers to letters which they have written to their friends. I have concluded therefore to make a final effort to communicate with my "loved ones at home" and to cast it like "bread

––––––––––

[98] Thomas Sparrow Papers, #1878, Southern Historical Collection, The Wilson Library, University of North Carolina, Chapel Hill, North Carolina.

upon the waters"[99] hoping that it may reach you after many days.

My letter, committed to the care of Commodore Stringham, who was every inch a gentleman, you received no doubt. I then expected to be conveyed to Bedloe's Island, but we were all brought here instead thereof. There is, as you well know, no pleasanter nor prettier spot than this, & we are permitted on parole of honor to pass at pleasure over most of the Island. Our quarters are comfortable, and we have added to the usual army rations, such articles of food as were necessary to make our table quite equal to what we had at home. So you see there is no likelihood of your husband's starving.

I have had letters from many friends & visits from several. Among the latter, were two old college friends from Trenton, N. Jersey, & Rev. Mr. Wall from Philadelphia. We are allowed to receive letters, not anonymous, but not to see friends.

My wardrobe has been fully supplied by Messrs. W. & J. Bryce of N. York, except a few articles rec'd within a few days from your Uncle J. M. Blackwell. He writes me every day or two & is as usual exceedingly liberal in his offers. "Aunt Jenny" is to do some shopping for you & the girls, when I receive notice to leave, which I hope will be very soon. Write me a list of what you would like to have for yourself & for them.

My health has never been better. My cheerfulness you know I never lose. Among the officers captured at Hatteras are some very excellent & agreeable gentlemen, & to these have lately been added Col. Pegram & Capt. De Laguel, captured at Rich Mountain in Virginia. With Com. Baron, Col. Bradford, & such gentlemen as these, we have no lack of good society.

You need therefore give yourself no concern about your absent husband, unless it be to cherish the natural wish that he may shortly join

---

[99] Ecclesiastes 11:1 KJV Cast thy bread upon the waters: for thou shalt find it after many days.

his family circle. To George, Nan, Jane, Maggie, Lizzie, Caddie, & little John, their father's sincerest love and blessing. Let George & the girls write in your letter to me. Remember that all you write will be read several times before it reaches me, & remember also to write your names & not simply your initials. <u>My men are all well</u>. Let this be known to their friends. Write to me at this place, & send your letters under cover to <u>Genl. Huger</u>[100] at Norfolk, with a request to forward.

Yours, T. Sparrow[101]

General Benjamin Huger
Courtesy Library of Congress LC-B813-1978 A

---

[100] General Benjamin Huger (November 22, 1805 – December 7, 1877) was born in Charleston, SC and graduated from West Point in 1825. In 1861 he joined the Confederate army after the fall of Fort Sumter. He became Major General in September, 1861 and commanded the Department of Norfolk and evacuated it as Union forces approached. He commanded Huger's Division at Seven Pines, and Seven Days. Kerry Webb, The Civil War Circuit website, "U. S. Civil War Generals: Benjamin Huger." www.sunsite.utk.edu/civil-war/generals.html.

[101] Thomas Sparrow Papers, #1878, Southern Historical Collection, The Wilson Library, University of North Carolina, Chapel Hill, North Carolina.

Fort Columbus
Governor's Island
September 28th 1861

My dear Annie,

 I have written you three letters since my arrival here. Two I did not send, seeing no prospect of their reaching you. One, written two days since and sent in a bundle with others, I fear will miscarry. I have concluded by way of experiment to write a few lines & send them in a single envelope, hoping that under some flag of truce they may be taken from Old Point to Norfolk.

 We are in comfortable quarters here, & have the liberty on our parole of honor, of the larger part of the Island. To the usual army rations furnished by the U. S. Gov. we have added others purchased in the city so that we are in no danger of starving. I sleep on a straw bed, cover with a heavy blanket, & use my overcoat for a pillow. Good enough for a soldier.

 Mr. Wall came from Phila. to see me last week. I did not see him, but he wrote me a note. I had a letter from him yesterday giving me gratifying intelligence from you & the family. He also promised to send me books for my own use, & others for the men in The Castle.[102] We have no lack of reading matter, & are supplied with the N. York morning papers. Tell the children that I have purchased for them several of the pictorial newspapers, with illustrations, which I will take home for their amusement.

---

[102] Castle Williams, popularly known as "the cheese box" because of its circular shape, was begun in 1807 and completed in 1811 after the designs of Lieutenant-Colonel Jonathan Williams. Two hundred feet in diameter, with red sandstone walls, forty feet high and eight feet thick, it is casemated with arches for three tiers of guns. Today Castle Williams is the disciplinary barracks of the U. S. Army. Source: Lou Gody, Editor-in-Chief; Chester D. Harvey and James Reed, Editors; *New York City Guide,* Federal Writers' Project, Random House, New York, 1939, p.414.

Castle Williams
(Looking southwest from Staten Island Ferry)
Courtesy of Jim Henderson, author, September 19, 2008

You recallest the round brown stone fort at the water's edge on this Island. There the privates of our command are quartered. The third tier of casemates are comfortable rooms, & furnished with stoves. Two of these are occupied by my men. They are not confined to the interior of the fort, and are quite comfortable. Measles are prevalent among the prisoners. Eight or ten of my men have had them, but are now well, or getting well. None of the <u>town </u>boys have been sick.

I had not a complete change of apparel when I reached here, but friends in N. York have supplied all my wants in this way. I have a common trunk pretty well filled. Aunt Jenny offers to shop for you & the girls. Write me a list of what you want, & she will get them. "Uncle Mack" is very clever, & writes every day or two. Offers me his purse, or any thing that he has. I received a <u>stately</u> letter from your "Uncle Robert," congratulating me on my captivity & <u>personal safety</u>. I replied in such terms as I thought his want of decency deserved, & have not since heard from him. I have heard through your Uncle James from the folks in Illinois. They were concerned about me, & wrote to know how I fare.

When you, George, Nan or Jane shall write, remember that your letters will be read before they reach me. Direct to me at this place, & enclose to General Huger at Norfolk, Va. with request to forward.

Your Husband,

T. Sparrow [103]

---

[103] Thomas Sparrow Papers, #1878, Southern Historical Collection, The Wilson Library, University of North Carolina, Chapel Hill, North Carolina.

October 2nd, 1861

Rev. Thos. G. Wall,

Philadelphia

Dear Bro: Upon the suggestion made by you a day or two since, I yesterday requested our Executive Committee to make a grant of $15 worth of our publications to the prisoners of war recently taken at Hatteras, and now imprisoned in the fort in New York Harbour. The package will be forwarded by Express at the expense of the Board.

In forwarding the package, I presume you will write to the prisoners, or to some one of your acquaintances among them. If so, will you please to assure them that this grant was unanimously and most cordially voted by our Committee, and that we all earnestly hope that the books and tracts will be not only instrumental in helping to while away the dreary hours of solitude and imprisonment, but also in bringing to one and all of the prisoners that light and hope and joy which comes from Heaven through the agency of the Holy Spirit, by the instrumentality of the truth.

We would be glad to receive through you, from the prisoners, some acknowledgment of the safe receipt and acceptableness of the package.

Very fraternally, yours in the Gospel,
W. E. Schenck, Cor. Sec.[104]

---

[104] Thomas Sparrow Papers, Collection No. 1, Manuscript Collection, J. Y. Joyner Library, East Carolina University, Greenville, N.C.

Thomas Sparrow Diary
Tidings from Home

Received a letter from Nan today, without envelope, which I copy, purposing to send the original to Illinois, enclosed in a letter which I have just written to Emma.

Washington, N.C.
October 10th, 1861

My Dear Father,

We received with much pleasure your interesting letter written September 28th. Of course every one in town had to read it, so many had friends & relations in <u>The Washington Grays</u>. That is the only letter we have received from you since you left the ship.

I should like very much to see illustrations of the bombardment of Fort Hatteras, though I don't think we need anything that Aunt Jennie could get for us, as your purchases last winter will provide us with clothing for this.

I am glad Ma's relations have been kind to you, though they only did as you had a right to expect. I have no doubt that you felt very grateful to Uncle Robert for his <u>interest</u> in your personal safety.

Through the kindness of Miss Lizzie, I still continue to take music lessons, and it is as ever my greatest pleasure.

Mrs. Parmerler desires you to tell Lieut. Shaw & Mr. Latham to write to her the same way you write to us. When you write again father, please mention your Ensign, his friends are anxious about him, having received no letters.

Mr. Wood has gone away, but Mr. Potts conducts the service every Sunday.

I almost forgot to tell you Miss Lizzie says she wants me to begin to play on the organ in Sunday School soon, so you know how I am progressing.

Aunt Maggie & Caly are still in Raleigh, though we receive letters from them.

As it would take too much time and space to mention the names of all who send their love to you, I shall only say, that all the family join me in much love to yourself. And now dear father good bye.

Affectionately your child,

Annie Sparrow[105]

—————————

New York

October 18, 1861

Capt. Thomas Sparrow

Dear Sir

By the kind permission of Col. Loomis, I herewith send some smoking tobacco & segars for yourself and companions, which please accept and oblige.

Yours Resp'y

G. Potter, Jr.

181 Front St.[106]

---

[105] Thomas Sparrow Papers, #1878, Southern Historical Collection, The Wilson Library, University of North Carolina, Chapel Hill, North Carolina.

[106] Thomas Sparrow Papers, Collection No. 1, East Carolina Manuscript Collection, J. Y. Joyner Library, East Carolina University, Greenville, N.C.

New York

October 18th 1861

Captain Thos. Sparrow

N.C. "Washington Greys"

Dear Captain:

Although I have not a personal acquaintance with you, I have made bold to send you a little box which I have made up containing some articles that I supposed might be serviceable. I should be very much in doubt as to the propriety of doing so under the circumstances, if it were not that, though unacquainted, a mutual friend, Mr. Demill,[107] encourages me to hope that you will accept what I send and thus afford me one of the most heartfelt pleasures of my life. Will you please deliver to Private S. Schenck what I have marked for him and the letter which I enclose herewith. Such of the other articles as you do not care to retain for your own or your officers' use please distribute among the men of your command in your best discretion and oblige.

Respectfully and Sincerely Yours,

A Friend

P. S. I am sorry to learn through your letters to Mr. D. that several of the North Carolina soldiers (twelve?) have died. I wish it were in my

---

[107] In the early 1800s Thomas A. Demill from New York settled in Washington, North Carolina and went into the general merchandise business. He was one of the founders of St. Peter's Episcopal Church. He is the father of William Demill who married Margaret Blount Hoyt. William and Margaret were the parents of Henry Churchill Demill who in turn became the father of the Hollywood "Great" Cecil Demill, famous movie producer of King of Kings and The Ten Commandments. Henry Demill was also the father of William Demill who was an established playwright with several solid hits and who was the father of Agnes Demill, a famous choreographer. Source: Ursula Loy and Pauline Worthy, *Washington and the Pamlico*, Washington-Beaufort County Bicentennial Commission, Edwards & Broughton Co., Raleigh, North Carolina, 1976, pp. 298, 441-443.

power to do much more than my very limited means allow for the survivors of them. Please acknowledge receipt of this letter and of the accompanying articles (of which a list is hereto subjoined) in some of your letters to Mr. Demill who is a particular friend of the writer and will forward me your letter.

The Madeira wine and the currant Jelly please distribute or cause to be distributed among your sick. I trust that Col. Loomis will not object to your receiving them when he knows they are for sick men who (as I suppose), are in actual urgent need of such articles. The jelly is home-made and I think I may venture to recommend it as being good. I believe it is often prepared for the use of the sick by dissolving in a tumbler of water and thus making a drink of it.

<u>List of articles in the Box sent with this letter.</u>

12 Pair white canton flannel drawers

6 Red flannel shirts

1 Coat

5 Vests

1 Pair of pants

1 Overcoat

1 Pair grey woolen knitted socks

36 Packs playing cards (for Whistle)

1 Piece old castile soap (for the teeth)

24 Pieces soap (for washing purposes)

6 Bottles Madeira wine (for the sick)

1 Stone pot currant jelly

2 Dozen combs

1 Dozen hair brushes

1 Colored cotton shirt

3 Colored cotton collars

1 Doz. Tooth brushes

2 Pair of boots

Some tobacco

(chewing & smoking – 8 or10 lbs. I <u>believe</u> in all)

2 Pair of men's shoes (fm. Mr. Demille)

<u>Books and Pamphlets (22 in number)</u>

Lectures on Dramatic Art and Literature (bound)

The Shakespeare Novels (unbound):

The Youth of Shakespeare

Shakespeare and his friends

The Secret Passion

Dickens Christmas Stories (unbound)

Sharp's Letters and Essays (bound)

Rewick's Chemistry (bound)

Russel's Ancient and Modern Egypt (bound)

One Bible (bound)

One Book of Common Prayer (bound)

The Second Adam and the New Birth (unbound)

Tract on the Sacraments (unbound)

The Christian Week (unbound)

Letters to a man bewildered among many Counselors (unbound)

Why I am a Churchman (unbound)

Day's Algebra (bound)

Merry's Book of Puzzles (unbound)

Greenleaf's Arithmetic (bound)

First Lesson in Perspective (bound)

Philip Augustus   Novel

Dombey & Daughters (unbound)

Sketches by "Boz" (unbound)[108]

---

[108] Thomas Sparrow Papers, Collection No. 1, East Carolina Manuscript Collection, J. Y. Joyner Library, East Carolina University, Greenville, N.C.

Capt. Thos. Sparrow

N.C. "Washington Grays"

Dear Captain:

I am very much pleased to learn today, through your letter to Mr. Demill, that all the articles contained on my list were received by you on Saturday and that "they are all acceptable." I only wish their quantity might have been more commensurate with the number of your men and that all the articles of wearing apparel were entirely new. There was one little parcel I remember putting into the box which I see has been omitted in my list by an oversight. It contained a few needles, some thread of different colors, tape, pins, etc. Such things are I suppose quite often in the hands of those men who are, like you and your men at present, separated from "home" and "its dear ones," whose gentle hands were wont in happier times to do their "mending" for them. I trust that the leading men on both sides will yield to the divine promptings which every living man I believe feels within him more or less strongly and frequently and will strip this war of as many of its hardships and cruelties as possible, by exchange of prisoners and in every other practicable way. I do not mean to imply that I think I see some prospect of an early exchange, for I know nothing whatever about it, one way or the other. I only hope so for the sake of the prisoners so far separated from their homes and families and cut off from all communication with them in considerable numbers on both sides. It would seem to me that an equal exchange in such cases as the present would be an act of humanity in no sense degrading or damaging to either side. With best wishes for the health and happiness of yourself and men, both in time and in Eternity, I remain,

Sincerely yours,

A Friend

P.S. I hope there will be no additions to your number (16) buried on Governor's Island. How many are now considered dangerously sick?[109]

———————

Fort Columbus

October 29th 1861

Capt. Sparrow has not language suitably to express to "his friends the Misses Kendell," his sincere thankfulness for the timely & welcome offering of an excellent comforter & pillow. This purpose to procure such necessaries would have been defeated by the unexpected order to pack up for Boston, but for the thoughtfulness of his new friends on the Island. For this act of kindness, the Misses K. will be held in lasting remembrance by Capt. S. and all his.

Most Sincerely

T. Sparrow

The

Misses Kendall

Gov's. Island[110]

[109] Thomas Sparrow Papers, Collection No. 1, East Carolina Manuscript Collection, J. Y. Joyner Library, East Carolina University, Greenville, N.C.
[110] Thomas Sparrow Papers, Collection No. 1, East Carolina Manuscript Collection, J. Y. Joyner Library, East Carolina University, Greenville, N.C.

Departure

At about five O clock P.M. we left the wharf. The ladies there, & on all visible parts of the Island waived their handkerchiefs to us as long as we were in sight. We responded with all our hearts. God bless the women. They are always on the side of the oppressed, the wronged & the captive! God bless the women! They are the best of Gods creatures in this world of darkness & of sorrow. They are our best companions & comforters next to that Friend "who sticketh closer than a brother."[111] In all my hours of sorrow, I find Him to be my best comforter & friend. If I know my heart, my love to Him is supreme & I look to Him with confidence to take care of my family, and to bring me out of all my troubles.[112]

————————

John Slidell and James Murray Mason, both former U. S. Senators, were appointed commissioners to the courts of London and Paris by the Confederate government – this done in hopes of cultivating the good will of England and France. They sailed from Charleston to Havana with their families and secretaries Messrs. Eastin and MacFarland, November 7, 1861 in the British mail steamer *Trent*. Captain Charles Wilkes (formerly commander of the scientific and exploring expedition around the world in 1838 – 42), of the *San Jacinto*, inter-

---

[111] Proverbs 18:24 KJV

[112] Thomas Sparrow Papers, #1878, Southern Historical Collection, The Wilson Library, University of North Carolina, Chapel Hill, North Carolina.

cepted the *Trent* and forced Messrs. Slidell, Mason and MacFarland to board his ship.[113]

When they arrived prisoners in the United States, President Davis had just inaugurated his retaliation for the mistreatment of the captive privateersmen. In a mingled flush of anger and joy, the House of Representatives at Washington passed resolutions to hold these diplomats as counter–hostages (Congressional Globe, December 2, 1861). But the ardor of the United States Government was very soon brought under control by the unequivocal demands of the outraged British Ministry, and no executive action was taken on the resolutions.[114]

––––––––––

Thomas Sparrow Diary
November 24th 1861 Sunday

Changes

While we were yet dressing this morning Col. Dimick sent for Col. Martin to notify him that he desired us to vacate our rooms for Ministers Slidell & Mason, & their Secretaries Eustis & McFarlen who had arrived during the night in The San Jacinto.

---

[113] Edward S. Ellis, A.M., *Library of American History*, Volume 4, The Jones Brothers Publishing Company, Cincinnati, Ohio, 1918, pp. 52-55.
[114] William Morrison Robinson, Jr., *The Confederate Privateers*, Yale University Press, New Haven, Connecticut, 1928, pp. 252-253.

Thomas Sparrow Diary
November 14th, 1861 Thursday

Autographs are the order of the day. Many of the officers have bought books, and some of the Marylanders are even getting the signatures of the men.[115]

Thomas Sparrow Diary
November 27, 1861 Wednesday

Written for Capt. John Lamb's Book of Autographs
Dear Lamb,

You have asked me to fill this page. What can I better say than to advise that you and I & our fellow prisoners cultivate patience and cheerfulness in our captivity. If to die for one's country be sweet, surely to suffer exile & imprisonment for it should not chafe us. Let us not therefore follow the example of the captive Israelites, who wept by the rivers of Babylon, & hanged their harps upon the willows in the midst thereof. Let us be stout of heart, take down our harps & tune them to the songs of our own bright South, cherishing the while the beautiful Jewish sentiment, "If I forget thee, let my right hand forget her cunning."[116] And if kind Providence shall spare us to a good old age, "shielding our heads in the day of battle,"[117] as we shall "totter down the hill John," you will take your little Lambkins on the knee, as I shall take my little Sparrow birds on mine, and we will tell to them "the story of our life

---

[115] Thomas Sparrow Papers, #1878, Southern Historical Collection, The Wilson Library, University of North Carolina, Chapel Hill, North Carolina.
[116] Psalm 137:5 KJV
[117] Psalm 140:7 KJV

From year to year, the battles, sieges,

Fortunes that have passed.

 Of most disastrous chances

Of moving accidents by flood & field,

Of hair-breath 'scapes; the imminent deadly breach,

Of being taken by the insolent foe,

And held in bondage, of our redemption thence.

 Let us in the further progress of this war of independence aim to deserve well of our country & then in after life these days of Captivity will recur to us like the memory of <u>joys</u> that are departed, pleasant tho' mournful to the soul."

Your friend

T. Sparrow

To Capt. John C. Lamb
Defender of Fort Clark.[118]

---

[118] Thomas Sparrow Papers, #1878, Southern Historical Collection, The Wilson Library, University of North Carolina, Chapel Hill, North Carolina.

Fort Warren, Boston Harbor, Massachusetts[119]
Courtesy of Wikipedia

Fort Warren Boston Harbour

Thursday Nov. 28th 1861

My dear Annie,

Dr. Pool of the Hertford Light Infantry leaves for N. Carolina tomorrow, & Col. Dimick[120] has kindly consented to allow us to write short letters by him to our wives & Mothers. I drop every thing to seize the opportunity. I have written to you as often as possible, but fear that half my letters have reached you. I have had but one letter from you, one each from George, Nan & Kate Carraway. Today I had a nice letter from Mary, & I am glad to learn that you and the children are well. You must be patient & cheerful, & I trust before long to join you at <u>home</u>. I need not say how anxious I am to see you all. Nan's letter I sent to Illinois. Just after the receipt of Mary's today, Mr. Langston,

---

[119] Main entrance of Fort Warren about 1861 – granite guard house on left and a wooden sentry box on the right. This Civil War fort was used as a prison for Confederate military and political prisoners. Source: Jay Schmidt, Fort Warren: New England's Most Historic Civil War Site, Amherst, New Hampshire, Unified Business Technologies Press, 2003.
[120] Col. Dimick was commander of the prison at Fort Warren, Boston Harbor, Boston, Massachusetts.

one of the political prisoners, brought me a long one from Sally. Two days since I received one from Sarah Waters. These two last I shall ask Col. D's permission to enclose in this. Sarah & Ed are keeping house near your father's, & <u>she</u> has become quite reconciled to Illinois. She sends much love to her Aunt Sally Ann, to Caroline, Brady & others. Your father & mother are well & so are all the rest. They think & talk much of you all, & your mother worries about the war & her children who are South.

My respects & love to Mr. Potts. John is well & received a letter from him a few days since. Wm. Patrick has a long letter from his sister last week. It was a great comfort to him as he was sick at the time. He is now quite well, & reads most of the time. Grimes is in the Hospital, but is not much sick. Will be out in a day or two. I left John Blount in the Hospital at Governor's Island, but had a letter from Dr. Sloan the surgeon two days ago, saying that he was up, & quite well. I have had no serious case of sickness. This is fortunate when so many have been sick, & twenty five have died. The deaths have been mostly among the men from the Roanoke & Albemarle Counties – half of all of them from Martin County. The boys have plenty of clothing & good quarters, & books to read, and are comfortable in all respects. My respects to Mr. Williams. Sam is the life of the Company, has not been sick a day, & has received his trunk. I see much of Howard Wiswall. He is an excellent young man, & I esteem him very highly. Thos. Bobbins, Thos. Latham, Schenk, Hall, Richardson, Lieuts. Shaw, Whitehurst, & Thomas all well & cheerful. So are Baynes, Little, T. Gray Latham, and all other members of the Company. I would mention all, but have not space. Let the people at home know that Mr. T. A. Demille of N. York supplied the wants of my Company, and sent vegetables & delicacies for all the men. As for myself I received letters from Baltimore, Philadelphia, N. York & other places, from friends who offered to do any thing for me within their power. I have wanted for nothing. I am remaining here with Col. Martin, Major Andrews & others, & occupy a very fine suit of rooms. Tell Nan that I am getting for her the autographs in a very pretty book, of all the most prominent of the prisoners here. It will contain some distinguished names: Mason, Slidell, Faulkner, Gov. Morehead, Commodore Barron & others. Love to George & all the girls & little Johnny. He has forgotten his father I fear. Love to Mary, Sister Ann, Jenny, Caddie & all friends. I have written so much that I fear it will not be allowed to go. God bless you & take care of you.

> Your Husband & Friend
> T. Sparrow

Mrs. Thomas Sparrow
Washington, N. Carolina
Expect to be exchanged soon.[121]

Thomas Sparrow Diary
December 3rd 1861 Tuesday

A Good Sell

Capt. Johnson informed us last night, that he would be permitted today, to introduce a lady to our acquaintance, holding out the idea by innuendo that it was to be a friend of his from Boston. It was a leading topic of conversation last night but he refused to tell any one who the lady was to be. This morning Lassell & Poole were up by times cleaning up & putting the room in order. The windows – mantle – books – table - & every thing was put in nice order. Lamb, Allen, Poole, & others washed & shaved up after breakfast, dressed in full uniform

---

[121] Thomas Sparrow Papers, #1878, Southern Historical Collection, The Wilson Library, University of North Carolina, Chapel Hill, North Carolina.

& sat down to await the arrival of the lady. When Capt. Johnson & I left Mr. Mason's room we went to Lieut. Whitehursts room & he borrowed a book called "The Lady in White." Going to our own room, he knocked at the door & when admitted held out the back of a book in which was the picture of a "lady in white," & introduced her as his expected friend. The scene that followed may better be imagined than described. Suffice it to say, the disappointed young men soon doffed their new clothes. Mr. Warfield was in the room at the time & almost died with laughter.

—————————

Fort Warren, Boston Harbour
Sunday, Dec. 8th 1861

My dear Annie,

Two hundred & fifty of our men & some of the officers are to go home, on parole, until exchanged.[122] Among the privates are twelve of my Company, John Potts & Thos. Latham of the number. The list is made up of the married men, & the men & officers who have been sick & all are in feeble health. As my officers & myself we are all in excellent health. None of us go, and as so few of the Company have been sick, a small proportion only of them are to go. It will not be many weeks before all will follow. I had promised my boys a Christmas dinner in Washington, but this promise I shall hardly be able to fulfill, though some will be there to enjoy a dinner with their friends on that

—————————

[122] At the start of the Civil War a formal exchange for prisoners of war was not arranged because President Lincoln did not recognize the Confederacy as having wartime rights. However, after the defeat of Union forces at the 1st Battle of Bull Run, with a large number of Union prisoners held by the Confederacy, the U.S. Congress requested that Lincoln take measures to effect an exchange. On July 22, 1862 a formal Prisoner Exchange System was agreed to by the two governments. *Civil War Records, "Prisoner Exchange System." www.civilwar.bluegrass.net December 30, 2010.*

day. Col. Martin & Major Andrews go out of my room, & I shall take Lieut. Whitehurst & Whitehead in their places. Had I been offered the choice of going home, I would not have gone & left my men here. Much depends on keeping them in good heart, & were I to leave them, they would soon become disheartened. Earnestly, therefore as I long to be at liberty & to see my wife and children, dearer to me now than they have ever been, I would not forsake my men to see them.

We have an old school Presbyterian Preacher here from Charleston (near Harper's Ferry) Virginia, who preaches for us every Sabbath. He was taken at Boliver Heights,[123] while attending the wounded. His name is N. G. North. He is much beloved & does good among us. The prisoners & garrisons all attend his preaching. I am just from church, & brought with me Thomas Latham, to see my rooms. They are three in number, (two opening into a third) with a closet. They are handsomely finished: our closet is never without crackers, cheese, bologna, sausages – fruit cake – plain cake – coffee – tea – loaf sugar – whiskey & wines – the gift of ladies & other friends in N. York. We have received two boxes of cake even from Boston. So we are not allowed to suffer for the want of good things. We have two meals a day in the eating room – one at 9 o'clock, & another at five. We receive rations & add to them other things, so that we live very nice.

---

[123] Bolivar Heights Battlefield known as the Battle of Harpers Ferry was fought September 12–15, 1862, as part of the Maryland Campaign of the Civil War. Principal Commanders: Col. Dixon S. Miles (US); Major General Thomas J. Jackson (CS). Learning that the garrison at Harpers Ferry had not retreated after his incursion into Maryland, Lee decided to surround the force and capture it. On September 15 after Confederate artillery was placed on the heights overlooking the town, Union commander Col. Miles surrendered the garrison of more than 12,000. Jackson took possession of Harpers Ferry, then led most of his soldiers to join with Lee at Sharpsburg. After paroling the prisoners at Harpers Ferry, A. P. Hill's division arrived in time to save Lee's army from near-defeat at Sharpsburg. National Park Service, U.S. Department of the Interior, National Historical Park, CWSAC Battle Summaries., www.nps.gov/faqs.htm.

We have near a thousand prisoners here, many of them among the ablest & best ever of our Confederate States. I know them all, & some of them know quite intimately. We have a little world of our own here. Col. Dimick who has charge of the post, is a kind Christian gentleman & every body respects him. We make the most of our unfortunate condition and long for the day when we shall be set free. Our independence is <u>certain</u> and will be speedily acknowledged. Rely on this. Our people however have nothing to hope for from the <u>spirit</u> of the North. It is thoroughly united & hostel. They will not leave an effort untried to <u>crush</u> us, but their rotten Government will break down before Spring. They will not be able, with all their boasts, to get funds to carry on the war, & keep their sinking ship afloat.

Dr. Poole went home a week since & I wrote you by him. By Willie Clark of Greenville I wrote & sent some coins for the little children & a book to you. By Mr. Hoskins, a preacher, I sent a little pocket Testament with gilt edge to Maggie. I sent some rings made by the men, & some other trinkets for you & the children. You must divide them as you think best. I sent some little pincushions by Dr. Brown of Greenville who has no doubt been to see you before now. I hear quite often from Arcola & will take the letters home with me. Sarah Waters has written me a long letter for her friends in Washington. She is very comfortable & quite contented with the prairie, but very anxious to see her old friends in Washington, especially Mrs. Tayloe. I would send these letters but fear to trust them to other hands. I will be sure to take them myself. I have a pretty book of autographs for the girls & some books for Nan & George. I have an abundance of good clothes & plenty of blankets. I wrote out at Fort Columbus a narrative of what I saw of the bombardment & capture, & have kept a dairy ever since. Both of these I will try to take home with me. I received kind letters from Kate Carraway & Sister Mary, & would have answered them but could write but once a month & then six lines. These I thought I should devote exclusively to you. I hope to see you all before long. My love to them, & to Jenny, Sally Ann, Elisa Ellison, Lib Tayloe & all my friends. To Sister & Jenny & Boberdean, you can learn all that you may wish to know of me from the boys, who will go to see you. I shall take for you some needles & the like. This letter is to go by Thomas Latham. I learn that they are not to get off before Tuesday or Wednesday. If so I will write by John Potts. God bless you my wife. Love to George, the girls & little ones. Kiss them all for their father.

Your Husband T. Sparrow [124]

Fort Warren, Boston Harbour
Dec. 11th 1861

Dear Annie,

We have a rainy day & are all within doors. I wrote you on Sunday, supposing that the boys would get off at least by Monday. There is some doubt now whether they go this week, as there is some difficulty about getting transportation. The Lincoln Congress have passed a resolution favouring an exchange, & it will not be long before all of us are at home. I will write again if they should not come tomorrow. I received a letter from Sallie yesterday & send you this & three other letters from Arcola. The one from Sarah Waters you will take to Mrs. Tayloe as it is written mostly for her & friends. I send by John Potts, Thos. Latham, Powell, Hawkins, others of the boys, the following books for you & the children, together with a small looking glass,

---

[124] Thomas Sparrow Papers, #1878, Southern Historical Collection, The Wilson Library, University of North Carolina, Chapel Hill, North Carolina.

some rings made for me by the boys, two puzzles, all of which you will distribute to suit yourself. The books were sent by Mr. Wall, and are "House on the Moor," "Castle Richmond," "Sketches by Boz," Atlantic Monthly, Two numbers of Harper, one small Bible for Maggy, & Newtons Letters. The last are a present from Rev. N. G. North who is a prisoner here. I have not read it but have no doubt you will find it excellent. I have written to N. York for shoes for all of you. I knew your number & Nans & Janes, but the rest will have to be guessed at. I have no doubt that shoes are scarce & high at home. I shall carry you an assortment of needles, cotton, silk, soaps, & the like of which I have procured from time to time. Mr. Demill & Thos. Telfair send me these things. I have also an ounce or two of quinine, which I shall endeavor to carry home. I wish I had the means of writing to sisters Ann & Mary, Kate, E. Ellison & other friends. You must give my love to all and tell them I am obliged to them for all kindness to you, & their letters to me. George I doubt not is a good boy. I hope he will stick to the Sunday School & church, & to fall into no bad habits. I have requested our Adg. General to pay you $110 per month which with care will support you. I would have ordered the whole $130 to be paid to you, but have contracted bills for clothing here which I wish to pay. Mr. Wall has been very kind & bought me in Philadelphia a full uniform suit, including shoes & cap. I have rec'vd. letters & acts of kindness from all directions. Mr. Gilbert Potter of N. York went to see me at Gov's. Island, but was not allowed to converse with me. B. Bateman, Ms. Abbott's brother was with him. He sent me a fine cane, which is a pipe. I shall take it to George. Langue, Annie Whitemore's husband, sent me a comfort, blanket & pillow & the Misses Kindall on Gov's. Island sent me a pillow & comfort. Uncle Mack has been urgent in his kindness & writes to me very often. I requested you in one of my letters to send the enlistment for the war to Raleigh, so that if I were to remain a prisoner longer than April, <u>my pay</u> would go on. If not sent, give Henry Respass' to his Mother Mrs. Latchwell.

Love to all,

Your Husband, T. S.[125]

Thomas Sparrow Diary

December 11th 1861 Wednesday

Raining to day and all hands confined to quarters.

Spent much time in Moore & Grimes & in Com. Barrons room. Capt. DeLaguel is up & bright. I rejoice at it, for I love him as a brother.

There was boisterous shouting & singing at the men's quarters night before last & Col. Dimick had then all drawn up yesterday morning to talk to them. This he did kindly as he does all things. At breakfast to day the men gave me an account of it. They were singing Dixie in the dining hall, much to the annoyance of the sentinels near there. They sung also the following lines.

"We Carolina Boys went down to Hatteras,

And didn't care a d___ if they did shoot at us.

The Indiana Boys went down to Hatteras,

And slept upon the sand without any mattress."

This infuriated them & the soldiers of the garrison raised a hurrah for Lincoln, whereupon our boys rallied out of quarters and raised a loud shout for Jeff Davis. I talked with the Col. about it & he seemed much amused at the incident.

---

[125] Thomas Sparrow Papers, #1878, Southern Historical Collection, The Wilson Library, University of North Carolina, Chapel Hill, North Carolina.

Thomas Sparrow Diary

December 17th 1861 Tuesday

The most exciting day we have had in the fort. Prisoners of all grades are wild with joy & look & act as if <u>they</u> were Masters of the fort. England demands Mason & Slidell & an apology, or threatened war! "Blessed be the Lord, who teacheth my hands to war, & my fingers to fight."[126]

The two hundred & fifty left. I parted gladly with the boys from Washington but yet with some emotion. All got off at 2 O clock & the fine Bark Island City cast off her lines & was towed out of the bay.

I cannot describe my parting with Col. Martin. It was outside the Sally Port, near the Guard House, in sight of the wharf. He embraced me, & was able to speak – I could not utter a word, but choked with emotion. He is a charming man & I love him as I do an own brother. His last words were, "Sparrow my dear friend pray for me."

Col. Dimick allowed all the remaining privates from Hatteras to go upon the Southern Ramparts to see their comrades sail. They gave cheer after cheer, which were responded heartily from the decks of the Bark. Most of the officers & many of the political prisoners were on the ramparts cheering with them. Mr. Mason was among the number. He has been exceedingly cheerful during the day.

The Bark moved slowly forward down the bay, all sails set, while the weather was bright & charming. Our good wishes & our prayers went with them. At the same time the English Steamer Europa, with the bearer of dispatches to Lord Lyons, steamed majestically by the fort & up to Boston.[127]

---

[126] Psalm 144:1 KJV.
[127] Thomas Sparrow Papers, #1878, Southern Historical Collection, The Wilson Library, University of North Carolina, Chapel Hill, North Carolina.

Europa of 1848
(One of the earliest known photographs of an Atlantic Steamship)
Wikipedia Creative Commons: RMS Europa

Thomas Sparrow Diary

December 19th 1861 Thursday

Wrote a long letter to Elisa Harvey, Illinois, & enclosed to her Nan's last letter. I copy here extracts therefrom.

Nan's Letter Dec. 2nd, 61 "Aunt Maggy and Caly think of coming over this winter. I hope they will, for it will contribute much to our spending a cheerful and happy Christmas; but there will always be a vacancy in our circle, which can be filled by no one but yourself, my father. I sit by the fire these cold nights and hope you and the prisoners are warm & comfortable. I know that God will bless all who are kind to you and them. I always think that when I am thinking of you, you are thinking of us all at home. . . . Liz talks a great deal about her old dad, & Cad wishes he would come home mighty bad."[128]

---

[128] Thomas Sparrow Papers, #1878, Southern Historical Collection, The Wilson Library, University of North Carolina, Chapel Hill, North Carolina.

Barque, June 1859
Courtesy of Wikimedia Commons

On board Barque[129] Island City

Off Fort Monroe

December 22nd 1861

Dear Sparrow and all my old roommates –

I rejoice to be able to give you the gratifying intelligence that we have all arrived here safely after our sea voyage. Our sick have much improved and contrary to my expectation we have not buried any body in the great deep. We made the run in exactly 5 days, the most of which was spent in getting clear of Cape Cod and its surroundings, but after we once shook off Massachusetts our noble Barque shot off like an arrow from the bow and rolled off nearly 300 miles in 28 hours. We should have been in last night but could not get the pilots out, though we were off the Cape at 3 o'clock p.m. yesterday ready to come in. Of course the pilots got no blessings from us, particularly as they also detained us about three hours today so that the flag of truce boat did not have time to go up to Cranez Island & back before night. We go in the

---

[129] A barque also bark. A sailing ship with from three to five masts, all of them square-rigged except the aftermost mast which is fore-and-aft rigged. *The American Heritage College Dictionary,* Third Edition, Houghton Mifflin Company, Boston, New York, 1993.

morning at 10 o'clock, so say the officers here and Genl. Wool[130] has not taken a look at our rags and will not have them examined tomorrow, which will expedite matters and save a great deal of useless work to his officers.

General John E. Wool
Courtesy Library of Congress LC-USZ62-18161

Mr. Casey has been unremitting in his attention to the prisoners and added yet more to the obligation they are under to him, and although very sick himself, he has always <u>promptly</u> <u>crawled</u> out to aid the sick and help them as much as possible. Such a sick crowd in the cabin perhaps never was seen. I was sick incessantly for two days but crawled about eating & giving it up, repeating the operation time after time until I got hold of a <u>cod-fish</u> which stuck. When codfish became popular and Cahoons had one under his head, Shannon on the shelf near and Tyler not only on his bed & shelf, but his pockets full of the article, you never saw the like. Johnston suddenly became enamored

---

[130] General John E. Wool (February 29, 1784 – November 10, 1869). When the Civil War began, Wool at age 77 was the oldest general on either side of the war. He was widely considered one of the most capable officers in the army and a superb organizer. In the early days of the war, Wool's quick and decisive moves secured Fort Monroe, Virginia for the Union. Source: Ezra J. Warner, *Generals in Blue: Lives of the Union Commanders*, Louisiana State University Press, Baton Rouge, Louisiana, 1964.

of the salt cod. The effect was surprising. Poor Martin was sick all the time up to the last day when he resorted to cod also and improved immediately. Today we had our first real state dinner two turkeys, game & champagne. There have been many funny things, but I cannot tell them now. Here we are safe under the guns of the Minnesota in the midst of what Old Purbis calls the "Bulk heading squadron" which he declares he will "knock all to smash if they don't get out of the way and let us go up to Dixie."

He says "the d____d blockheaded squadron had better keep out of his way for he expects to be a Commodore yet and he'll give them h___l if they trifle with him." The boys are on deck tonight singing some very fine songs which sound delightfully. They have not struck "Dixie" yet though the ** & - line the shore all round south of us. I suppose their respect for the Sabbath restrains them. Martin declares he had rather have stayed at Fort Warren 2 months longer than have taken the trip. For myself I confess I would have done and endured a great deal more. We have talked about you, across the cabin "as rolling on restless pillows" sick and sore we came, we have tried to think what you were doing and saying and how you were located since we left, and our hearts still fondly turn to you and send our yearning hopes for your speedy deliverance. Lt. Casey says he will deliver our notes. I wrote he could also give expression to our well wishes and earnest desires for your safe return home. You must consider them sent herewith. Tell Sutton I have heard from Ben and he has got home safe - With love to all, and assurances that I will do all I can for you. I am truly your devoted friend.

Lt. S. G. Andrews [131]

---

[131] Thomas Sparrow Papers, Collection No. 1, East Carolina Manuscript Collection, J. Y. Joyner Library, East Carolina University, Greenville, N.C.

Fort Warren, Boston Harbour
Tuesday, Dec. 31ˢᵗ 1861

The last day of the old year – an eventful year – the most eventful of the century. The great American Republic has been divided, and a nation has been born in a day. A great Southern Republic, destined I believe under God, to be <u>one</u> of the purest & best Governments of the earth – free from the vices & corruptions of the old.

How little do we know what a day may bring forth? How little twelve months ago, with my happy family in Illinois, did I imagine that on this day, I should be a prisoner of war, in one of the strongest forts of the U. States? Yet so it is. All events are in the hands of Providence, & he disposes them to suit his wise designs. I am fully convinced that God's hand is in all this war, and that great good to His church & the nations of the earth is to be the result. I am as firmly convinced that these troubles among the nations, are to precede the downfall of Romanism & Mohamedism, & usher in the dawn of the Millennium.

My captivity has brought me nearer to God my Saviour, and I find Him to be my best friend in every adversity and in every trouble. As the years pass away & I grow older, my prayer is that I may grow better & wiser, & that God will enable me to provide for my family & to rear my children in his fear. Last night & the night before I dreamed of seeing my beloved Annie, dearer to me than all the earth beside. My thoughts have been much turned on home, yet I wait on God to restore me to my home in His own good time.

I have been much to the hospital today. Jacob Woollard is very ill and I fear will nor survive. Oliver and Turner are also very sick.

I am to go into my old room up stairs when Messrs. Mason and Slidell depart. This is settled.

Spent an hour in Capt. Johnson's room this P.M. in conversation with Mr. Harrison – the wise & excellent – for he deserves the name. He gave me an account of their political clubs – & a dissertation on Tariffs.

Col. Dimicks band arrived this afternoon, so we shall have musick.

I close the year with a prayer for the prosperity of my country, the success of her arms, & the happiness of my family.[132]

––––––––––

Captain Sparrow and the remainder of his Company were paroled and exchanged at Fort Monroe, Virginia about February 3rd, 1862.[133] After their return the Company was reorganized and sent to the Cape Fear where they assisted in building the forts on that river, being for some time at Fort French. A short time later, Captain Sparrow was promoted to Major (January, 1863) of the 10th Regiment of Artillery, and for some time, had charge of the city garrison at Wilmington, remaining there during the yellow fever epidemic.[134]

––––––––––

Tarboro
July 20th, 1862

Dear Annie,

You will be surprised to hear from me at this place. I am summoned to Wilmington on a General Court Martial, presided over by Col. Levinthorp, which will last some weeks. Most of the members

[132] Thomas Sparrow Papers, #1878, Southern Historical Collection, The Wilson Library, University of North Carolina, Chapel Hill, North Carolina.
[133] Dr. Louis H. Manarin, Compiler, *North Carolina Troops 1861 – 1865 A Roster, Volume 1 Artillery,* State Division of Archives and History, Raleigh, North Carolina, p. 158.
[134] Annie Blackwell Sparrow (Mrs. R. H. Lewis), *Recollections of the Civil War,* Thomas Sparrow Papers, Collection No. 1, East Carolina Manuscript Collection, J. Y. Joyner Library, East Carolina University, Greenville, N.C.

board in the town. I go each night to my Battery, returning next day. In the intervals of the session each member is at liberty to go where he sees fit, & after the adjournment yesterday I found most of the members were going off on the railroad. I thought it would be a good time to visit Nan, & so came here last night. I dined with her at Mr. Owen's today, & after dinner took her to Mr. Hank's where she now is. I am writing in Capt. G. H. Brown's office, on the same lot. Sally Ann Carraway sent for me a short time since & I took her also to Mr. H's where I left her & came here to write. Nan looks very well, and is growing quite fleshy. She is very anxious to see you & the children, & I am hesitating as to the propriety of sending her home to Washington. Her vacation commences next Thursday week (the 1st of August) and George's about the same time. Mr. & Mrs. Hanks wish Nan to stay with them & she will go there on a visit until I can determine what to do with her. I have some thought of sending both George & her to Morganton to their Aunt Mary's. The objection is to the cost. Then I think of sending Nan to see you, trusting to the chances of getting her out again. She is much attached to Mr. & Mrs. Owen, & I wish her to continue at school.

I am at a loss to know what to do with George, unless I take him to my camp & into my tent with me. He is very much dissatisfied at Hillsboro & says he cannot study. I have received his report, & will send it to you when I get back to camp. I wrote him a permit the other day to visit his aunt at Graham. I think I will order him to go to my camp at Wilmington after the close of his school until I can make further arrangements for him. It will cost less to support him there.

Mr. Selby has sold your quinine for $35, but has not sold the Buttons. I can sell them at Wilmington for $5 per Doz. & I think even more than this. I shall take them there, sell them & send him the money & he is to procure for you <u>State</u> Notes. He can send them he says at almost any time. I will sell the balance there also & add this to the amount. I have not lately drawn any pay, but shall do so the first of the month, & will send you the larger part of it. Write me what you get to eat & how you fair. Also how the children are off for shoes. I will try to send you some. Did you get the box of sugar? It was sent from Greenville. I can continue to send you almost any thing you want. Love to Sister. Tell her to write me what she wants. Don't under any circumstance, part with your gold, nor the <u>Brandy</u>. The latter had better be bottled. How is your garden? I hope you have a good one. Every thing is high at Wilmington & I live very plainly in Camp. I shall try to buy some butter, eggs, & vegetables here.

We have lately taken Murfreesborough, Tennessee near Nashville, & shall soon have the State. Jackson is again in the Valley after Pope[135] this time, & we shall soon have Washington & Baltimore unless McLellan leaves the James River. We have whipped the whole Yankee fleet at Vicksburgh & run them down the river. The Yankees tremble in their shoes & soon their game will be over. The prospects of the Southern Confederacy were never so bright as at this time.

I long to see you & the little ones & Maggy and Jenny. My love to them all. I have my new uniform, trimmed with red, & it cost just $100. I had to buy Buttons, not getting those sent Nan in time.

Love to Sister & Cad. Farewell. Write as often as you can.

Your Husband,

T. Sparrow

I have written in great haste.[136]

---

[135] Union General John Pope, born Louisville, KY, March 16, 1822. Source: Thomas, Dean S., *Civil War Commanders*, Thomas Publications, Gettysburg, PA, 1988., p 54.
[136] Thomas Sparrow Papers, Collection No. 1, East Carolina Manuscript Collection, J. Y. Joyner Library, East Carolina University, Greenville, N.C.

Uniform of Major Thomas Sparrow
Courtesy of North Carolina Museum of History

Wilmington, NC
July 26th, 1862

My dear Annie,

    I saw Mr. Proctor to night at Daniel Reid's room just from below. He tells me that he can probably send a letter to you next week & I therefore hasten to write you a few lines though it is quite late. I wrote you from Tarboro on Sunday by Mr. Van Nortwich & suppose you have received the letter. I enclose with this a late letter from Nan & one from George. Also some scraps from the papers which I suppose you will find interesting. We have met with a procession of glorious achievements in Tennessee & Kentucky & one even in Indiana. We have run the Yankees entirely out of the State of Arkansas. The foreign press is at last <u>unanimous</u> in our favour, & so are all the nations of Europe. The Despots and Vandals also pollute our soil & desecrate our homes. Many will tremble in their shoes. A day of reckoning is near at hand for the scoundrels in Beaufort County who have joined the enemy or given him aid & comfort. They will have to leave the country or grace a limb with their worthless carcasses.

I received today your welcome letter of the 9th telling me of the receipt of the sugar, & the excellent health of all the children & the splendid appearance of our boy. Since I have been living in town away from the duties of the camp, you have been in my dreams at night & my thoughts by day. I long most earnestly to see you all, & to be with you at <u>home</u> in peace once more. My sincerest love to Sister & Jennie & all the children. Tell John his Pa wants to see him in jacket & trousers very much.

On coming from Tarboro I found that the General commanding the department of N. Carolina had appointed me Judge Advocate of the General Court Martial[137] sitting here. It imposes on me immense labor, & taxes all my exertions. We have tried more than a dozen cases, & have yet <u>eighteen</u> or twenty to try. I am living with Capt. Andrews, in the Methodist Parsonage, a fine large house, keeping house together, he and I. I have invitations to several other places. Van Aswinges – Jas. Willards – Capt. Muses & elsewhere.

My Company is now quite large, & I have a splendid Battery below here, made so by myself mostly.

I have sold the six doz. Buttons for $30 & the balance for $15 & send the amt. $45 to B. M. Selby who will send it to you in N. Carolina

---

[137] Judge Advocate: an officer acting as prosecutor at a court-martial. *The American Heritage College Dictionary*, Third Edition, Houghton Mifflin Company, Boston, New York, 1993. .

money. I do not add to this any money of my own, supposing that you wish to make perhaps a different use of this. I shall draw funds soon, & send you most of that, in bills you can make use of. Let Sister have what she may require. I am quite largely indebted to her. Tell her that Elisha is working in the Blacksmith shop in Newbern, so James Howard informed me this afternoon. He is here working on Gunboats.

I must close. Write as often as you can, & may your God & my God, watch over & protect you.

Your Husband,
T. Sparrow [138]

---

[138] Thomas Sparrow Papers, Collection No. 1, East Carolina Manuscript Collection, J. Y. Joyner Library, East Carolina University, Greenville, N.C.

Made when he was inau-
gurated as Governor, 1862.
Z. B. Vance, 1862

Governor Zebulon Baird Vance
37th Governor 9/08/1862 – 5/29/1865
43rd Governor 1/01/1877 – 2/05/1879
Courtesy of the North Carolina Office of Archives and History
Raleigh, North Carolina

Always a man of the people, in war and in peace, Zebulon Baird Vance is probably North Carolina's best known and most beloved governor. A mountain man, born May 13, 1830 in Buncombe County, Vance's unexcelled gift of wit and stump-speaking oratory, forever endeared him with the people.

His earliest political connection was with the Whig Party and when war was eminent, he urged that North Carolina call a convention to demonstrate that the State did not want secession. Vance remained firm against secession until President Lincoln called for troops to coerce the seceded states. With war inevitable, he quickly reversed his position. Organizing the "Rough and Ready Guards" in May, 1861, he was commissioned captain and shortly joined the 14th Regiment under W. D. Pender. Brief as his military career was, he saw much action, at Hatteras, at New Bern, and in the Seven Days Battle before Richmond. In 1862, however, the old-time Whigs and former Unionists nominated and overwhelmingly elected Vance as governor.[139]

---

[139] Beth G. Crabtree, *North Carolina Governors 1585-1975*, North Carolina Division of Archives and History, 1974. p. 95.

Defences of Cape Fear
Major Thomas Sparrow
Wilmington, October 5th 1863

Head Quarters
Defence of Wilmington
October 5th 1863

Special Orders
No. 29S

Major Sparrow is released from duty for the present with the line. He is assigned as Special inspector of the Ordnance & Munitions of the different forts, batteries and defences.

Major Sparrow will examine each gun and magazine, commencing with the defences of the harbors – see that they traverse well – and report defects. Whether the magazines are in proper condition, the ammunition ready, in good order, the supply such as is needed, the crew of the guns instructed in their duties. To this and all commanding officers of forts or batteries will on the requisition of Major Sparrow afford him every facility in their power.

Major Sparrow will make his report direct to the commanding General and as often as circumstances will admit.

He will commence the duty named above with Fort Caswell and from thence will continue by Smithville to Fisher and thence up the river.

By command of
Major Genl. Whiting
Maj. & A.A. Genl. James H. Hill[140]

---

[140] Duties included Fort Anderson, Fort Campbell, Fort Caswell, Fort Davis, Fort Fisher, Fort Hatteras, Fort Lee, Fort Pender. Thomas Sparrow Papers, #1878, Southern Historical Collection, The Wilson Library, University of North Carolina, Chapel Hill, North Carolina.

Chapter 4

Hillsborough Military Academy

Captain Sparrow enrolled George in Hillsborough Military Academy in May, 1861, much to the chagrin of George. From a carefree country lifestyle, he was thrust into a military environment where following rules and regulations were demanded. There was constant worry about his Mother and family.

Hillsborough Military Academy
Cadets in Formation
Courtesy of North Carolina Collection,
University of North Carolina at Chapel Hill Library

Hillsborough Military Academy
Cadets at Barracks
Courtesy of North Carolina Collection,
University of North Carolina at Chapel Hill Library

Hillsborough Military Academy was founded by Colonel Charles Courtney Tew who was born in Charleston, South Carolina October 17th, 1827. Col. Tew entered the Citadel, Charleston, South Carolina March 20th, 1846 forming one of the original number of twenty cadets composing the nucleus of the Academy. He graduated with First Honors in 1846 and was called at once to serve his Alma Mater in the branch of the Academy at Columbia, South Carolina. As an officer of the Arsenal he gave valuable assistance in putting that School upon a course of prosperity. After spending a year in Europe, he returned and was appointed to the Citadel Academy where he served as superintendent from 1857-59.[141]

---

[141] John Payre Thomas, The History of the South Carolina Military Academy, Walker, Evans & Cogswell Co., Publishers, Charleston, South Carolina, 1893, pp. 130-131.

Cadet Charles Tew while attending The Citadel
Courtesy of The Citadel Archives and Museum
Charleston, South Carolina, Charles Courtney Tew Collection

As the 1850's drew to a close, Tew dreamed of establishing a military college of his own – a school that would become North Carolina's own prestigious version of the Citadel. He put his dream into action, establishing the North Carolina Military Academy – soon to be known as the Hillsborough Military Academy.

Tew started construction in 1858 for his North Carolina Academy while still at the Citadel and moved to Hillsborough with his wife Elizabeth Faust Tradewell and their children.

The commandant's house was built in March 1859 and on August 14, 1859 Freemasons from Hillsboro's Eagle Lodge laid the cornerstone for the barracks. Three stories tall and 217 feet long, it was immediately the most impressive structure in the region. A rambling 190-foot long wooden structure housing an infirmary, surgeon's office, mess hall and kitchens were constructed behind the barracks.

When Tew's Academy opened in January, 1860 a United States flag flew peacefully from the barracks tower.[142]

Colonel Charles Courtney Tew
Courtesy of North Carolina Division of Archives and History

Hillsboro Military A.

May 24, 1861

Dear Father

You will see by my letter that I have arrived at the end of my journey safe and sound, but I cannot say that I am much pleased with the prospect. You know you told me when I left that this would be the case, but it is not that that makes me think as I do. I do not think the school is what it is represented to be, we have only about thirty boys and small ones. I think the charges are to high also. I sent you a circular of the school so that you can tell all about the charges yourself. I did not get a

---

[142] Robert E. Ireland, *Civil War Times,* *"The Tar Heel Citadel,"* May, 2001, p. 41.

chance to deliver those letters to Dr. Jones and Mr. Norwood but shall do so tomorrow, that being Saturday. When I left home I forgot to ask you one question that is how long do you want me to stay? One session or one year embracing two sessions? I meet some few of my acquantences here but the most of the boys are small and poor companions at the best. I have not much time so "good bye" and "write soon" to

> Your affectionate Son
> Geo. A Sparrow

P.S. When you write please tell me all about Washington and the Yankees.

Envelope addressed to Captain Thomas Sparrow

HILLSBOROUGH, N. C.

Military Academy,

You may send me a few postage
stamps as they are hard to get
here, that is if convenient.

Hillsborough
May 29 1861

Dear Father,

I received a letter from you this morning and seeing it postmarked
"Wilmington" could not imagine who it was from until I saw your well
known and familiar handwriting. I was very much surprised expecting to hear from you below Greenville. How do you like the change? I
have written to you several times since I left you but I think it doubtful wether you have received any of them or not as you said nothing
about them in your letter. I am very glad to see that "Annie" is getting
along so well at school and that she is so much beloved and I hope that
she may not out rival me in her good conduct and I am determined to
do all in my power to get along well with every body though that is
almost an impossibility in a military school as the boys are compelled
to report one and another for the most trivial things. You did not tell
me in your letter wether the company was with you or not? Are they? I
should like to know. I hope you did not have to quit that, if not I think
the boys would like it. When I first came here I took your advice and
formed no acquaintances but what I thought were of the right stamp.

There are one or two boys here from <u>Tarboro</u> who are very nice, gentelmanly fellows. Battle and Powell are their names. Then there is Mr. Clark's son from Greenville. Since comtemplating things I have fully awaked to the responsibility that is resting upon me as an "oldest son" and you may rest assured "Dear Father" that I will try all in my power to fill that station which as you say is a very important one indeed. Such a large family and no one to depend on but you and in the war at that. I could not read your letter today without shedding tears. No one can appreciate a parent until they are separated from them and to be separated from family and friends under such circumstances as these are would melt a heart of stone. I am very glad indeed that you feel "proud" of me and may God grant that you may never have cause to feel otherwise is the earnest prayer of your son.

George A. Sparrow

P.S. I am very much obliged to you for your kind offer for anything that I may want but I am happy to say I want <u>nothing</u>. Write soon and tell me all the news especially from the vicinity of Washington and home.

————————

When Superintendent Tew left for an Army assignment in May, 1861, the Academy closed down so George returned home to Washington and helped his family.

Washington N.C.

June 5, 1861

Dear Father

We received your very welcome letter together with the Basket this morning for which we are very much obliged. The children were very much tickled with the eggs that you sent them, and liked the candy that you sent them on account of it coming from Captain Sparrow. I am very glad to find that you are so popular among your men. In fact Captain Sparrows name is on every ones lips as a model officer. This war, if it should last, will memorialize your name at least around this section of Country. I am very busy now all the time and scarcely find time to write a letter. There is no one here but Mr. Telfair and myself now. I do most of the writing now. We are all well and in good spirits at home.

Give my love to Mr. Schenk and Mr. Ellison, and tell them to write to me and anything they want that I can get for them I will do so willingly. You also might tell them to write to Mother.

Your Obedient Son,

George A. Sparrow

————————

Washington N.C.

July 26, 1861

"Dear Father"

Mother received a letter from you yesterday by Mr. Myers and the box of mullets that you sent, she made the desired disposition of them. They were very nice and we are all very much obliged both for the fish and the letter. I suppose it is not worth while to write you a long letter as Annie and Jennie can tell you all the news. I shall try and send you all the Papers from the commencing to the ending of the Battle at "Manassas"[143] but every one is so much excited and so anxious about the News that I think it doubtful whether I can or not. I suppose you have heard that there has been a big fight but none of the minute particulars. You can form no idea of what a terrific Battle it was they say. It excels the Battle of Waterloo in respect to fury. They fought like dogs on both sides.

Battle of Manassas
Courtesy Armchair General and History

---

[143] The Battle of First Manassas July 18-21, 1861 also known as the Battle of First Bull Run was the first major land battle of the armies in Virginia. This battle claimed the lives of approximately 4,700 soldiers. After a 4-day battle, the introduction of Confederate reinforcements forced a retreat of Union troops back to Henry Hill. This battle convinced the Lincoln administration that the war would be a long and costly affair. McDowell was relieved of command of the Union army and replaced by Major General George B. McClellan who set about reorganizing and training the troops. Source: National Park Service, U.S. Department of the Interior, National Historical Park, CWSAC Battle Summaries. www.nps.gov/faqs.htm.

General John Daniel Imboden
Courtesy Ware Family Genealogy, December 6, 2010

Capt. Imboden [144] told me he saw one of the soldiers who was in the fight who came home in charge of Col. Fisher's body (from this state) who was killed in the fight. He says that when the command was given to charge that celebrated "<u>Sherman's Battery</u>" that the men in order to get to it had to climb over dead bodies breast-high and when our men got close enough he saw they dropped their muskets and went at them with "Bowie" Knifes. Some of them killed the men at their guns with the exception of a few, and he says that the whole road along toward Alexandria was strewed with dead bodies. While I am writing the New Berne stage has arrived and brings the News

[144] John Daniel Imboden (February 16, 1823 – August 15, 1895) was a lawyer, teacher and Virginia state legislator. During the Civil War he received a commission of captain in the Staunton Artillery of the Virginia State Militia, commanded the unit during the capture of Harpers Ferry, was commander of an artillery battery at the First Battle of Bull Run (Manassas) and promoted to Colonel of the 62nd Virginia Mounted Infantry. He fought with Major General Stonewall Jackson in the Valley Campaign and was promoted to Brigadier General in 1863. Trevor N. Dupuy, Curt Johnson, and David L. Bongard, The Harper Encyclopedia of Military Biography, Harper Collins, New York, 1992.

Joy W. Sparrow

that the <u>Proud Flag of the Confederate States</u> is waving over Alexandria. I dont know wether it is so or not. <u>God</u> grant that it may be is my earnest <u>Prayer.</u> This Battle and glorious Victory at Manassas has raised and inspired the whole South and in less than two weeks every man woman and child in the Confederate States will be <u>under</u> Arms. President Davis[145] in his late message[146] has called for a corresponding number of men which is 500,000 men. Half a million, Well! All I can say is he will get them and as many more if he wants them. As for money he doesnt say anything about that except that he has got as much as he wants and furthermore he says that every Southern man is willing to take Treasury Notes for every cent he owes in the world,

---

[145] Jefferson Davis (6/3/1808-12/6/1889), son-in-law of President Zachary Taylor, was born in Todd County, Kentucky, graduated from the United States Military Academy, West Point, New York in 1828. He served in the Black Hawk War in 1832, was elected as a Democrat to the 29th Congress; commanded the First Regiment of Mississippi Riflemen in the war with Mexico; was appointed to the U.S Senate to fill the vacancy caused by the death of Jesse Speight and was subsequently elected in 1847 and served until 1851 when he resigned. Davis was elected to the Senate again in 1857 and served until January, 1861. On February 18, 1861 he was chosen President of the Confederacy by the Provisional Congress and elected for a term of six years. He was captured by Union troops in Irwinsville, Georgia, May 10, 1865 and imprisoned in Fort Monroe. Library of Congress, *Biography: Jefferson Davis, (1808-1889).*

[146] Jefferson Davis' Telegram to Samuel Cooper after First Manassas. Received at Richmond July 21, 1861. "Night has closed upon a hard fought field – Our forces have won a glorious victory. The Enemy was routed & fled precipitately abandoning a very large amount of arms munitions Knapsacks and Baggige – The Ground was strewn for miles with those killed & the farm houses and Grounds around were filled with his wounded - The Pursuit was continued along several routes towards Leesburg & Centerville until darkness covered the fugitives - We have captured several field Batteries & Regimental Standards & one U.S. Flag . Many prisoners have been taken - Too high praise cannot be bestowed whether for the skill of the principal officers or for the Gallantry of all the Troops …" Source *Transcribed from the National Archives, RG109, Documents in the Official Records, Series 1, Volume 2, p. 987.*

on the whole it is an able document.

Your Obedient Son
George A. Sparrow

Jefferson Davis
Courtesy of Library of Congress LC-B8172-2021

Washington N.C.
July 26 1861
4 P. M.

Dear Father

Since writing to you this morning I have learned some important news which for fear you will not hear I will write. I am very glad to inform you that the regiment of Zouaves is formerly commanded by Col. Ellsworth[147] and numbering some 1200 men now numbers "200" all total quite a decrease. It is said that in the retreat of the

---

[147] Elmer Ephraim Ellsworth was a colonel of Chicago's National Guard Cadets and introduced his men to the Zouave uniforms which French colonial troops wore. President Lincoln nicknamed him "the greatest little man I ever met." On May 24, 1861, the day after Virginia seceded, President Lincoln observed from the White House a large Confederate flag prominently displayed in the neighboring town of Alexandria, Virginia. Ellsworth offered to retrieve the flag for Lincoln and was killed with a shotgun blast to his chest after cutting it down Source: Wikipedia: Ruth Painter Randall, *Colonel Elmer Ellsworth: A Biography of Lincoln's Friend and First Hero of the Civil War*, Boston: Little Brown, 1960.

Federal Army that they were overtaken by a Body of Texas Rangers and literally cut to pieces. In a letter from the President which I saw this morning he estimates our loss in killed at 500 and 1500 wounded "No Prisoners" and that of the Enemy is estimated at from <u>seven</u> to <u>eight thousand</u> killed and wounded and an immense number of Prisoners besides which the Confederate captured "<u>sixty one</u>" pieces of artillery among which is Sherman's Battery, 20,000 stand of "<u>Arms</u>" all their wagons and bags. And as the President said in his speech enough Provisions to last 50,000 men some time. General Scotts[148] <u>carriage</u> and <u>horses</u> together with his sword which was presented to him by the Seivells of Virginia was captured. A great many of the U. S. Senators were out in Arlington Heights and vicinity near the Battlefield to witness the defeat of the Rebels and for that occasion was prepared a Sumptous Banquet in a house near the Battle and on the retreat of their men and the pursuit of ours came very near being captured. Three of them were captured besides a great many Baskets of champagne with all the sumptuous Dinner. "<u>Poor Fellows!</u>" I wonder if they didn't get hungry before they got <u>home</u>.

Your Obedient Son
Geo. A. Sparrow

---

[148] General Winfield Scott was known as "Old Fuss and Feathers" for his equal love of discipline and pomp. Scott by 1861 had served in the military for more than fifty years and under fourteen U.S. presidents. He was the last Whig Party candidate for U.S. president and was commanding general of the United States Army at the beginning of the Civil War; a native of Dinwiddie County, Virginia, he remained loyal to the Union. Source: Peter Carmichael, Senior Editor, Eberly Professor of Civil War Studies, West Virginia University, *Encyclopedia Virginia*, Virginia Foundation of the Humanities, Charlottesville, Virginia.

Annie Blackwell Sparrow, George's Mother

George, age 15, felt he was shirking his duty staying at home while so many of his age were going off to fight for their country. With a burdened heart his mother yielded a reluctant consent to his urgent entreaties, and gave the last she had to the holy cause. Annie recalls: "I shall never forget the day my brother left with his battery for Fort Fisher. They marched through town, flags flying, men bright and brave and wild with enthusiasm. My brother was sitting on one of the guns, looking so young and so ignorant of all he was afterward to undergo. We watched them from our porch, proud of the brave and willing spirit that sent them to do their duty, but with tear-dimmed eyes for the vacant places by the firesides, and the uncertainty of their coming back to fill them."[149]

George enlisted in "Kennedy's Artillery" on September 23, 1861 in Beaufort County and was mustered into Confederate States service at Washington, October 14, 1861, for twelve months as "Captain Charles P. Jones Company Light Artillery N.C. Volunteers for local defense and Special Service in the county of Beaufort and counties adjacent thereto."[150]

——————————

In Camp
April 22nd 1862

Dear Mother

Captain Reid is here and leaves this morning sometime for Washington and thinking it a good chance to write I will write you a short letter. I should have written you a long one yesterday but I felt so badly that I could not write that being the day in which we were to elect our

---

[149] Annie Blackwell Sparrow (Mrs. R. H. Lewis), *Recollections of the Civil War,* Thomas Sparrow Papers, Collection No. 1, East Carolina Manuscript Collection, J. Y. Joyner Library, East Carolina University, Greenville, N.C.
[150] Dr. Louis H. Manarin, Compiler, *North Carolina Troops 1861-1865 A Roster, Volume 1 Artillery,* State Division of Archives and History, Raleigh, North Carolina, 1988, p. 272.

new officers. Capt. Ives and Lieut. Rumly both declined being elected and now they are going to leave. I cannot stand it any longer to be under men whom I do not consider my <u>equals </u>let alone my <u>superiors </u>is to me very <u>humiliating</u> and I am determined in my purpose to get out of it if I can. I think that Father can assist me in it if he will. The only way that I can get out of it now is by getting some position above the one I now hold, for by the late act of Congress I am held in it <u>nine</u> <u>months</u> longer anyhow, and if I had to stay in this company that much longer I should be miserable in the extreme. I <u>loved</u> Capt. Ives and so did all his men. Tell Mrs. Blount that Jimmie says send him his <u>fiddle </u>by Capt. Reid and look on his other one and get the strings and put on the one she sends. If you get a chance you can send me a couple of calico shirts. I do not want anything else unless you can buy me some stationery. I will save all my money and bring it home when I come and give it to you. Mother you must not feel badly because I have written you such a <u>doleful</u> letter. I am well and fat weighing a <u>hundred</u> and <u>forty-five</u> pounds. Capt. is about to leave so Good bye. Write soon to

Your Soldier boy

<u>Georgie</u>

Army of Pamlico

At camp near Kinston

April 22, 1862

————————

Captain Sparrow was exchanged from prison in February, 1862. It must have been decided that it was in the best interest for George to return to Hillsborough Military Academy which had reopened in May, 1862 with Major William M. Gordon[151] as Superintendent. He

---

[151] Major William Milburn Gordon (9/6/1830 – 2/14/1907) was born in Warrenton, Virginia, an 1852 graduate of Virginia Military Institute (VMI). He was married to Georgia King and had eight children. Source: VMI Archives and Records Management, Virginia Military Institute, Lexington, Virginia.

Joy W. Sparrow

remained there until November, 1862. During this session George saw many of his friends go to war and many were killed on the battlefields. Washington, N.C. was captured by the Yankees. At first Superintendent Gordon was very tough on the Cadets but loosened up as the session went on. The Cadets did have a little fun with the Nash School girls and George enjoyed his visits with Uncle Henry and wife[152] in Graham.

Receipt for Clothing Deposit
Signed by Major William Gordon

"During his time at Hillsborough Military Academy, George ran away twice to join his father (at Wilmington), having been sent back both times by his father. On the third 'running away' to join his father, George was permitted to stay and was given the job of carrying water to the soldiers."[153]

---

[152] The wife of George's Uncle Henry was Martha Clark. Source: Sparrow Family Records.
[153] As quoted in letter dated February 25, 1968 from Elizabeth Sparrow Watkins to Joy Sparrow.

Dear Father

I have written you once or twice before this week, but to day being Sunday I thought it was a good opportunity to write home, or to you at least for a "<u>home</u>" is a thing that I cannot claim now, it is only when I think of this that I feel dissatisfied. I think to be in my countrys service and near you is <u>preferable </u>to any thing on earth, but then I can put up with anything knowing that it is your <u>wish</u>. I want to say to you that to succeed in getting any of my things out of the hands of the Yankees do not send them to me as I requested you, for we are only allowed to wear clothes furnished us which are 2 Brown Linen jackets, 4 pair B. L. pants, 2 white jackets, 2 pair white pants, shoes and cap, a great uniform aint it though. I suppose anything else cannot be had these times. I went to <u>church</u> this morning for the first time in a long while and heard a regular war sermon by the Methodist Minister. We have 3 churches here in operation now and I shall hereafter go to my own church exclusively. Father I have one request to make of you and that is should Mother and the children succeed in getting out of Washington you will send for me to come home and see them. They are all the time in my mind. I can not think of any one else and lately it seems as if I have an evil foreboding that some thing was going to happen to them though I hope it is false. When you write to Annie in Tarboro tell her she must write to me very often as I have no doubt you will be so busy that you cannot do so yourself and I shall always be anxious to hear from "down below" as they say. I should like to stay here until the end of this session 31st of July and then get the place of Drillmaster in the Army. Most all the old cadets have that place and rank a Lieutenant, and any one who stays here "two months" and tends to his business will be well qualified for that office. We have the strictest sort of discipline. You can write to me and tell me what you think of this plan and what you intend doing. Give my love to "all" the Grays and any of my friends that you may see and write immediately to

Your Affectionate Son

Geo. A. Sparrow

Direct Cadet Geo. A. Sparrow

Hillsborough Military A

Hillsborough N Carolina

Major Gordon Is Superintendent

Hillsborough

Sunday, June 1 1862

Dear Father

I received a nice long letter from Annie yesterday of four pages. She did not say much about the Yankees in Washington though one of the boys got a letter from Greenville that said they were fortyfing the town. I do not place much confidance in it, at any rate I hope they are not. I got a sight at some Yankees yesterday morning, about 250 passed through on their way to Washington on parole. They are passing through all the time on their way down there. Yesterday I saw Lieut. Primrose and Ed Harvey, the latter told me that he had been ordered to report to you at Wilmington but had gone to Gen'l Holmes in Goldsboro and been detached. I do not know where Lieut. Primrose was bound. It was reported here yesterday that McClellan was falling back from Richmond and that Jackson was in Maryland. I hope it may be so though I doubt it very much. You can hear almost anything now a days. Father dont you think if Mother only knew it and wanted to do so that she might write to Grandma by giving it to one of those paroled Yankees and let him put it in one of the Northern Post Offices. There would not be anything in that would there? I thought that Greenville was bad enough about hearing news but this is worse. We might hear some thing if we could go down town but we are not allowed to go out of the barracks except on Saturdays and Sundays. I think I should much prefer to go to a civil school. I don't like the idea of being under such restriction and then I think I could learn more too. You know you asked me in your last letter to write you freely to tell you the truth. I think things are badly conducted and I am satisfied that a boy cannot learn much except drilling and the only one they teach of that is infantry. I have studied the best I could though since I have been here and got very good marks and shall continue to do so as long as I stay here. It is almost impossible for one to study times like these. Sometimes I will be studying my lessons hard and before I know it my mind will be on the war and my lessons forgotten but I suppose I can overcome this after a while. Major Gordon the Sup. is not liked half so well as Col. Tew was nor do they think he is as smart a man. It is getting most breakfast time and I shall have to quit. Good bye. Write soon to

Your Affectionate Son

George

Joy W. Sparrow

HILLSBOROUGH, N. C.
Military Academy,

Hillsborough
June 2 1862

Dear Father

I received your welcome and long letter this morning and was a little surprised not thinking I could get an answer so soon being only two days coming. I am very glad that you are so near me. My head is so completely upset by a report that reached here this morning that there had been a big battle in <u>Virginia</u> near Richmond[154] and our <u>Army</u> victorious that I scarcely know what to say. I hope this report may prove true though I am afraid it will not. I am glad to see that all of my letters have been forwarded to you from Tarboro. I was afraid you would not get them. You say that the boys are with you and all well – hard at work mounting guns. I think that will suit them better than "retreating from a <u>drove</u> of cows," don't you think so? Is your friend Major Andrews with you or not? Poor man I sympathyse with him in his "misfortunes." When I was in Goldsboro his name was on every

---

[154] The Battle of Seven Pines also known as the Battle of Fair Oaks or Fair Oak Station took place on May 31 and June 1, 1862 in Henrico County, Virginia as part of the Peninsula Campaign. Principal commanders were US Major General George B. McClellan and CS General Joseph E. Johnston (seriously wounded during the action) and Major General G.W. Smith. Although the battle was tactically inconclusive, it was the largest battle in the Eastern Theater up to that time with estimated 13,736 casualties Source: CWSAC Battle Summaries: Seven Pines, National Park Service, U.S. Department of the Interior, www.nps.gov/faqs.htm.

tongue and he was branded as an "arrant Coward." When Lieut. Allen read your letter he laughed immoderately and said he intended to tease you about it as long as you lived. Aunt Maggie and Cora are at Graham about 20 miles from this place and I have no doubt would be very glad to see me. (I know I would them) but I cannot see them. We are not allowed to leave barracks except on Saturdays and Sundays and then we are marched in and then right out. It gives me a great deal of happiness to hear that Mother and the children are well and "<u>unmolested</u>." I was afraid they would trouble her on your account and then my fears were strengthened by hearing that they were cleaning out the jail for "<u>female prisoners</u>." While in Goldsboro I saw some of those people that were released from New Berne among them Mrs. Roberts and son. They would not tell anything in regard to the Yankees. Where do you intend carrying Ma if she should succeed in getting out of Washington? Do you look for an engagement at Wilmington soon? Should you have any action there you may expect to see me as soon as the cars can carry me so that if anything should happen to you I will be there to see to you. While at Tarboro on my way up here I found a letter in the office from Aunt Mary Burbank that had been written nearly one month and it was a very pretty letter, as soon as I arrived here I answered it but have not heard from it yet. There are a great many refugees in Hillsborough from all parts of the state about 40 families, and a large female school so you see there are plenty of people here but it would be all the same to us if there were only 2. Cora Blackwell is coming here to school so I understand. Your old friend Miss Konlac of Portsmouth notoriety lives here and has a brother in this school. One of my room mates[155] is a son

---

[155] George's roommate at Hillsborough Military Academy was John Caldwell, son of Governor Tod R. Caldwell. John was killed in the Battle of Gettysburg fighting for the cause of the Confederacy. Source: Biography, Gov. Tod R. Caldwell, The News Herald, June 8, 1922.

of Todd R. Caldwell[156] whom I have heard you speak of so much he was in the house of Commons with you. Letter writing is rather cheaper here than else where. We (that is the Cadets)

Governor Tod R. Caldwell
*Courtesy of the North Carolina Office of Archives and History
Raleigh, North Carolina*

---

[156] Tod Robinson Caldwell (b February 19, 1818, d. July 11, 1874) was born in Morganton, North Carolina, attended the University of North Carolina at Chapel Hill, was a solicitor for Burke County, and was a member of the General Assembly for a number of sessions. As Lieutenant Governor he became governor upon the impeachment of Governor Holden and was elected governor in 1872. His areas of interest were the state debt, finances, and the public schools which had been closed in 1863 for a lack of money. His appointment of Stephen D. Pool as superintendent of public instruction and passage of a bill providing private aid for public schools hastened the re-opening of the schools. Governor Caldwell died before the end of his term of office. Source: Beth G. Crabtree, *North Carolina Governors 1585-1975*, North Carolina Division of Archives and History, 1974, pp. 100-101 .

only have to pay fifty cents a quire for such paper as this and then it is so <u>convenient</u>. I can get an answer to any of my letters in from 2 to 4 days. Major Gordon the Sup. is very rigid and carries every thing out to the very letter. We are under the strictest sort of discipline imaginable and then such <u>eating</u>!! But I suppose this is customary in Military schools. We had quite a rain and thunder storm here last night and I laid in my bed and thought of you hoping that you had good comfortable quarters. It is very warm to day and I have just returned from drill where I had a pretty hot time I can tell you in the sun. We only have two classes in school 5 & 4. I am in the 5 and making very good progress but in consequence of the "<u>War</u>" there is very little studying done, indeed times are different for <u>schoolboys</u> from what they used to be. Give my best love to all the Grays and to all my friends. Are you anywhere's near Captains' Whitehurst and Hardings Companies. Good bye. Write Soon to

Your Affectionate Son,
Geo. A. Sparrow

Joy W. Sparrow

HILLSBOROUGH, N. C.
Military Academy,

Hillsborough Penitentiary
June 4, 1862

Dear Sister

Cadet Powell leaves today for Tarboro and as I have some spare time I have concluded to write you a letter although you owe me one. Since I last wrote to you I have received a long letter from Pa enclosing one from Mr. Myers to him in which was a little news from Washington the first I have heard since I arrived here. Father says that Mr. Hanks is engaged daily in carrying paroled prisoners from Tarboro to Washington and that he instructed him to bring Mother away if she wanted to come. I hope she may come. I cant see how she does to stand it. Staying there now must be <u>terrible indeed,</u> if she does succeed in getting out of Washington. I intend to see her at any rate. I got a nice long letter from Aunt Mary a day or two since. She is very well and sends love to you and <u>Mary</u> <u>Pauline</u> <u>Potts</u> the "<u>Anchoress</u>." There is quite a large female school here and it has a large number of girls. They call us the <u>Penitentiary</u> boys, and we call them the <u>Factory</u> gals. We never get a chance to see them except on Saturdays and Sundays. Your Aunt Cora is coming here to school so I understand. She and Aunt are at Graham twenty miles from here. I suppose you have heard that Fathers old friend the Hon. Edward Stanly[157] has been appointed <u>Provisional</u> Governor of this State by the Federal Government. I was very much surprised when I heard this. I thought he was a man of more sense but never mind, this war was not destined

Governor Edward Stanley

to last always and if in the end the South should come out victorious which she is certain to do, then <u>Mr. "Governor Stanlys"</u> career will prove of short duration for it will end in <u>shame</u> and disgrace to him. I hope he may meet his reward as an <u>ignominious</u> traitorous son of the Old North State. We received news last night of the great battle near Richmond and of the success of our army and it has so excited me that I have not been able to study a bit since. Ever since last night my lessons have been what schoolmasters generaly call "<u>outrageous</u>" and so was every student in school. The 4th N.C. Regiment Col. Anderson, this one Capt. David Carter was in, suffered very much in this late battle but I do not know who was killed and who was not.

---

[157] Edward Stanly (1/10/1810 – 7/12/1872) was born in New Bern and represented the southeastern portion of North Carolina in the U. S. House of Representatives for five terms. In May, 1862 Mr. Stanley was appointed military governor of North Carolina by Abraham Lincoln only to have him resign in January, 1863 following a bitter attack on the president's emancipation proclamation. Source: *Biographical Directory of the United States Congress: Stanly, Edward* and Norman D. Brown, *Edward Stanly: Whiggery's Tarheel 'Conqueor*, University of Alabama Press, 1974.

Joy W. Sparrow

General Bryan Grimes
Courtesy of the North Carolina Office of Archives and History
Raleigh, North Carolina

Bryan Grimes[158] from Washington is in the same regiment. Your Uncle William Sparrow[159] was in the fight, also he was attached to a battery of Light Artillery. I have not heard from him since the battle. Aunt Mary told me she got a letter from him some time since and he was within four miles of Gen. McClellans Army. Two long trains of

---

[158] General Bryan Grimes (11/2/1828 – 8/14/1880) was born on the family plantation called "Grimesland" in Pitt County, N.C. He joined the Confederate Army as major of the 4th North Carolina Infantry and saw his first combat action at First Manassas in Virginia. Grimes fought in nearly all of the major battles of the Eastern Theater of the war and was the last man in the Army of Northern Virginia to be appointed by Robert E. Lee as a major general. Source: John H. Eicher and David J. Eicher, *Civil War High Commands,* Stanford, CA, Stanford University Press, 2009, pp. 279, 810.

[159] William was George's uncle, brother of Thomas Sparrow. He served in the Confederate Army until discharged in 1862 because of poor health. He returned home to Hyde County and died in 1862.

Yankees prisoners from Richmond have just passed by here. Give my love to all my friends and <u>particularly</u> to <u>my "Cousin Sid</u>." Write soon to

Your Aff. Brother
George

Hillsborough,
Saturday, June 7 1862
Tower cell no. 3

Dear Father

You cannot imagine my surprise and delight this morning on seeing a letter from Miss Martha Fowle. Knowing as I did that she was in Washington I am very glad to find that things are not so bad as I feared they might be and that the family were all well and getting along so well. I received a very nice clever letter from Uncle Henry (in Graham) this morning in which he urges me to come up and see him and says that it will afford him a great pleasure to contribute to my welfare and happiness in any respect he says that it is only <u>fifteen</u> miles from here to <u>Graham</u> and he does not see why I cannot come up and spend the day with him. He offers as one inducement a <u>horse</u> and <u>buggy</u> and as another he says <u>Miss Julia Mitchell</u> is on a visit and sends her respects to me and says she would be happy to have my company in a horse back ride any day. That alone would induce me to go if nothing else. She is about my age and used to be my old "<u>sweet heart</u>." If you will write me this week and just write a <u>furlough</u> on a piece of paper I can go up any Friday evening and come back Monday morning soon so that it would not interfere with my studies in the least. Major Gordon would be willing anyhow but he does not permit any Cadet to leave town without permission from his parents. I wish you would do this. I have seen a paper containing a list of casualties in the 4 N.C. regiment. Col. Anderson and I see that Capt. Carter was <u>seriously</u> wounded and "<u>Tom Perry</u>" and "<u>Eddie Redding</u>" killed. I was very sorry to hear this, it only leaves one <u>officer</u> in Carters company. The same paper says that <u>Major Grimes</u> of Pitt displayed great bravery during the action. He had two horses shot from under him and while on foot <u>seized</u> a flag the bearer of which had been killed, and planted it on the breastworks amid a perfect storm of grape and canister.[160] I think that old Washington has contributed his <u>full share</u> in the great <u>battle</u>. I have not heard anything from Marshes company. Have you heard anything from Uncle William since the battle. I got a letter from Aunt Mary a few days since and he was within four miles of McClellan's Army attached to a battery of <u>Light Artillery</u>. I think he was in the battle. Do you know anything about Branch's Brigade? Was it in the engagement? I saw Mr. A. A. Willard in town this morning but did not get a chance to speak to him. He was in an omnibus[161] on his way to the depot. Do you ever get any papers, if you do I wish you would send me one occasionaly.

---

[160] A cluster of small iron balls used as a cannon charge. *The American Heritage College Dictionary*, Third Edition, Houghton Mifflin Company, Boston, New York, 1993.

[161] An omnibus was the first mass transportation vehicle in America. It looked like a stagecoach and was pulled by horses. Source: About.com/inventors.

THE BATTLE OF TRANTER'S CREEK, NEAR WASHINGTON, NORTH CAROLINA, ON JUNE 5, 1862.—SKETCHED BY MR. A. WEBB.—[SEE PAGE 413.]

Battle at Tranter's Creek near Washington, N. C
*Courtesy of the North Carolina Office of Archives and History
Raleigh, North Carolina*

Col. Singeltary was killed down at Tranter's Creek[162] in an engagement with the enemy. Did Miss Martha Fowle tell you wether Ma knew where you and I were at? I wish you would buy some two or three dollars worth of postage stamps and send me and I will send you the

---

[162] The Battle of Tranter's Creek was fought on June 5, 1862 in Pitt County, North Carolina. On June 5, Col. Robert Potter, garrison commander at Washington, North Carolina, ordered a reconnaissance in the direction of Pactolus. The 24th Massachusetts under Lt. Col. F.A. Osborne, advanced to the bridge over Tranter's Creek, where it encountered the 44th North Carolina, under Col. George Singletary. Unable to force a crossing, Osborne brought his artillery to bear on the mill buildings in which the Confederates were barricaded. Colonel Singletary was killed in the bombardment, and his troops retreated. The Federals did not pursue and returned to their fortifications at Washington. National Park Service, U.S. Department of the Interior, National Historical Park, CWSAC Battle Summaries: Tranter's Creek, www.nps.gov/faqs.htm.

money as soon as I get mine from Kinston. I am looking for it daily. Love to all the boys. Good bye Write soon to

> Your Affectionate Son
> George

P.S. If you can purchase any stationary in Wilmington cheap I wish you would send me some as I am entirely out. Can you not get some from off "The Mariner."

HILLSBORO' MILITARY ACADEMY.

REPORT upon the Recitations and Conduct of Cadet *G. A. Sparrow* of the *5ᵗʰ* Class for the four weeks ending *June 27ᵗʰ*, 1862:

MERIT MARKS FOR RECITATIONS.	Number Attainable.	Number Received.
IN MATHEMATICS,	45	29.25
" FRENCH,		
" LATIN,		
" ENGLISH BRANCHES,	15	13.50
"		
" *Geography*	15	12.75

DEMERIT MARKS FOR DELINQUENCIES IN CONDUCT:

Number at the date of last Report, *4*

Number at present, *28*

N. B.—Any Cadet who may receive more than 200 demerit marks in one academic year, shall be suspended.

Respectfully,

W. M. Gordon

Superintendent H. M. A.

Governor Edward Stanly Entering Washington, North Carolina
Courtesy of the North Carolina Office of Archives and History
Raleigh, North Carolina

Hillsboro M. A.

July 11 1862

Dear Father

Your letter containing one from Mother also a newspaper, was received yesterday. I was very glad to hear from you. I had been looking for one some time. I had seen <u>Gov.</u> <u>Stanlys</u> <u>speech</u> before and had it preserved in my trunk and I hope that at some future time I may find issue for it if the war ends soon and the south comes out <u>victorious</u>, which she is certain to do. <u>Then</u> "<u>Mr. Gov. Stanly</u>" will find that his speech will prove "<u>a thorn in his side</u>." One of the Cadets has just handed me a letter from Mary Ellison, she says that two young men left "Salem" to join your company. Sam Masters was one of them. The other one is a young man from "Salem," and his name is "Lemly." Mary says he is not quite eighteen and has never been much among strangers and consequently his Mother feels very anxious about him.

She made her (Mary) promise to write you and ask you to look out for him and take care of him, and I repeat the request, for since I got the letter one of my room-mates tells me that he knows him well, and that he has got two "beautiful and amiable" sisters. His family is quite wealthy. I was down at the train the other night and saw Sam Waters just from the battle field of Richmond also Mr. Ives of New Berne. He told me that he saw three men in Goldsboro on their way to join you. Our session is up now in a short time and there is some prospect of our having a holiday of ten days. I can then visit all my relatives around here, that is with your consent. It will cost very little. If convenient you can send me some money in your next so that I can pay my promised visit to Aunt Maggie. I wish you would write on a scrap of paper to Mr. Gordon permission for me to go up to Graham next Saturday. I did not show him your letter.

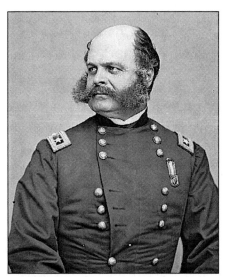

General Ambrose E. Burnside
Library of Congress LC-B8172-1625

It was reported here a few days since that Burnside[163] was evacuating New Berne. If this be so they will evacuate W. also. I hope they will. "Good bye."

Your Affectionate Son,
George Attmore Sparrow

Write immediately
Before the end of session
Aunt Mary would like to hear from you. She is in Morganton.

Hillsboro M. A.
July 14 1862

Dear Father

I wrote you a letter some few days since, and have not heard from it yet but necessity or rather circumstances compel me to write this one. A few nights since, myself and several of the "Cadets" considered by all to be the best boys in school "one of whom stands first in school," went down to the depot to see the train come, and while we were gone the officer of the guard visited and reported us absent from barracks half an hour, for which offence "he put us all under arrest, and the sintinels that let us pass he sent them home." He has decided our case and came

---

[163] General Ambrose Everett Burnside (5/23/1824 – 9/13/1881) was a Senator from Rhode Island, born in Liberty, Indiana. He attended a seminary at Liberty and Beach Grove Academy and graduated from the United States Military Academy at West Point in 1847. During the Civil War he entered the Union Army in 1861 as colonel and commanded a brigade at the first Battle of Bull Run. He was commissioned brigadier general and major general and resigned in 1865. He served in the United States Senate 1875 – 1881 as a Republican. *Biographical Directory of the United States Congress: Ambrose Everett Burnside, (1824-1881).*

very near sending us home, but this is not what I want to say. I only mention this as an instance. What I wish to tell you is this, you know you asked me in all your letters to be frank. I will try and be so at least, but to my subject I must tell you that I think it is throwing money away to keep me here, not that I do not appreciate your kindness in sending me to school or that I do not try but simply because I "<u>cannot</u> <u>study</u>." There is not a cadet in school that studies, it is impossible to do so now. I want you to send me a discharge as soon as you get this. I do not think either, that the school is a good one either. Only two days since, a Cadet officer kicked a private while on post, a son of "Col. Cowan" by the way a fine boy. The private was sent home and the officer came out all right. This aroused the boys and caused several to be sent home, and more than one half are going to leave in a few days. But dear Father, you and I both will have the satisfaction of knowing that ever since I came here, I have been praised by the Supt. for my strait forward conduct and besides I think I will stand third or fourth in my class. I asked Major Gordon for a discharge but he would not grant it unless by your consent. I told him just what I have told you. Please answer this immediately and send me a discharge.

> Your Affectionate Son
> George A. Sparrow

Answer by next mail.

HILLSBOROUGH, N. C.
Military Academy,

Hillsborough

July 21 1862

Dear Father

I was very much pleased this morning to receive a letter from you containing the welcome intelligence that you wanted me to come to Wilmington. There are several Cadets here from there that are going home in a few days and I shall have plenty of company. One received a discharge by the same mail that I got my letter. This session ends on next Thursday 31st of July one week from to day. I shall have ample time to hear from you before then. I saw Aunt Maggie yesterday morning. She is looking for you to come up but as you are so busy about the Court Martial I suppose it will be impossible to come now. I know very well that it will cost too much to let Sister Annie spend her vacation in Morganton but could she do so, she would find it a very pleasant tripp indeed. We have a good many friends and relations there now. Aunt Mary's family, Cousin Fannie Grist, Mr. Blackwell, Mr. Williams and Cousin Fannie Jarvis from New Bern and a good many other families that I could mention. One of my roommates a son of Todd R. Caldwell has been urging me to go up to Morganton and spend some time with him. As the mail goes off shortly I am compelled to close, hoping that I may tell you more in "propria personae" in a few days. Write soon to

Your Affectionate Son

Geo A Sparrow, Cadet H. M. A.

Hillsboro Penitentiary
Hillsborough,
July 27 A. D. 1862

Dear Father

I presented your letter to Major Gordon this morning and he says that it is perfectly satisfactory but he will like to have things done in order, and requested me to write you and ask you to enclose a note to him in my letter telling him to let me come home. The school is breaking up very fast indeed and at the end of the session I don't think there will be a sufficient number of boys left at the end of this session to continue the school. <u>Please</u> <u>answer</u> "<u>immediately</u>" and send the note to Major Gordon.

Your Affectionate Son
Geo. A. Sparrow

Please do not fail to send in my letter a <u>discharge</u> to Major Gordon. Nothing could induce me to stay here longer than this session. You may look for me on next Saturday certain. Love to Ed Geer and all the boys. Goodbye.

Goldsboro, N.C.

August 22 1862

Dear Father,

Mr. Alfred Stanley has just arrived here from Washington. He mailed some papers and letters to you in Tarboro. He says there are only 200 Yanks in Washington and a force of 871 good men will take the place. He is now waiting to see General Clingman[164] on this business I suppose. I have just seen Sam Schenck, Mr. Harvey and a good many friends that I know. This is a good chance for your Company to show their valor. I have no doubt from Mr. Stanley's description that the Gen. will send a force down immediately and if you want to go now is your chance. Please mail to me any of my letters that you may find in the office.

Affectionately Your Son

Geo. A. Sparrow

---

[164] Thomas Lanier Clingman (July 27, 1812 – November 3, 1897) was born in Huntsville, N.C. and educated by private tutors and in the public schools in Iredell County, N.C. He graduated from the University of North Carolina, Chapel Hill in 1832; studied law; was admitted to the bar in 1834 and began practice in Huntsville. He was elected to the State house of Commons in 1835, the State Senate in 1840, elected as a Whig to the 28th and 30th – 35th Congresses. He was appointed as a Democrat to the U. S. Senate on May 6, 1858 to fill the vacancy caused by the resignation of Asa Biggs. He was reelected and served through March 28, 1861 when he was expelled from the Senate for support of the rebellion. He then served as a brigadier general in the Confederate States Army. *Biographical Directory of the United States Congress 1977 – present, Thomas Lanier Clingman (1812-1897).*

General Thomas Lanier Clingman
Courtesy of the North Carolina Office of Archives and History
Raleigh, North Carolina

Hillsboro Military Academy

August 27 1862

<u>Dear</u> <u>Father</u>

The letter you mailed me from Wilmington was from Ma and contained several messages to you. In the first place she says that she sent me some clothes by one of your men. Do you know who this was or have you seen anything of the carpet bag of clothes. I wish you would inquire around and see if you can trace it out. Clothes are an item these days. Mother says that Mr. <u>Stanly</u> is in Washington but that his visits there do not help their situation any but make things worse. She says she had rather apply to <u>Abe Lincoln</u> for a favor than to the <u>Hon. Edward Stanly</u>. She says "say to your Father that Mr. Stanly is as cute and cunning as any Yankee he ever saw." He arrived here last Friday afternoon and Saturday morning Dr. Wheeler and himself went over the bridge, soon after the Cavalry followed. They staid sometime and the <u>Cavalry</u> brought them back. I can't mention names but it is thought by several gentelman here that they went to meet "<u>Satterth-waite</u>" and "<u>Warren</u>." Sunday morning Mr. <u>Stanly</u> went over the bridge again, at 9 Oclock met <u>Fred Grist</u> on the other side and remained until One when he returned. He sent down here for <u>Tankard </u>to come and see him and sent in the country for Jack Cherry and <u>Henry Hodges</u> and then refused to let them return without taking the Oath of <u>Neutrality</u>. Ma says that she got Mr. Alfred Stanly to apply for her to get a pass to go over to Cousin Ben Tripps and Gov. Stanly would not permit her to go. She says that she has bought several things from the Yankees but it was only in cases of extreme necessity. I would send this letter but I want to show it to Aunt Maggie. Write soon to

Your Affectionate Son

Geo. Attmore Sparrow

––––––––––

Hillsboro Military Academy

September 7, 1862

<u>Dear</u> <u>Father</u>

Your letter of yesterday has just been handed me by one of the Cadets, and although it is now most 9 Oclock and I have very little time I hasten to reply hoping that you may receive this while in Tarboro. It was here yesterday by telegraph from Goldsboro that Washington had been captured by our troops and as a matter of course I have been in a state of great excitement and anxiety ever since, until I got your letter tonight.[165] I could scarcely refrain from leaving here and going there immediately. When you get down to Tarboro and Washington should be taken or anything should have happened to any of the fam-

–––––––––––––

[165] *Recollections of the Civil War* by Annie Blackwell Sparrow in Chapter 6 Unsung Heroes describe the terrible battle of September 6, 1862.

ily you can telegraph me to come down. I feel very anxious about it and should my presence be needed I beg you to let me know so that I may come down immediately. I am very glad that my last report was so satisfactory and I hope they may continue to be so. And in regard to my <u>demerits</u> you need not think anything of them for I can assure you that I have got as few as almost any Cadet in school that has been here the same length of time. Very few boys go to a Military school without getting a good many demerits. It is almost impossible. If you bring Mother out of town please do not bring her here to live. Upon consulting with Aunt Maggie she seems to think that you could live much cheaper some where else. I think so to, and besides I do not fancy the house that you would have to live in. It is an Old Hotel and very unpleasantly situated, and in fact I know if you were to see it you would not live in it. I wish you would go to Morganton. I think it would be cheaper and there Mother would have so many Friends there. Well the drum is beating for tattoo[166] and the boy leaves with the mail in about ten minutes. So Good Bye. Don't forget the bag of clothes. She gave them to one of your men.

Your Affectionate Son
Geo. A. Sparrow

Capt. T. Sparrow
Co. K, 10 Reg., N.C. Troops

––––––––––

Hillsboro M. A.
September 16 1862

Dear Father

Both of your last letters have been answered in this but recently my time has been so completely occupied and my mind so unsettled

---

[166] A signal sounded on a drum or bugle to summon soldiers or sailors to their quarters at night. *The American Heritage College Dictionary,* Third Edition, Houghton Mifflin Company, Boston, New York, 1993.

that between the two I could not do it. Your last containing all the particulars of the fight at Washington was I think the most welcome letter I ever received for it conveyed to me the news that my Mother and Sisters were <u>safe</u>, something that I did not know untill the receipt of your "favor." I was aware all the time that they had had a fight and that our forces "<u>as usual</u>" had been victorious but could learn nothing in regard to the safety of our family. My anxiety during that time can be better <u>imagined</u> than <u>described</u>. It was reported how at one time that the town had been shelled without any warning being given to the women and children. I was so worried when I heard that that I was very strongly tempted to telegraph you asking permission to come down. The suspense was terrible. At the same time that we got the news Aunt Maggie received a letter from <u>Grandpa</u> telling her of the death of his son Johnnie and as you might expect this was a sad blow to all the family and particularly to his Sister Maggie. Having no children of her own she idolized him. I suppose he wrote to Mother informing her of the fact. The manner in which he died[167] made it so much harder to bear. The very idea of having one so dear to us perish by drowning is in itself awful. Grandpa's letters were written beautifully and I think if there are any <u>good</u> <u>Christians</u> in this world he is one. I would give you all of the particulars of my <u>Dear</u> Little Uncle's death but the last time I saw Aunt Maggie she told me that she would do so, and I suppose has by this time. He was drowned in the Okaw River. I never was more surprised at anything in my life than I was at Hannah Selby's death. Truly can it be said that "death spares neither young nor old." Cut down in the very flower of youth and prime of Life her fate was indeed a sad one to all who knew her. The very day that I received

---

[167] Ironically, George had a son who was drowned in the Pamlico River at the age of eleven while riding his bicycle and rode off the end of the bridge into the river.

Joy W. Sparrow

your letter I was talking about her to one of my friends and little did I think that I was "then" talking of a corpse. As you say her death will be a terrible blow to her parents. She was a perfect Idol to both. My time passes much more pleasantly now than it used to. The first thing that improves our condition is the change in Major Gordon. He is now almost a different man. He has actually deviated from his former ways so far as to give a party of us permission to go over in town and serenade the "Young Ladies" twice and stay untill one o clock. And in the second place I have since coming here this time become acquainted with a good many Young Ladies at the "Factory" (alias Mrs. Nash's school) and this makes time pass much more pleasantly. I think that Young Ladies Society ought to be cultivated by every young man of any standing or position in society. It has such a good influence over his manners and makes him so much more refined. And nowhere can it profit a boy more that at a school of girls like that where almost every character and disposition of the female sex is spread out before him. And one other great inducement in my visiting there is, it is a Presbyterian School out and out. Mrs. Nash has about 90 scholars. Cora attends her school. Cora Blackwell wishes to go up to Graham next Friday evening and come back Monday morning and wants me to accompany her. Major Gordon is willing that I should go, he lets George Attmore go quite often. Please write me in time to make the trip on Saturday. Did you hear anything from my clothes? Not time to write more at present. Write soon to

Your Affectionate Son
George A. Sparrow

The Nash School[168]
Courtesy of The Alliance for Historic Hillsborough
Hillsborough, North Carolina

Hillsboro M. A.

September 30 1862

Dear Father

I arrived here at 2 P. M. today from Graham where I spent part of Friday, Saturday and Sunday. My tripp was a very pleasant one and I enjoyed myself much better than I had anticipated. But my enjoyment was cut short on my return to Hillsboro. Instead of finding the gay <u>lively</u> crowd of boys that I left I found the school converted into a "<u>house</u> of <u>sorrow</u>." Mrs. Tew had just received the confirmation of Col. Tew's death and numbers and numbers of the Cadets had lost <u>friends</u> and relations, some brothers and some Fathers. Death hath made sad

---

[168] It is believed that "The Nash House" was built in 1766 by Isaac Edwards, secretary to Governor Tryon. In 1807 it became the property of Chief Justice Frederick Nash and later was operated by his daughter and a niece as the "Select Boarding School of Misses Nash and Kollock." Source: Allen Alexander Lloyd, *History of the Town of Hillsboro*, 1948-1949, p. 35.

ravages in our ranks. I have felt very uneasy for the last two or three days on your account. I hear that the yellow fever is spreading very rapidly and I am so afraid it will get among our troops. I heard that as many as 17 died in Wilmington in "<u>one day</u>." Uncle Henry is very nicely fixed up in Graham. He has a nice comfortable little house, three or four servants, and two horses. And what is better than all a nice wife. I like her almost as well as any aunt I have. He (Henry) is not doing any thing at present except trading. He makes something that way occasionally. Father, I wish you would try all plans in the world to get Mother and the children out of Washington. I feel <u>very uneasy</u>. It seems as if I have a presentiment that something will happen to them if they stay there. It seems to be the impression of everyone almost, that the Yankees not being able to accomplish anything in the field, will as soon as our rivers become navigable for their Gunboats <u>penetrate</u> as far inland as possible and <u>destroy</u> and <u>devastate</u> all that falls into their hands. A gentelman who left New Berne a few days since says that the Yankees are building light draft vessels. I suppose with the intention of going up Neuse River. Should you write to Ma soon say to her for me that if possible I should for her to send my trunk containing "<u>all</u>" my winter clothing out by Annie when she comes. Good Bye. Write soon.

Your Affectionate Son
Geo. Attmore Sparrow

––––––––––

Hillsboro, M. A.
October 3 1862

Dear Father

Your letter of the 29th Sept. was received this morning and was very gladly welcomed by me. I was very sorry to learn of the death of Mr. Vanamridge and Dr. Dixon. They were both of them very nice gentlemen and the latter will be a great loss to the people of Wilmington. He was an esteemed and eminent man in his profession. Major Gordon left this morning for Maryland to try if possible to recover the body of Col. Tew. His loss is a sad one to our state both as Principal of this school and as a talented and accomplished officer. He was shot through the head by a Minnie ball. His family is here. I am glad that you have at last discovered my carpet bag of clothes. I wish you would send them to me by express. It will not cost you much. Who brought them out of Washington? Mother will find her new home a very pleasant one. I expect at any rate it is a much nicer one. Do you know wether she intends keeping it any length of time. I hope she may for she has got one of the nicest neighbors in the world in Mrs. Fannie Bryan. While I was coming from Graham on Monday last I saw Capt. Samuel Waters. He is now Capt. Of a company and has charge of the Yankee prison at Salisbury.

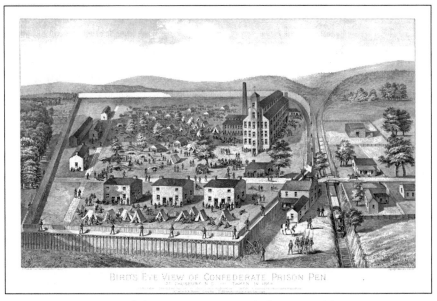

Confederate Prison at Salisbury, 1864
Courtesy of the North Carolina Office of Archives and History
Raleigh, North Carolina

He has been offered a position on General Lee's staff as Major but was on his way to Richmond to try and get a furlough to recover from the effects of his wound and if successful to accept the position. Tom Blackwell passed through here a few days since wounded in the leg. He was wounded in the battle of Sharpsburgh.[169]

Battle of Sharpsburg
Bodies of Confederate Dead Gathered for Burial
Library of Congress LC-B8171-0557

---

[169] Battle of Sharpsburg (a.k.a. Battle of Antietam) fought on September 17, 1862 near Sharpsburg, Maryland was the culmination of the Maryland Campaign of 1862, the first invasion of the North by Confederate General Robert E. Lee and the Army of Northern Virginia, and was the first major battle in the Civil War to take place on Northern soil. The twelve hour battle began at dawn and for the next seven hours there were three major Union attacks on the Confederate left. After clashing for over eight hours, the Confederates were pushed back but not broken, however more than 15,000 soldiers were killed or wounded. National Park Service, U.S. Department of the Interior, National Historical Park, CWSAC Battle Summaries: The Battle of Antietam, www.nps.gov/faqs.htm.

Battle of Sharpsburg (Antietam)
Artist Unknown
Showing the Union Advance on the Dunker Church

You say you have been over to Tarboro. While you were there did you get those <u>toothbrushes</u> that Hall promised you? If you did I wish you would send me one by the carpet bag. I have tried everywhere and it is utterly impossible to get one for love or money. I am glad that there is some chance for your promotion. I think it ought to have been done a long time since, for I don't think there is a man in service that is more deserving of promotion than you are and I sincerely hope that General French will do so. Father dont you think you are very imprudent in going to Wilmington among the yellow fever. (I wish you would not do it any more for you might take it.) Were you not very sorry to hear of Gen. Branch's death. It will be a sad blow to his family but he lived long enough to redeem his character and make for himself a name. He is spoken of in the paper as having acted very brave in every engagement. Love to all the boys. Write very soon.

Your Affectionate Son
Geo. A. Sparrow

General Samuel Gibbs French (1818-1910). Despite his Northern birth Samuel G. French joined the Confederate Army and rose to the rank of major general. The New Jersey native and West Pointer (1843) was wounded at Buena Vista while serving as an artillery officer in Mexico. Transferring to the quartermaster department in 1848, he resigned as a captain eight years later and spent the next five years managing his Mississippi plantation. When war began he answered the call and his N.C. assignments included: commanding Department of North Carolina and Southern Virginia (February 17-26, 1862); commanding District of the Pamlico, Department of North Carolina (March 18-20, 1862); commanding District of the Cape Fear, Department of North Carolina (March 20 – September, 1862); commanding French's Command (North Carolina), and Department of North Carolina and Southern Virginia (September, 1862 – April 1, 1863). In the early part of the war he served in Virginia and North Carolina before being dispatched to command a division under Joseph E. Johnston in Mississippi. As such he took part in the unsuccessful attempt to free the garrison at Vicksburg. (French, Samuel G., *Two Wars: An Autobiography.*)[170]

---

[170] Stewart Sifakis, *Who Was Who In The Ciil War,* America by Facts On File, Inc. New York, New York, 1988, p. 229.

General Samuel Gibbs French   General Lawrence O'Bryan Branch

Courtesy of the North Carolina Office of Archives and History
Raleigh, North Carolina

General Lawrence O'Bryan Branch (1820 – 1862). Branch was a veteran of the Seminole War and had embarked on such civil pursuits as law, journalism, and politics. Upon the secession of North Carolina he resigned from Congress and joined the South. Branch was defeated by Burnside's expedition at New Bern on March 14th and a few days later was replaced by General French and later General Holmes. Sent to Virginia in May, his brigade acted as a link between Johnston's army on the Peninsula and J. R. Anderson's command facing McDowell near Fredericksburg. Merged into the newly created Light Division, he fought at Hanover Court House, the Seven Days, and under Jackson at Cedar Mountain, 2nd Bull Run, Chantilly, and Harper's Ferry. In Hill's charge to restore the Confederate right at Antietam, Branch played a leading role but was killed by a sharpshooter once the lines were stabilized. (Freeman, Douglas S., *Lee's Lieutenants*).[171]

---

[171] Stewart Sifakis, *Who Was Who In The Civil War*, America by Facts On File, Inc., New York, New York, 1988, pp. 69-70.

General Theophilus H. Holmes
Courtesy of the North Carolina Office of Archives and History
Raleigh, North Carolina

General Holmes (1804 - 1880), a North Carolinian West Pointer (1829), had won a brevet south of the border and fought the Seminoles and Navajos before resigning on April 22, 1861, as major, 8th Infantry. Joining the Confederacy, his North Carolina assignments included: commanding Department of North Carolina (March 25 – July 17, 1862); commanding Reserve Forces of North Carolina (April 18, 1864 – April 1865). Placed in command along the Rappahannock in Virginia, he took a small brigade of two regiments to join Beauregard at Bull Run but did not get into the action. He led a division to join Robert E. Lee in June 1862 for the Seven Days but performed poorly (due to partial deafness). Lee replaced him the next month but Jefferson Davis found him a place west of the Mississippi. There he was in overall charge as a lieutenant general during the defeat at Prairie Grove. Holmes was pleased when E. Kirby Smith arrived to succeed him. Retaining command in Arkansas, he directed the unsuccessful attack on Helena. Smith felt that Holmes was too old and slow and informed the Richmond authorities. An incensed Holmes resigned. Davis then put him in charge of organizing the reserves in North Carolina, a duty he performed for the remaining year of the war. (Freeman, Douglas S., *Lee's Lieutenants*).[172]

H.M.A.

Oct. 27 1862

Dear Father

I have been anxiously looking for a letter from you all this week but this far have not received one. I have heard nothing from Wilmington in several days and of course feel very anxious about you. But I put my trust in Providence. I feel satisfied that he will keep and protect you from all harm. Major Gordon has informed me this morning that my deposit money has amounted to $89.00. This leaves $9.00 due on that. Our winter uniform cost $18.00 for jacket and pants. Aunt Maggie told me yesterday that she had written you a long letter. I am glad of this for I cannot write myself as often as I could wish on account of my time being so much occupied. The weather up here has been <u>very cold</u> indeed for the last week or two and I have been very much in want of my overcoat. I am sorry that I ever left it in Wilmington. Please send it to me as soon as an opportunity occurs. Mary Ellison says in one of her letters that Mr. Fred Grist is dead and that Mrs. Havens has lost her little Mamie. I almost hate to hear from home now on that account. Every letter brings to us the intelligence of some of our friends. This war is a sad thing for us all. Mrs. Jennie Bonner has a little girl named Eliza Ellison. This is her second baby. Mrs. Ellison's family are going to move down to Wilson in a few weeks. Our session is up now, in little

----

[172] Stewart Sifakis, *Who Was Who In The Civil War*, America by Facts On File, Inc., New York, New York, 1988, pp. 315-316.

less than two months and I have proposed a plan to spend my vacation which I think is a good one provided it should meet with your approval. It is this. The session ends on the 2nd of December, it is then only a few days to Christmas and Uncle Henry has invited me to spend that time with him in Graham. Aunt Maggie and Cora will be there. After that I have promised to stay sometime in Raleigh with Chas. McKinnon. Aunt Mary has also written me to come and see her, so you see it will not cost me much more than to stay at Wilmington with you. I hope you may succeed in getting in some profitable business so that you may make something. I intend after this war to use all my energies to make something for the family so they will at least be <u>independent</u>. Love to all the Washington Greys. Good Bye. Write soon.

Your Affectionate Son
Geo. A. Sparrow

––––––––––

Hillsboro Military Academy
October 30, 1862

Dear Father

Your kind favor of the 28th came this morning and was as your letters always are gladly welcomed by me. From your long silence I was afraid that something was the matter but I am happy to see that all is right. You must have had a very pleasant time while General Raines was on a visit to your camp. To a "<u>gentelman</u>" one of the greatest deprivations of "<u>camp</u> life" is the want of associates. Has Lient. Whitehurst returned to the company yet? If he has not you must be somewhat short of officers now as Lient. Thomas is away also. If he has not returned to camp and is any where in the vicinity of Washington I wish you would write and ask him if possible to get some of my clothes for me at the same time that he gets your things. I shall need them this vacation.

And if he should succeed in getting them I would like particularly to have a pair of shoes that are at "home." You must have misunderstood my meaning when I spoke about what Nan said in her letter. I did not mean that they would ever want anything as long as you could send it to them, what I meant was this. That if they could not receive means from you any other way that I was willing to risk my self in carrying it to them. I do not anticipate that this will happen but still if it should and things were to come to such a pass that it were impossible to keep them supplied then I have not forgotten what is due to a "Mother" from her son. Although it may be for the best that they should stay in Washington and that I am incapable of judging I do not doubt but still the thought of having them and all that is dear to me completely in the power of such vandals as the Yankees is enough to make any boy's blood boil with indignation and make him think only of "revenge." No doubt this school will be discontinued next session and then should you give me your consent I can doubtless obtain a situation as Drillmaster at Raleigh. This will at least enable me to get along without any cost to you. Father to be candid with you I do not like the idea of being such an expense to you as I am. I feel that in doing so I am depriving my Mother and Sisters of their just dues. I can take care of myself, they cannot. These are the only reasons that prompt me to persist contrary to your wish in entering the Army. And besides I shall be "<u>eighteen</u>" in July anyhow. I wish you could get into some money making business and resign your position in the Army. If I have said anything in this letter that you think I ought not to have said then I hope you will forgive me, for I can assure you the only thing that prompted me to do it was <u>gratitude</u> to you and Mother. If you are not willing for me to enter the Army in the capacity of Drillmaster, I can go during my three months vacation. I think that through you and with a <u>good</u> recommendation from Major Gordon which I can get, that Gov. Vance would give me

Joy W. Sparrow

that commission. If it was only for a short time I should like to be of <u>some</u> <u>service</u> to my Country.

When you write please send me some stamps and a little money. The stamps cannot be had here, and the other is hard to get anywhere. "<u>Please write soon</u>" to

Your Affectionate Son

Geo. A. Sparrow

––––––––––

Hillsboro Military Academy

Hillsboro, Nov. 1, 1862

Dear Father,

Your very kind letter of the 29th was received this morning and as you desire I will answer it immediately. The Ten Dollars ($10) was received for which I have to return my thanks. In my letter to you I did not mean that you were to send the money for my winter uniform. I merely told you what they cost. I wrote you a long letter yesterday which to day I am very sorry for. I had a severe attack of what is generally termed "Blues" and consequently you must take no notice of what I said. Do not take any notice of it and answer it as you would any one of my letters. After sealing my letter to you yesterday I inserted a small slip of paper containing some news that I had just heard. Since that I have seen Mr. Collier from Goldsboro and he says that it is certainly so, that the people of New Berne have either to take the oath of <u>alligeance</u>[173] or leave. He saw a good many people from there himself. I am sorry that Ma could not get permission to come out and see Lieut. Whitehurst.

––––––––––

[173] The standard loyalty oath was given to all released prisoners, civilian or military. It pledged that one would hereafter be loyal to the U. S. Constitution, its government, and its policies. Source: William L. Richter, *The A to Z of the Civil War and Reconstruction,* The Scarecrow Press, Inc., Lanham. Toronto. Plymouth, UK, 2009, p. 430.

I am under many obligations to you for your kindness in sending my overcoat and things and in buying me the vest. I shall be on the lookout for them. I would write more but have not time. Write soon to

Your Affectionate Son

Geo. A.Sparrow

———————

Hillsboro Military Academy
November 9, 1862
Study Hours, 9 P. M.

My Dear Father,

Your kind favor of the 4th containing Twenty Dollars ($20) and in answering it allows me to express to you my "sincere thanks" for your kindness in supplying my wants so well and you may rest assured that I duly appreciate your kindness. The bag of clothes that you sent has also been received. Uncle Cis brought it up from "Goldsboro" on Friday night last. We have heard to night that the enemy are at Scotland Neck with "sixteen thousand" (16000) troops and that a battle is expected in the eastern part of this state daily. I of course feel very anxious to hear something from there. On hearing that the state was invaded and that strenuous efforts were necessary to prevent their farther advance inland, and that serious apprehensions of an attack upon some of its most important places were felt, the Cadets of the H. M. A. deemed it their duty to assist in driving the invaders not only from our soil, but from their very homes and firesides. And in view of this they have agreed "en masse" (or at least 70 which is by far the larger half) to form themselves into a company or Cadet Corps to aid in the expulsion of the enemy from our state to serve for the period of one month or longer if necessary. We purpose to go independently having nothing to get from the state except our knapsacks. They have already tendered the Captaincy and 1st Lieutenant to two of our officers (which I think are in every respect competent) and they have accepted it upon conditions that we gain the consent of Major Gordon, this one already, "<u>provided</u>" the Cadets gain the consent of their parents. I have taken no steps, nor will I, untill I hear from you. In my own mind I have no doubt that the whole thing will prove a <u>failure.</u> I anticipate having a very pleasent time this winter and more especially from my visit to Graham. Uncle Henry has one of the nicest wives I ever saw and they are both anxious for me to come. Miss Cora and Miss Julie Mitchell are going up with me and a good many ladies from Hillsboro will be there also, so you see I will not want for company. If you hear from home please let me know.

Yours Affectionately

Geo. A. Sparrow

––––––––––

H. M. A.,

Nov. 28, 1862

My Dear Father,

Your favor of the 24 was received yesterday morning and at the same time I received one from Washington which I enclose in this. Since receiving your letter I have heard that there was a large fleet in Wilmington and that you were looking for an attack daily, but do not place much confidence in the report for I thought had there been any truth in it you would have written me about it immediately. I am very much in hope that you may succeed in communicating with Ma. If you do you can let me know and probably by the same plan I can see her also. She is very anxious to see both of us and I have no doubt it would make her feel much more satisfied. You mentioned in your letter Mr. Telfair being near Washington and his wife being at Mrs. Vanor-

lucks. Dont you think that in the same way you could communicate with Mother and probably bring her away, that is if she wants to come, and I think from her letter that she does. I shall write her a long letter to day and as soon as you receive this I want you to answer it so that I can send her the letter. I know of no other way to get it to her. I received the brush and combe at the same time I did the other things. It is cold and my hands are so numb that I cannot write. Write soon.

Your Affectionate Son

Geo. A. Sparrow

Chapter 5

Soldier Boy

After leaving Hillsborough Military Academy, George re-enlisted in 2ⁿᵈ Company G, 36ᵗʰ Regiment, N.C. Troops (2ⁿᵈ Regiment N.C. Artillery) in New Hanover County July 14, 1863 for the war after being discharged from Company K, 10ᵗʰ Regiment N.C. State Troops (1ˢᵗ Regiment N.C. Artillery). Transferred to Company D 13ᵗʰ Battalion N.C. Light Artillery October 9, 1864. Captured and paroled at Goldsboro in May, 1865.[174]

Even though at times George was homesick and downcast, he remained a true patriot to his beloved South.

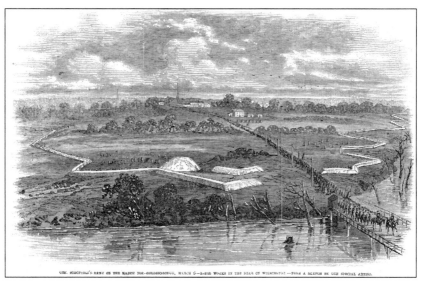

General John M. Schofield's Army Leaving Wilmington
on their march to Goldsboro to meet Sherman
*Courtesy of the North Carolina Office of Archives and History
Raleigh, North Carolina*

---

[174] Dr. Louis H. Manarin, Compiler, *North Carolina Troops 1861-1865 A Roster, Volume 1 Artillery,* North Carolina Division of Archives and History, Raleigh, North Carolina, pp. 60 & 279.

In Camp Near Kinston
April 26/63

Dear Father

I wrote to you while you were at Washington and have not received any answer to my letter but being so busy all the time accounts for this. It is raining quite hard to day and not having any thing to do I thought I could employ my time most profitable by <u>writing home.</u> I find <u>camp</u> <u>life</u> to be very monotonous on such days as this and the only thing that I can resort to is my <u>writing desk</u>. I heard from Jennie and Mother a short time since and answered both of their letters the same day by Sargeant Judkins who left for Washington after some deserted men. Since this <u>conscript</u>[175] bill has been passed there is a great deal of dissatisfaction among the twelve months men, and some have tried to <u>desert</u> but have been caught and brought back. I hope they will get their just dues. I think that any man who can complain at a measure like this when he knows that we were forced into this thing and have got to get out and the only way is to fight out cannot be a true man or at least has not got the love for his country that he ought to have. A flag of truce went down to New Bern yesterday to carry the child of Col. <u>Roberson</u> his wife is already there, her father is a Col. in the Federal Army and her brother a <u>Captain</u> and I understand that General Burnside is intimately acquainted with her, at any rate he refuses to parole him and he is to be sent North. This is likely the work of his wife's relations. I saw yesterday a demonstration of <u>Yankee</u> cowardice that is

---

[175] Because of recruiting difficulties, an act was passed making all men between the ages of 20 and 45 liable to be called for military service. Service could be avoided by paying a fee or finding a substitute. The act was seen as unfair to the poor, and riots in working class sections of New York City broke out in protest. A similar conscription act in the South provoked a similar reaction. *The American Civil War:* Conscription. www.us-civilwar. com/1863.htm.

a <u>steel</u> <u>breast plate</u>. It is made in the form of a vest and covered with blue cloth. It looks very well on a man. It was brought from New-berne by Mrs. <u>Guthrie</u>. She says it is worn by a great portion of the federal officers. I had seen accounts of it in the papers <u>frequently</u> but did not believe it until I had seen an actual demonstration, "<u>brave</u> <u>soldiers</u>." It looks very <u>much</u> <u>like</u> subjugating the South with such men as those!! Don't it? I am getting very tired of the K. L. A. I should like very much to get among <u>gentelman</u> once, if it should be my unhappy lot to have to remain in this company which I hope and pray it may not be. I shall always do my <u>duty</u> as a <u>soldier</u> and a man but further than that I do not intend to have anything to do with <u>Officers</u> <u>nor</u> <u>men</u>. They can tend to their business and I will tend to mine. I do not think I have been treated right at all and if there is any possible chance to get out of this company I shall most assuredly do it. I wish you would write me and tell me what you think about it. Since Capt. Ives and Lieut. <u>Rumley</u> left I do not think there are more than <u>six</u> real <u>gentelman</u> in this whole <u>company</u>. I see some of my acquaintance very often and when I go to Kinston I see Mr. <u>Harvey</u> <u>generally</u> with a <u>Female</u> strung on <u>his</u> <u>arm</u>. When I first met him on the street he did not seem to care about recognizing me and would not had I not spoke to him. Capt. Latham[176] has got a fine battery of <u>eight guns</u> and every thing ready for another

---

[176] Alexander C. Latham born in Craven County resigned as 1st Lieutenant in Company B, 10th Regiment on February 4, 1862 and was appointed Captain of this company January 20, 1862. He resigned September 16, 1863 to resume duties of sheriff of Craven County. Source: Dr. Louis H. Manarin, *North Carolina Troops 1861-1865 A Roster, Volume 1 Artillery,* State Division of Archives and History, Raleigh, N.C. 1988, p. 465.

fight. They say that John Potts[177] makes a fine <u>Officer</u>. Write as soon as you get this.

Your Affectionate Son
George A. Sparrow

Direct to me
Care Y. T. Adams
36 Regiment Artillery

Not Dated

Dear Father

Please send me a certificate like the one you gave me when I left. I lost that one. It was a fortunate thing for me that I had one or I would have had trouble. General Hill now has a guard that accompanies the train and they require papers from every one citizen as well as soldier – if a citizen to show he is not a conscript, and if a soldier, a furlough or orders.

Very Sincerely Your Son
George A. Sparrow

---

[177] John R. Potts (9/23/1839 – 5/8/1864), born in Beaufort County, was appointed 1st Lieutenant January 20, 1862 at age 22 and was appointed Captain September 16, 1863. When Captain Alexander Latham's company of light artillery known as "Branch Artillery" resigned, Potts was promoted and the company became known as "Potts Battery." He was killed in action at Spotsylvania Court House, Virginia. Source: Dr. Louis H. Manarin, Compiler, *North Carolina Troops 1861-1865 A Roster, Volume 1 Artillery*, State Division of Archives and History, Raleigh, N.C. 1988, pp. 464 and 594.

Green Wreath, Pitt County
May 15th 1863

My Dear Father

I arrived here this morning about 9 P. M. on the boat and succeeded in getting my two boxes and Aunt Annie's trunk safely to their destination. Thinking that you would be glad and anxious to hear of their safe arrival I concluded to write you immediately. On my way down I met Lt. Stephen Sparrow and he accompanied me down, he will remain with us a few days. Mr. Foreman[178] is not here at present having gone to Tarboro yesterday but will return on Sunday. I procured some fishing poles this evening and tomorrow we will try the <u>fish</u>. All the family are well and send love. I can think of nothing to write now that would interest you but will write more shortly.

Your Affectionate Son
George A. Sparrow

Green Wreath, Pitt County, North Carolina

---

[178] William Joseph Foreman was the plantation owner at Green Wreath.

My Dear Mother

I wrote you a few days since, but as Jennie was writing this morning, I thought I would write a note and put in her letter. Providence permitting I will get off from here next Wednesday or Thursday by leaving then it will allow me a weeks time. I am at a loss to know how to get to Tarborough unless I go with Tucker and he charges Five Dollars ($5). I had to pay him that to come down. Please write me immediately. It has rained almost incessantly ever since the day I came down. I am anxious to get back to Camp so that I shall have something to do. I am sick and tired of doing nothing. Mr. Foreman is in Tarborough and it is very lonely. Enclosed is a letter from Uncle Henry. Nan opened and answered it. I am heartily glad that this is the last time that I shall have to ask you for any assistance in the way of money for when I reach Camp, then I can take care of myself or rather the Government does it for me, and besides I shall be able to add something though it be but little to the support of the family. Give my love to Pa and the children.

Your Affectionate Son
Geo. A. Sparrow

I am <u>marking</u> all my clothes

——————

Camp Holmes Landing
July 15th 1863

Dear Father

I arrived here safely about 5 P. M. yesterday, and joined the Company last night. I am satisfied that I have done well, and shall be contented to remain. There is in the Company about 110 men, Louis Reid, Carney Bryan, John Selby, Jimmie Blount, Ed Small and myself mess and tent together. If you move to town I would be glad to have any of your mess things you can spare if you will send them to Willards store I will get them. Please send me a few clay pipes. Write to me

    Your Aff. Son

    George

––––––––––

Camp Holmes Landing

July 31 1863

My Dear Father

    The stationery and stamps that you sent me were received and I am very much obliged to you for it. If I had waited a few days it would have saved you that much, as I am supplied with paper as "for the war." I feel pretty tired and worn out today after my labor yesterday helping to unload a schooner that went ashore at the inlet. She was loaded with assorted cargo goods of every description. She came direct from New York, and the cargo was marked Port Royal South Carolina, and the Captain of her says he was bound for this inlet, and that his cargo was for the Government and he was a Government agent. The camp is full of cheeses, lemons, corned beef and all sorts of eatables. We use lemonade now in lieu of water. I would liked to have gotten a cheese and some things to send you but I could not get them without "pressing" them and that I would not do. I send you a dozen and a half lemons, a box of Colts pistol caps and a small comb. The lemons you can use to make lemonade and the caps will do for your pistol. They are very nice ones. Our mess is provided with a great many little niceties that were given to us, such as mustard, concentrated milk, coffee, rice, beef and the like. The schooner is now safely moored two or three miles up the sound. I was very much surprised to hear of the death of Uncle Henry. He was my favorite of all the family. I shall miss him very much. I have seen Yankee papers of the 17th. I suppose you have later. All the boys send their respects. Should any letters come for me please drop them in the office. It will save you trouble. Write me.

Your Affectionate Son
Geo. A. Sparrow

––––––––––

Camp Holmes Landing
Sunday August 23 1863

Dear Father

I would have written you some time ago but have been on pickett for the last week and had no writing materials, all of them being at Camp. Before this reaches you, you will doubtless have heard of the affair last night. I will tell you all of it that I know. I was not there being down at the station and when I arrived at the Camp all was over. A steamer came up the beach yesterday evening about sunset and anchored about opposite to where the schooner lay in the sound and it being such a common occurrence no one anticipated any danger from her. And all on board went to sleep as usual except of course the sentinel on deck. We had down there the 1st detachment Crawly Reid, Capt. Adams and Lt. Latham. The Yankees had their barges and about sixty men. They hauled them across the beach and came up on the left of the schooner and flanked there on land and were taking them all by surprise. The first they knew of their approach was their shooting at the sentinel on deck. They took Crawly and Lt. Latham but they escaped from them. They burned McMillans salt works, still, and all the houses around there. We had three horses burned to a coal, and five or six others burned very badly, cut up our harness and carried off three of our men and succeeded in burning the schooner. I never heard before in my life on putting an Artillery Company on Pickett <u>without</u> <u>arms</u>. This is the result of it. Goldsmith and his vessel turned out to be more harm than good. This was the <u>third</u> attempt to burn her. I shall return to the station today. Love to all at home when you write.

Your Affectionate Son

George A. Sparrow

Camp Pettigrew[179] Topsail

October 2nd 1863

My Dear Father

Your letter of the 30th sent by Sergt. Judkins has been received. I was very glad to hear that you were well. A day or two ago I sent by one of our wagoners a bundle containing three letters, one to you and two to be mailed. By your not saying anything about them I presume you did not get them. He says he left them at your office. In the letter I asked you to procure me if possibly some flour, crackers or something of the kind (flour if you can get it from the commissary). If you can get the things send me a bill and I will send you the money. If you get them send them to Brannans. Doctor Latham is in a hurry or I would write more. I am well. Write me if anything of interest transpires. I hope it may be so about your promotion.[180]

Sincerely Your Son

George A. Sparrow

Major Thomas Sparrow

Wilmington

---

[179] Camp Pettigrew is in Tyrrell County, N.C. and was named for Confederate General J. Johnston Pettigrew. *North Carolina Division of Parks and Recreation, Raleigh, North Carolina.*

[180] Thomas Sparrow was promoted to Major on January 9, 1863. Dr. Louis H. Manarin, Compiler, *North Carolina Troops 1861-1865 A Roster, Volume 1 Artillery,* State Division of Archives and History, Raleigh, N.C. 1988, p. 158.

Camp Whiting, Lockwood[181]
March 29th 1864

My "Dear Father"

The wagons leave for town in a few minutes and one of the Corporals has promised to take a letter for me. If you can sell that blue cloth coat of mine for a good price I would like for you to do it as it is entirely too small for me and if I go home I want to try and have me a suit made while I am down there. Capt Adams requests me to say to you that if you think there is any chance for him to get his Battery down to Tarboro or Greenville please use your influence to get it there.

Very Sincerely Your Son

Geo. Sparrow

––––––––––

Green Wreath Pitt Co
April 19th 1864

My Dear Father

I arrived here yesterday evening at 5 o'clk P. M. tired and worn out with walking. Wrote you short letter from Tarboro. I heard there that Jasper Keech intended to announce himself as a candidate for the Commons and intended to run on a ticket with you, defeat it if you can. I would not run on a ticket with such a <u>fool</u> as he is. Mrs. Mayo and Miss Bessie Joyner are spending the day here. The family are all well and send love.

Very Sincerely

Your Son

Geo. A. Sparrow

––––––––––

[181] Camp Whiting, Lockwood Folly River, a short tidal river near Supply, North Carolina in Brunswick County. Source: Wikipedia: Lockwood Folly River.

Green Wreath

April 20/64

Dear Father

Don't you think you might get me an extension of my furlough for 5 or 10 days. I would like very much to remain until the events of the troops in this section are over and besides I want to have my suit made and will hardly have the time. You might get Maj. Venable to do it. Got trunk this morning. All safe.

George

Chapter 6

Unsung Heroes

With their young men away at war, Washington and Beaufort County came under the heel of the Union Army. When New Bern fell on March 14, 1862, the Georgia regiment, under Colonel McMillen, evacuated Washington. On March 20th, the U. S. Transport Guide, with a convoy of gunboats, left New Bern for Washington. When the gunboat Delaware with two companies of the 24th Massachusetts entered Washington, they found the town evacuated by its defenders and abandoned by about three-quarters of its inhabitants. Many had left and found refuge with friends and relatives further inland.

Union forces continued to occupy Washington from the end of March, 1862, until April 20th, 1864.[182]

Life was not easy for the women and children who were left behind when husbands and sons went off to war. In their own words Annie Blackwell Sparrow (Mrs. R. H. Lewis) and Elizabeth Sparrow McCord, daughters of Major Thomas Sparrow, recall some of their experiences during the Civil War.

---

[182] Col. C. Wingate Reed, *Beaufort County Two Centuries of Its History,* Edwards & Broughton Co., Raleigh, N.C., p. 184.

Excerpts from
Recollections of the Civil War
by Annie Blackwell Sparrow

"After the fall of New Berne, our town was evacuated by the Confederate forces including a Georgia regiment. On March 20, 1862, the 24th Mass. Regiment on a Transport Guide, and two gunboats were sent to Washington from New Bern. This expedition was stopped by a blockade which had been erected in the river a few miles below the town by our forces. One gunboat, however, with two companies, succeeded in passing the blockade and landed at our town. I had been sent to a neighboring town to school soon after the return of my father from prison, and was not at home at this time, but my mother was still there with her younger children. Consternation spread among our people when the dreaded enemy was at last in our midst, and we all expected little less than a general massacre. However, "even the devil is not as black as he is painted," and some of us still live to tell the tale of life in a town garrisoned by the enemy. At this time, however, the Yankees only spent a short time, and after marching through the principal streets, flaunting their colors, they all returned to New Bern. Soon after this, a permanent garrison occupied the town and held it until the spring of 1864. The gunboats were anchored in the river in front of the town, and our people were most uncomfortable and unhappily situated. Burning with love for the southern cause, our people were obliged to be most particular in giving expression to their patriotic feelings. Ladies and girls went out very little as the rude stares of the soldiers and the often unpleasant remarks were very hard to bear as we must. Singing southern songs in private parlors was prohibited, and on one occasion, an officer called to tell my mother that if her daughters sang any more southern songs in their parlor, they would be arrested and put in jail. Considering it of all glorious things, the most glorious to suffer for our cause, I was anxious to repeat the offense, but my mother firmly forbade it.

No letters could be sent or received except through military headquarters, and were of course, opened and read. But we were fortunate – my father being a lawyer had clients and friends in the country around the town, and they brought us letters in various ways. Of course they were all stopped, questioned, and searched as they came through the outposts. But they managed to elude the vigilance of the guards, and brought us letters hid in the bottom of a basket of eggs, and in their shoes, tacked inside their bonnets, and one colored man brought us a letter from my father tied inside his cravat. This last named affair brought us into trouble as it was reported and distorted, we supposed by our cook. A report went to headquarters that my father had written that he would slip in the town that night and spend several days with his family, hidden, of course, by them. The next day, a squad of soldiers commanded by a traitor, a low fellow to whom and to whose family my parents had often given charity before the war, came to our home and searched it thoroughly, and most impudently and offensively, being very rude to my mother. The man in charge said to the soldiers as they entered, "If you find that d….. rebel, shoot him on sight," and before this the wife and children had been kind to him.

Across the street from us, on the corner, was a small house occupied after the town was garrisoned by a class of women whom I blush to name. They sat on the porch day and night, and always some soldiers were with them. So offensive was the proximity that we kept the windows closed next to them and passed the street by another way. But at the sight of any of us in the yard or garden they would sing loudly, "Hang Capt. S...... on a sour apple tree." My mother went on one occasion to headquarters to ask permission to spend a day outside the town with country friends, having received notice from my father that he would be near the town on that day. But the general in command had been informed that my mother was sending and receiving letters to and from friends outside the lines, not only for herself but for many others, and he could not find out how. So her request was refused in such a rude and insulting manner that she returned to her home, burning with indignation and outraged pride. Among other things the general told her that she was a "rebel mail bag." We children were very proud of this and considered it a grand title.

The report that my father would come in to see his family was not so improbable a thing as it seemed, for on several occasions our men outside did elude the guards and get inside the town, and on one occasion a Yankee sentinel was killed by one who slipped in at night.

General James Green Martin
Courtesy of the North Carolina Office of Archives and History
Raleigh, North Carolina

Joy W. Sparrow

About four o'clock on the morning of September 6, 1862, a Confederate Company commanded by Gen. J. G. Martin[183] attacked the town. There was then a garrison of ten companies and there were two gunboats in the river. Our men surprised the pickets and dashed into the town, captured four guns and some prisoners. For three hours the fight waged fiercely and our men gained some advantage. Imagine our fright and our hopes when we were awakened by the noise of the fight, not knowing at first what it was. Peering through the closed shutters, early dawn as it was, we could at last distinguish dashing past, the grey uniform we loved so well. How madly our hearts beat and how earnestly we prayed. A Yankee gun was planted on our corner just a half block away, our men and another gun firing upon it. Our hopes were high, but our men labored under a great disadvantage. At one time they met four companies of cavalry and a battery all ready on their way to march to Plymouth. This with the shot and shell from the gunboats decided the day, and our brave men withdrew after a hotly contested fight. The gunboats threw many shots into the town and afterwards into the woods beyond. Our part of the town was badly injured. As the shells went whizzing over our roof, my mother assembled us all in a

---

[183] General James G. Martin (February 14, 1819 – October 4, 1878) born in Elizabeth City, N.C. was a West Point graduate of 1840. While serving in the Mexican War he lost his right arm after it was shattered by grapeshot. Due to the loss of his arm, he became known by the nickname "Old One Wing." In 1861 he offered his services to North Carolina and was commissioned captain in the Cavalry. He was later appointed adjutant general of North Carolina. At his suggestion, blockade running ships were first employed to bring supplies to the Confederacy from Europe. On September 28, 1861 he was appointed commander-in-chief of the State forces with the rank of major general of militia. Martin was able to raise 12,000 more men than the state quota. After Martin had completed his work he applied for duty in the field, and in May, 1862 was promoted to brigadier general in the provisional army. In August, 1862 he was given command of the district of North Carolina with headquarters at Kinston. Source: http://thomaslegion. net/martin.html, biography at Thomas' Legion. *General James Green Martin Biography.*

room downstairs. With her weeping children around her, she besought God to protect us. We were on our knees when a shell went crashing through the roof of our house and we clung together in speechless terror. But not our mother. Perfectly cool, calm, and quiet she showed not one sign of fear for herself. She thought only of her children and invalid sister. The next day, or rather that day, was a terrible time. We kept our shutters tightly closed for outside the streets swarmed with angry men, and the army's most offensive and threatening remarks were made for our ears. All day the soldiers were picking bullets from the planks of our house where they were imbedded during the firing. It was told by the Yankees that our women fired upon the Yankee soldiers from the windows on the morning of the fight. It was utterly untrue, but notwithstanding, squads of soldiers (rude) were sent throughout the town to search for firearms. My brother had left his gun with which he hunted as a boy, and fearing that its presence in the house might be construed to our discomfort, my mother carried it upstairs to the garret, ripped off a plank from the floor and hid the gun there. Soon afterward our house was filled with rough men. Nothing was sacred to them. Bureau drawers and trunks were all opened and thrown on the floor. Everything was ransacked and then with sneers and jeers left us to restore as best we could, order in our disheveled home, for wrecked it was. The shell had so torn and shattered the roof that a hard rain demonstrated the fact that we could no longer live there in comfort. Representing this at headquarters we were allowed to move to another house in another part of the town. During the September fight, several of our men were killed; they claimed to have found twelve wounded and to have taken twenty prisoners. I never knew the truth, for we were not allowed to visit or to nurse our poor men, glad as we would have been to have spent our whole time with them, and to have given them of our best, poor and small as that was. One poor old woman

Joy W. Sparrow

who pled curiosity as her excuse, did get into the hospital, and stayed there and nursed them faithfully and lovingly, though pretending that she regarded them in the light of enemies. Her bones now rest in the cemetery near those of the men she cared for and under the shadow of the monument "To Our Confederate Dead."

Some months after the siege, my mother received through what we called her underground mail, a letter from my brother stating that he would be in the vicinity of the town on a certain day and would wait her coming at a farmhouse three miles in the country, hoping she could obtainpermission to spend the day out of town. A pass was secured for her and one of my sisters who was under twelve years of age by a friendly acquaintance who had some influence at headquarters. Going to one of our merchants who was not far from us, my mother bought a pair of boots, socks, underclothes, coffee, sugar and several other articles, all of which we conveyed to our house surreptitiously and at different times. To none of her children but the little girl who was going with her did she tell any of her plans. Early on the morning of the day they were to start, she took my sister into her room, locked the door and there proceeded to dress herself and daughter with the articles she wished to carry out. Hoopskirts were then worn and without them her plan would not have been feasible. The boots she hung, one on each side, inside the hoopskirt, and the other articles were so securely and ingeniously arranged under their clothing that after she was through, there was nothing unusual in the appearance of either of them. Thus burdened, they passed safely through the sentinel and walked three miles without any accident. My brother was awaiting them and after they had dined with kind friends, my mother proposed a walk in the woods on the pretence of a private and uninterrupted talk. When in a pine thicket, my mother and sister began to untie and display their treasures to the delighted eyes of the half-clothed, half-starved soldier boy. They were hidden in the woods. The next morning my brother gathered his stores together and returned to the army. To the honor of the little girl in this story, be it said that she did not breathe one word of the contraband goods to any human soul until after we had left our home and were outside of the Yankee lines.

Gen. Daniel Harvey Hill
Courtesy of the North Carolina Office of Archives and History
Raleigh, North Carolina

On the 30th of March 1863, Gen. D. H. Hill[184] gathered in all about 9,000 men around there and began a siege. He was trying, not only to capture the town and garrison, but collect supplies for our hungry armies. Our men were all around the town and had temporary forts on the other side of the river opposite the town. Our forts held in check for a while the gunboats and transports that were trying to

---

[184] Daniel Harvey Hill (July 12, 1821 – September 24, 1889) was born in York District, South Carolina to Solomon and Nancy Cabeen Hill. He was known as an aggressive leader, and as an austere, deeply religious man, with a dry, sarcastic humor. Source: Hal Bridges, *Lee's Maverick General: Daniel Harvey Hill*, Lincoln: University of Nebraska Press, 1991.

get up to the relief of the garrison. These gunboats daily engaged our batteries. Our men guarded the roads leading from the town to New Bern so that no help could come to the garrison from that point. The Yankee gunboats threw shells across the town, hoping to hit our troops on the land side. And our own batteries across the river, in firing at the gunboats at the wharves, sometimes sent the balls too far, and they fell in the town, damaging houses, but there was no one killed.

At the beginning of the siege, Gen. Hill had asked the commandant of the garrison that the women and children be allowed to leave the town, but this was refused. So dangerous was the firing from the gunboats, and from our own forts, that the people who had cellars and basements lived in them during the whole siege, inviting as many as they could accommodate to share their security. We had no cellar, but a kind neighbor who had quite a large one, offered us a place in his. The firing began at dawn and ended at sunset, so we felt secure at night. As we could, the ladies of the two families cooked enough to last during the day, and as early as possible, we moved to our underground retreat, where with rugs, chairs, books, and sewing, and dolls for the children, we managed to while away the days. Loving the southern cause with all our hearts, it was trying to remain inactive, afraid to say one word of what we felt, thinking of, loving and praying for, our brave men who were so near to us and yet so utterly separated from us. One morning very early as my mother was dressing hastily in order to get down into the cellar, a ball came crashing through the front of the house, on into the bedroom, through the headboard of the bed where my little brother was lying about two or three years old, then fell into the back yard. Covered with splinters, plaster and dust, the little fellow raised up and cried out, "Oh, mamma, I'ze struck." The ball came from a battery of Whitworth guns directly across the river, and we afterwards learned that my father, who had obtained leave to come down and see if he could learn anything of his family, was at that fort and was directing the firing of that very gun at that very time. After the siege was over my mother buried the ball in the back yard, dug it up after the war was over and we returned to our homes, and it now is in the possession of the boy who was struck. It has served as a plaything for his son, and namesake of the soldier who sent it speeding towards his son.

Being unable to blockade the river successfully, and having also received orders to send a part of the besieging forces to help the army of Northern Virginia, Gen. Hill raised the siege on the 15th of April, 1863 and our hearts were almost broken by our disappointment. Our artillery did good work. One of the gunboats was hit during the first four days of the siege by ninety-eight shots from the battery of Whitworth guns. Another steamer was hit forty times. After quiet was restored, we all came out of our holes in the ground and settled again sadder than ever in our homes. The men of the garrison were very much incensed by this attack and we soon began to feel the effects of their anger. A proclamation was issued to the effect that every Southerner over twelve years of age must take the oath of allegiance to the United States Government or leave the town within ten days. The order was sent to every Southern home, and sent consternation and dismay to all hearts. Many of our people could not go away. All they had was in our little town, and they had no means and nowhere to go when they left their homes. Those who stayed took the oath with the mental reservation that they did not mean it, that an oath under such compulsory circumstances was not binding, and they all disregarded it at the very first opportunity. Friends came to my mother urging her to submit to what they considered the inevitable, representing to her that she was more comfortable where she was and safer than as a refugee with six children to look after, and her husband and oldest son in the army and unable to help her. But she said that nothing would induce her to say that she would be loyal to the United States, and that she would not give help to her own people. So we prepared to leave our home with no idea where we would go or what would become of us. Just before the ten days expired, soldiers, officers, I think, were sent around to the different homes to ask the result of the order for exile, and my mother expressed in most emphatic terms her determination. Every night after it was dark, my mother and her children had been engaged in carrying to the neighbors who were going to stay in town such things as we most valued and could carry ourselves. My parents had never owned but three slaves and the only one remaining to us was a poor crippled girl about my own age whom my mother had raised with her own children and who had no kin or friends but us. No Negroes were allowed to go with their owners, and it was well for us that this was the case as our poor servant would have been a great burden. My mother left her provisions to this girl and left her in the care of some Negroes who lived near us. We heard that she went to New Bern soon after we left her, and did not live long, missing, no doubt, the comforts to which she had been accustomed. On the morning of the day on which we were to leave our home, an ambulance wagon was driven to our door to carry us out of town, and a squad of soldiers came with it. We were allowed to take two trunks of clothing and two feather beds, the latter tied up in quilts. Poor Jane, the Negro girl we were leaving, clung to my mother's skirts in distress, and when obliged to let go, fell on the floor of the hall with cries of despair. We children were all crying, but there were no tears in my mother's eyes. They were bright and flashing with indignation which nothing but the thought of her children enabled her to suppress. The soldiers stood around the porch jeering and laughing in evident enjoyment of the scene. As we went out, they went in and nothing of what we left in our home did we ever see again. It was the same case at all the homes of all the other refugees. The Yankees shipped north all they wanted and what they did not care for was given to Negroes of the town. The ambulance carried us a mile from town, and there, with many other families of loyal friends, we were left to fare as best we could. We were in the large yard of a farmhouse, and it was a pitiful sight to see a family here and there over the lawn sitting on their trunks and wondering what would become of them. The situation soon became known through the surrounding country, and farmers who could, came, or sent, for the refugees, and during the day all found shelter. A generous friend whose house was already filled, gave us a warm welcome, hospitality and kind sympathy. But we were still far away from my father, and my mother was anxious to get within the Confederate lines so that she might communicate with him. Accordingly, she expressed with deep gratitude for the kindness of our hosts, a desire to reach Tranter's Creek, where were our nearest picket lines. Mr. G. could furnish only a cart to carry our trunks and bed, and so we all walked the seven miles to the creek, the younger children occasionally being given a rest on the loaded cart when very weary. Oh, with what joyful hearts did we see the grey coats of our beloved soldiers, all heroes to us. God bless the living and dead. But we were still separated as the bridge over the creek had been burned and the black cypress water rolled between us. The soldiers were eager to help us, and soon procured canoes and transported us onto what seemed a happy land. I remember sitting on a log and recounting to the interested men, some of them almost as young as I was, our experiences while living among the enemy. Col. Ferebee[185] and his regiment were encamped near the creek, and hearing of our condition, he came to offer to my mother every service in his power. She asked him to send word to Col. L., an old friend of my father's, that we were there and homeless, which he immediately did. Soon after, Col. L.'s carriage and wagon for our baggage arrived and we were most warmly welcomed by the kind friends who could not do enough for us. Two of the children broke out with measles, and we were obliged to trespass on their hospitality for about two weeks. None of us can ever forget their unvarying kindness, and warm friendships formed between the young people, which have lasted until the present day, when grey hairs are worn by those who were children then. My father was then stationed at Wilmington, and as soon as possible, he procured a leave of absence and came to Col. L. to make some arrangements for a home for us."[186]

---

[185] Colonel Dennis Dozier Ferebee (11/9/1815 – 4/27/1884) was born in Currituck County, N.C. and graduated from the University of North Carolina in 1839. He was a farmer, lawyer and legislator (five terms in the North Carolina House of Commons and a member of the 1861 Convention that voted for secession.) Ferebee opposed secession as unconstitutional, maintaining that the Constitution of the United States "is not a league of confederacy but a government founded on the adoption of the people" and "no state authority has the power to dissolve these relations." He lost his point, of course, and like the majority of his fellow citizens, wholeheartedly cast his lot with the Confederacy and joined the Southern army. Source: William S. Powell, Editor, *Dictionary of North Carolina Biography*, Vol. 2 D-G, The University of North Carolina Press, Chapel Hill, N.C., 1994, pp. 187-188.

[186] Thomas Sparrow Papers, Collection No. 1, East Carolina Manuscript Collection, J. Y. Joyner Library, East Carolina University, Greenville, N.C.

An Addition to the Writings of Annie Sparrow
Written by Annie's Sister, Elizabeth Sparrow McCord in 1938

"My sister died before she finished her war memories – and I was too young to remember anything but childish happenings. Mother and we children were still at Colonel L's where she left off. A young planter in an adjoining county hearing that we had been driven out of our home town – got word to mother that we could have his plantation house. He and another soldier were home from the hospital in Richmond – until they were strong enough to join Lee in Virginia. Col. L. drove us to a nearby town (1) where Mr. F. (2) and his servants met us with a big wagon and two white mules and a carriage and apron of shiny black horses. We drove eight miles to the plantation. It was named Green Wreath – and it was a lovely name for it. The big colonial house stood in a marvelous grove – with apple and peach orchards on both sides of it – and the white road winding up to the door. There was an overseer's house on one side of the yard – which Mr. F. and his friend occupied. His housekeeper had one room in the "Great House" as the Negroes called it. We soon settled down – and the happiness of us children knew no bounds. Out of the Yankee lines – with woods to roam in – berries to pick and fruit of all kinds to eat. We would tie our sunbonnets upside down on our backs – fill them with apples and munch on them all the time. There were several hundred Negroes on the plantation who had to be fed and cared for. Mother would buy "cow peas" and bacon when she could and sometimes sweet potatoes with Confederate money. The farmers had no salt to save their meat – but father (3) would get a little to mother sometimes – as she could buy food for us. He had the soldiers at Fort Fisher fill all the receptacles they could get with water from the ocean, and when the water evaporated it would leave a little salt. We went barefooted all the time – summer and winter. The road in front of the house was beautiful white sand – and some cold days we three little girls would go out at noon and sit in the road and cover our feet with the top of the sand which the sun had warmed. The Yankees would every now and then raid thru the country stealing hogs, chickens, horses and anything to eat. The Negroes ran in one night saying the Yankees were only a few miles away. Mr. F. and his soldier friend took their guns and went in the woods to hide. The Yanks swarmed all over the place – filled the house, stole all our silver – and took a gold pin mother was wearing in her collar. She asked the man please not to take it and he said "shut your damn mouth – where's your watch?" She told him that her husband and son were both in the Southern Army and had more use for their watches than she did. She had three in an inside pocket to her underskirt. My eldest sister – then 17 – married the young planter and we moved to a town nineteen miles away. We found the Yankees there in full force – but father had yellow fever with his soldiers down on the Cape Fear River – and was sent home sick. He had the unloading of the blockade steamers at Fort Fisher which Mrs. Mitchell tells about in "Gone WithThe Wind." We had no coffee during the whole war – and mother and the older girls would cut sweet potatoes in little cubes, dry them – parch them, grind them and make coffee. I remember one week we had nothing to eat but sweet potatoes – and I thought I never would eat another sweet potato – but I have.

When father heard that some Yankees were hunting for all the Confederate Officers who hadn't surrendered and given up their swords and would be in our town a certain day – he walked two miles to the Tar River – took a canoe and paddled twenty miles down the river and staid all day. His sword is now in the History Building in Raleigh, N.C. with his coat. In time we went back to our home town (4) – with no clothes, no house – no money and no furniture. When the Yankees left our town they set fire to it and very few buildings were left. It was a Chicago Regiment. A good neighbor saved a mahogany Napoleon bedstead – a cradle and a dining table for mother.

Granny[187]

(1) Greenville, N.C.
(2) William Joseph Foreman
(3) Thomas Sparrow
(4) Washington, N.C.

---

[187] Grimes-Bryan Collection #16, East Carolina Manuscript Collection, J. Y. Joyner Library, East Carolina University, Greenville, N.C.

The following story was taken from the *History of First Presbyterian Church, Washington, North Carolina:*

"Since at least the 13th century, bells have been calling worshipers to prayer. No one could imagine a church without a bell, so naturally a necessary part of the original equipment of our church was a bell. One of the great sacrifices made by this congregation was the gift of this bell to the Confederacy. Churches all over the South gave bells to be made into bullets during that sad period. Of the church bells left in Washington it is recorded that one of them rang continuously as Yankee fire consumed the town.

After the Civil War, Presbyterian women initiated a project to collect scrap metal all over the ruined town. The object was another church bell. In 1872 the thousand pounds deemed sufficient had been collected and the Trustees of the church sent it north on one of the Fowle sailing ships to be cast. It was arranged that the bell would be picked up on a future trip, however, that trip was a disastrous one. The vessel, the "Catherine Johnson," on her return voyage wrecked off the coast of Hatteras with the Presbyterian church bell on board. The ship's valuable cargo was lost! Astoundingly enough, that thousand pound bell was washed ashore and salvaged. Presbyterians never doubted that it was saved by a miracle. That bell hangs in our steeple today." P.M.W.[188]

---

[188] *The History of the First Presbyterian Church, Washington, North Carolina. 1823-1973*, Washington, N. C

Chapter 7

The Vilest Sinner

Author C. Wingate Reed describes the sad state of affairs when General Lee surrendered on April 9, 1865 and the Confederacy collapsed. General Johnston surrendered two weeks later and within a few days Governor Vance was captured near Statesville and all semblance of Civil government in North Carolina vanished.

General John McAllister Schofield took command of the captured State of North Carolina. Police forces under the command of Union officers were established in every county.

Weary, defeated, and discouraged men in tattered gray began to struggle home. Some rode on horses or mules, far more made the long, discouraging trip on foot. Near twenty out of each hundred who had gone so bravely off to war did not return. Their blood hallowed the soil of half a hundred battlefields from Georgia to Pennsylvania and from Maryland to Texas.

Those who had left the prosperous and thriving town of Washington, North Carolina came home to a burned-out skeleton of a town, peopled by few more than 500 grim-visaged men and women and a scattering of hollow-eyed, hungry children.

Small farmers faced huge problems. Cattle and stock were gone, cribs and smokehouses empty, buildings and fences run down, and land grown up in weeds. Plantation owners lost their able-bodied male Negroes; huge acres of land were now a burden rather than an asset, and taxes continued to be levied against them.[189]

---

[189] C. Wingate Reed, *Beaufort County Two Centuries of its History,* Edwards and Broughton Co., Raleigh, N.C. 1962, pp. 192-194.

Scarcely had the war ended when dishonest white men – mainly from the North – and ignorant Negroes got control of the State governments in the South, and for many years longer that section suffered almost as much as it had during the war. Everyone now believes that, had Lincoln's life been spared, he would have saved the South from such a calamity.[190]

"At home on sick leave when the war ended, Major Sparrow refused to surrender and paddled twenty miles in a small boat in order to escape with his sword. So adamant were his loyalties to the Confederacy that for several years after the war, according to one writer, 'he led a laborious life as a farmer rather than take the oath of allegiance.'

Afterwards, in partnership with James Edward Shepherd who was later a Supreme Court Justice, Sparrow resumed his law practice in Washington and during the sessions of 1870-72 and 1878-80 served as a conservative Democrat in the General Assembly."[191]

George, not trained in any profession and having had farm experience in Illinois, became a tenant farmer. His letters show that he rented land from sister Nan who had inherited part of the Green Wreath Plantation, and rented land from Dr. Selby at Lake Landing, Hyde County. While here, with encouragement from friends, he decided to study law. Just how long George farmed and boarded with Dr. and Mrs. Selby is not known.

In 1874 George married Susan Selby Brown, daughter of Sylvester T. and Elizabeth Bonner Brown. Seven children were born in Wash-

---

[190] Waddy Thompson, *The First Book In United States History,* D. C. Heath and Company, Boston, Mass., 1929, p. 314.

[191] Article by W. Keats Sparrow, Professor at East Carolina University, in *Dictionary of North Carolina Biography,* Edited by William S. Powell, Volume 5 P-S, The University of North Carolina Press, Chapel Hill, N.C. , 1994, p. 407.

ington, North Carolina between the years 1875 and 1887: Thomas, Sylvester Brown, George Brown, Annie Mariah, Annie Foreman, Elizabeth Bonner, and Minnie Shepherd.

George passed the bar exam and became a law partner with his Dad practicing law for sixteen years, serving as a Solicitor for eight years.

The 1870's must have been a trying time for George and his family. As the letters show, drinking became a problem but with a father's "tough love" and by the grace of God, George realized there was hope for change.

———————

Major Sparrow's address to the Negroes expresses the struggles of the South and gives encouragement and hope for both blacks and whites.

Major Thomas Sparrow's Address to Negroes
July 4th 1867

We celebrate a day of glorious memories, Joy and Celebration.

By Providence of God you are interested participants. Why do we celebrate this 4th day of July. Why is it the Nation's holiday? I will tell you.

Several hundred years ago this country was a vast forest inhabited by Indians. English & other people settled and drove out the Indians. Thirteen States formed colonies or dependents of Great Britain. Your race brought here in British ships from Africa to cultivate the soil & clear up the forests. England began to oppress the states, taxed them without their consent – sent them to England to be tried – would not allow them representation – quartered soldiers on the people. The States complained only to be oppressed and treated a lot worse.

What was to be done? They resolved to rebel & to throw off their oppressive government of Great Britain. A congress of delegates from all the states went to Philadelphia. George Washington was there, Benj. Franklin, Thos. Jefferson, John Adams, Patrick Henry were all there, great and good men. On the 4th day of July 1776 just 91 years ago these great men made what is called a Declaration of Independence. They resolved to separate from Great Britain, to be a separate nation, & pledged their lives & honor. They established in this Declaration certain great principles. That all men are born free & equal. All just government is by the consent of the governed – the people. When governments become oppressive, it is not only their right, but their duty to rebel & throw off the oppressive government. The oppressed people & not the oppressors are to judge of this necessity. This Declaration hastens with shouts of joy all over this land, celebrated by bon fires & illuminations ever since. Hailed with joy by other oppressed nations for it brought the people their rights.

A bloody war of eight years followed. Washington led our Armies, & God fought on our side. Our people were poor & suffered for the want of means to carry on the war. Our armies were small & our soldiers suffered from cold & hunger & nakedness. They lived on roots and left the tracks of bloody feet upon the snow. Yet they triumphed. The great rebellion became a success. At Yorktown in Virginia Lord Cornwallis surrendered to General Washington. Peace followed & a nation was formed.

Now you are here today celebrating the Nation's jubilee. Here as <u>freemen</u>. No one envies you this loss. No one would make you slaves again. All wish you well & desire your prosperity. They wish you to deserve freedom & to enjoy it. Here not only as freemen but as <u>citizens</u>. You can go to the polls with white men & vote for those who are to make your laws & to govern you. Shall you not always go as friends? Whether liberty and citizenship is to prove a blessing to you will depend upon yourselves. Here is unity with badges of brotherhood and sisterhood. Feeling our interest in each other. Societies formed to improve your conditions are praiseworthy. Care for the sick – the poor – the widows & orphans – the unfortunate.

To be good citizens you should be <u>intelligent</u> men and women. Therefore seek to improve yourselves. Educate your children – teach them virtue & honesty & industry. Then you will gain respect. All good men will bid you God speed & God himself will bless you. Not afraid of work. <u>All</u> your <u>efforts</u> at improvement can be made without collisions with your white friends & neighbors. They will assist & encourage you. You should seek their friendship not their amnesty. Distrust any advice or any movement intended to alienate you from the whites, come from what quarter it may.

We all inhabit the same country. <u>All</u> <u>Southern</u> <u>citizens</u>. Abraham & Lot agreed to separate. We cannot do this. Our fortunes bound up together. Interests are the same. We struggle on together. The North does not want us. It wanted you less. You could not go there to live; could not vote if you went. Mobs would drive you out of their towns.

Why so many of you here, in this poor country, so desolated? Why did you not go away when free? I will tell you. You love this land – you love this people – It is your country – your home – your people – Here you were born – were married – worshiped God – buried your children. You love these fields– these woods – this river. In these fields you tilled – you hunted in these woods – fished in these streams. These are the things that take hold of your hearts and our hearts. Memories that cannot be forgotten.

Ruth's language to her mother-in-law Naomi – "Entreat me not to leave thee, etc." Let there be no amnesty between us. No black mans party. No white mans party.

Don't you see that their prosperity & your prosperity are one & the same? If they prosper you prosper. If they suffer you suffer. If they remain poor, you remain poor. If their cotton is taxed $3 the bale, so is yours. Traders don't pay taxes, laborers and consumers pay them. The whole South is poor. Needs capital & labor. Forests – fields – railroads – churches – towns – all must work. Avoid two classes. Those who want your money & those who want your votes. If you wish good advice from a wise friend, look out a man who has no eye upon your purse & no interest in your vote.

God grant our wishes. Be perpetual & real. No word of bitterness between white & black. God grant you grown up virtues and honesty and prosperity to the end of the age. This being of the Lord.[192]

---

[192] Thomas Sparrow Papers, #1878, Southern Historical Collection, The Wilson Library, University of North Carolina, Chapel Hill, North Carolina.

Green Wreath No Ca
February 18 1870

Dear Father

I send you by Panins Flat the cow and calf, one barrel vinegar and one barrel Peas. I had intended sending a bale of Pea vines and one of shucks had he remained a day longer. The Pork was received. Please send bill and a barrel good ordinary flour say about $9.00. My hands want some occasionally and I want some that I can eat myself. Mr. Moore has a barrel common flour and I will take that and let him have the bal. you send for the table, he paying the difference in cost. I am progressing <u>splendidly</u> with my farm and my hopes rise every day. Write me if you can make any arangements about 1-1/2 Ton Grain. Wrote Nan today.

Sincerely Your Son
Geo. A. Sparrow

––––––––––

Green Wreath N.C.
March 16 1870

Dear Father

I send you by the Steamer one barrel and one bag peas. In the barrel you will find the Swingle-Tree belonging to Iveys wagon. The other pieces I could not find any where on the place. Take good care of the wagon. Mr. Jno Randall has promised me a pair of Goats for it and Mrs. Lewis told me today that she had the stamp in good order in Tarboro and would give it to Nan[193] when she made her promised visit. I will keep the "team" here and try and break them some (by driving

---

[193] Nan fell in love with the plantation owner William Joseph Foreman. They were married February 1, 1865, and to this union one son Ivey was born December 11, 1866. Sparrow Family Records.

with a line) before sending them down. Jno is large enough to drive them now and the boys can have quite a stylish turn-out to bring butter and eggs from down town. It will not take much to feed them and I will try and contribute that from here. Mr Cotton has backed out from planting the low ground as first proposed in cotton and corn and wishes to plant an oat patch there. Mr. Lewis requested me to write you and ask if you think it better than letting the land lie out. The present arrangement (if you think it proper) is for Mr. Moore to plant 8 acres of it in corn and he and myself to plant 16 acres in oats for the use of the team this fall – Mr. L. furnishing 1/2 the seed, doing 1/2 the labor and 1/2 and Mr. Cotton the remainder or as much of it as he chooses in oats. I think myself this would be a very good arrangement for me. It would not take my mules but two days work and I will have the benefit of 8 acres in oats. So if you like it you can get me 5 bushels seed (there being 3 bushels here now I can get) and I will plant with Mrs. Lewis. She is very much afraid and justly so. I reckon that we will not have forage enough for the year. If I should not need them for the team they always sell well. Mrs L wants you to write her by return mail (at Tarboro) so she can give Mr Cotton an answer – not being willing to do so until she hears from you. She told Cotton that she would hold him responsible for the rent any how. He refused to pay it – both got pretty warm and had a stout quarrel and Mr Moore says he thought they would fight. She and Mr Broaddus had it also, she forbidding him to cut any more lumber on "Williams" land after today. She only staid here part of two days but kept things stirred up. To me she was as always clever and had not a "single" word to say nor a suggestion to make. She brought down with her 5 Tons of the Pataksco Guano and says the Egecombe Farmers are buying a good deal. I wish you would hurry up mine. I told Jimmy to save me Mr. Wilson's cotton plows –

don't let him sell them.

Love to all

Aff Your Son

George A Sparrow

I neglected to say that all of us Cotton, Moore,
and myself of course pay rent to Nan.
Send Summer Oats.
4 No 50 Plow Points

Green Wreath No Ca

March 23rd 1870

Dear Father

I received three letters from you this morning dated 15th, 17 and 19. I think it would be better for you to direct them in future the old way. Since the mail carrier has stopped taking passengers, he is much more punctual in bringing the mail. All the things sent per Steamer were duly received for which I am very much obliged. The oats are all planted. My half will give me enough forage for this and part of another year. I am very anxious about Mother myself and should she get any worse want you to let me know. When you come up to Pitt Court I would like for you to come up here on Saturday stay over Sunday and take a look at my farm. Would be glad for you to come sooner if you could. Give my love to Mother and all the children.

Very Truly

Your Son

Geo. A. Sparrow

Green Wreath No Ca
April 2nd 1870

Dear Father

I have been or sent down to the Steamboat for the Grain ever since your letter was received telling me it would be up. If it is in Washington please try and send by Mondays boat. I am badly in need of it for 3 or 4 days. To day I commenced drilling manure and disking up and should it not come by Wednesday at least I will have to arrange some land without. With a big crop and no more team I have no time share. If any thing has happened so you cant get it let me know by Mondays boat. I send you three bales forage for the cow. I think they are worth as much as a bale of Hay and will save you that much. I shall look for you up during court week. I wrote Mother a few lines.

Very Sincerely
Your Son
Geo A Sparrow

P.S.
I had some iron cut off at Mr. Fulfords for flute Plows. The bill is two dollars or there about I think. Ask him to send that on Monday too.

G.S.

Green Wreath No. Ca.

May 2nd 1870

Dear Father

The 1/2 Ton Grain has been received (5 bags) and is in the ground. I like it very much, but it is no better than the Pataksco which Mr. Lewis bought <u>on</u> <u>time</u> and for less money. My hands will be planting up to the time of the arrival of the boat today and if Mr. Burbank's come I will finish this week. The cotton planted while you were here has made a splendid stand <u>every</u> <u>seed</u> coming up and some planted as late as last Wednesday I see this morning is coming up. The year promises to make an excellent one for cotton. Give my <u>best</u> <u>love</u> to Mother and all the family and tell them that in order to avoid all accidents of the kind that befell me when last in Washington I shall take good care not to repeat my visit to that place – nor to Judge J. B. Jones Honorable Court. I feel just as if I would like to be a second "Robinson Crusoe" or one of the crowded denizens[194] of some vast city <u>unknown</u>, where I could console myself with the thoughts that no multitude of eyes were bent upon me pitying, censuring and condemning. Were I to commit my thoughts and feelings to paper <u>now</u> they would rival even E. A. Poe's "Black Cat."[195]

Cotton will act as a <u>sovereign</u> <u>remedy</u>.

Very Sincerely

Your Son George

---

[194] An inhabitant or resident. Source: *The American Heritage College Dictionary*, Third Edition, Houghton Mifflin Company, Boston, New York, 1993.
[195] *The Black Cat* by Edgar Allan Poe is a short story of a murder by a man who will be hung the following morning for his crime. It is a study of the psychology of guilt. The murderer carefully conceals his crime and believes himself invincible but eventually breaks down and reveals himself, impelled by a nagging reminder of his guilt. *The Black Cat* first appeared in the United States in *The Saturday Evening Post* on August 19, 1843. Source: Jeffrey Meyers, *Edgar Allen Poe: His Life and Legacy,* New York City, Charles Scribner's Sons, p. 137.

Green Wreath No. Ca.

May 3rd 1870

Dear Father,

Two Tons Grain shipped by Messrs. Burbank and Gallagher is received and I am useing it as I did the other. Please ask <u>him</u> how he applys it, <u>wether in the drill with the Cotton or underneath.</u> I am trying some both ways, but would like to have his idea. I am more in heart daily about the Cotton Crop and do not doubt but (Providence favoring as it has so far) that I am whole footed. If you have not ordered the <u>Pork</u> please send me a barrel from Mr. Potts as it is essential. I should have it <u>now</u> and the difference in price will not be equivalent to waiting for it some time. Love to all.

Very Truly Your Son

George

My best hand Duke is in want of some meat, after this barrel is sent I can make out until near the end of the crop.

G. A. S.

Soon as I get some stamps will write Lizzie.

Please send me some Postage Stamps by return mail. My letters are all waiting on my table now for want of some and I cant get them anywhere around here. Get about one Dollars worth, 33.

Green Wreath, Pitt Co.

May 9, 1870

My Dear Father,

Yours of May 3 has been received as also one dated 5th accompanying a barrel Pork from R. Griffin & Co. Please accept my thanks for the barrel Pork and the promptness with which it was sent. As to the contents of the first I have not a word to <u>say</u> as that would only be adding insult to injury. That I deserved all that and more at your hands I too well know, but I doubt if you have suffered as much <u>mentally</u> as I have done <u>myself</u>. Since my "last disgraceful drunken debauch in W- and Greenville" and I can say with Shakes

"If hearty sorrow

Be a sufficient ransom for offence,

I tender it here: I do as truly suffer,

As e'er I did commit." [196]

I have used all the Fertilizer and trust it may do well. Thank Mr. B. for it and assure him that it <u>shall</u> be paid for in the fall, and as things now look I may be able to sell him a bale or two on my <u>own</u>. Give my best love to Mother and all the children.

I remain

Very Respt.

Your Unworthy Son

Geo. A. Sparrow

---

[196] Shakespeare's *The Two Gentlemen of Verona*. Act 5, Scene 4. Proteus begging Valentine for forgiveness.

Green Wreath Pitt Co. No. Ca.
May 15, 1870

Dear Father

You will find in the Library (at home) a work on "book keeping" bought by you when in New Bern once for me. Please send it to me by some good opportunity, together with a blank book about 12 inches long x 8 inches wide ruled in double money columns. The one I have is pretty well worn. I want to keep myself posted in book keeping if I can. The Reconstructed Farmer[197] has not been received yet nor published for this month I suppose. If you come across anything of note in your papers – that is worth knowing either in the Political, Literary or Agricultural World please send it to me occasionally, as reading is the only amusement I have here. My cotton the piece that old man Jacob tended last year (about 17 acres) is <u>splendid</u> and everybody that has seen it pronounces it as good a stand as they ever saw – this is the piece I composted so well and will no doubt make me 15 bags. I have got along with my crop so far beyond all my expectations, fearing as I did that I had too much. I have plowed and hoed all my corn over thoroughly once and will be able in a fortnight to get in it again. The piece of cotton planted while you were here has been chopped out 10 days and is about <u>eight inches high</u>. Tomorrow I commence putting it to a stand (16th May). Ask some cotton farmer in Beaufort if they can beat that. Farmers say that a <u>good </u>stand is 1/2 the battle – if that be true mine is half fought. I am going to nurse my crop as closely as possible and do not intend to leave it a day again until it is made and see if I cant disappoint <u>some</u> <u>of</u> my friends. All this cotton talk dont interest you I suppose. But just now I am so full of it that I cant think of any-

---

[197] *The Reconstructed Farmer* was devoted to the farm, the garden and household. James R. Thigpen and John S. Dancy, Editors & Publishers. Published in Tarboro, N.C. Cost $2.00 per annum in advance. Source: *The American Farmer*, June, 1869, Worthington & Lewis, Baltimore, MD. p. 373.

thing else to write you. By close applications for 7 months only I hope to <u>pay all my debts</u> and be a free man once more with some property – a thing I never had before. I hear from Nan about twice a week. She will stop here on the 24th. I have sent Capt Warner an order for some few articles – a coat, hat, and some pantloons, snuff for Tom and 2 Snuff for Nathan. Please get him to send them by Wednesday's boat. Give my best love to the family and Cousin <u>Emeline</u>. Would be glad to hear from some of them if they don't think I have done too much for them to write me. I have been confined to my bed for 3 days with a terrible boil on my right side which has kept me quite sick – it is better today – was out this afternoon. I am

Very Sincerely
Your Son, Geo. A. Sparrow

Falkland Pitt Co. N.C.
August 18th 1870

My Dear Father

I send Tom down with a mule and cart for the barrel Pork if it be in Washington, if not for enough to last me until its arrival – say 50 pounds. Tom wants "for himself" 2 shirts and a pair of shoes. Yours of the 16th containing one from Mr. Zophar Mills received. I think he is very much mistaken about crops here, at least. We would send some fruit, but there is none here now that would pay for transportation down. All well and send love to you and family. You say nothing about coming up. I would like very much for you to see my crops. Could you manage to come next week. You might get a seat back with us.

Very Sincerely,
Your Son, Geo. A. Sparrow

P.S. Please send me a box collar 14-1/2

Falkland, Pitt Co. N.C.

September 25, 1870

Dear Father,

The Pork, spits and brush all received. I owe Mr. Dill 9$ for storage, carts and on goods sent to Greenville. Please enclose or send it to him by Capt Howard. When you send the bagging and ties let me know if possible one tripp ahead so my cart will be there to bring it right out. Will save some charges. I am sick now though getting better. Love to all.

Your Son

Geo. A. Sparrow

Please send me about 15 or 20 stamps. I have a good many letters to write you & when I get out having no way to get any.

––––––––––

Falkland Pitt Co.

December 2, 1870

Dear Father,

The bundle of papers and letter sent per Mr. Satchwell has arrived and you will please accept my thanks for the same. Mrs. Lewis has at last rented the place to her entire satisfaction to <u>Mr. R. R. Cotton</u>. She gets the Plantation, (Moore) field, Low grounds, Pittman field, Broaddus house, store at the landing and every thing else, or in other words makes a <u>clean sweep</u> of everything <u>estate</u> and all for the sum of "One Thousand Dollars" per annum. She seems to have <u>ignored</u> Mr. Bray and your self entirely <u>as I always thought she would</u>. This of course relieves you, Nan or anyone else of all further say so in the matter except that you see the estate righted from Mrs. Lewis. I think I can make a trade with Mr. Cotton right here for what I shall have to sell. He has made me as yet no direct offer, but I think wants to buy me out. If he does and will give me my price I shall sell to him, which I think he will do. If possible I desire to close the business right here and as soon as my cotton is all picked and packed which will be about Dec. 27th I hope. What I shall do next year I dont know but I am not uneasy about that the world owes me a living. If I can get it, I hope with a "strong arm" and a stout back, I have learned to work. If you see any opening or hear of one please let me know. I hear from Mr. Mills frequently and he keeps me posted on the price of cotton. First cotton shipped him sold for "barely low middling" at 15-1/2 cents. Nets here about 14 cents, in amt. nets $169.00 by Mrs. Lewis. I do not regret now that I cannot remain here another year. I induced Mrs. Lewis to send (4) four bags of her cotton to Mr. Mills and she has given me permission to send some more next packing, am glad of it. Write me whenever you can. I will write you weekly hereafter. I want to get thro' by Christmas. Your prominence in the House has been noticed on all sides and I am repeatedly told of it – especially in the matter of contesting successfully the seat of the Col. Miller. Will be glad of a paper any time.

Very Sincerely
Your Son
Geo. A. Sparrow

Falkland, Pitt Co. N.C.
December 8th 1870

Dear Father

Yours dated 6th received today. Have written Mr. Jas. L. Fowle today that his one barrel pork, would be paid as soon as a sale could be effected of my effects, which is likely to take place tomorrow, provided Mr. Cotton will give my price. Everything (that's my effects) remain in "status quo" excepting one mule, Jack, that I have traded for a horse (stallion), 5 years old, that Maj. Peebles, Mr. Cotton and all my friends say is worth $175.00. If I cannot sell my mules and utensils for their worth in cash I shall endeavor to trade them to your advantage. I ask Mr. Cotton $300.00 outside my horse. Can I get it will be a good sale. Afterwards they may turn out some money. Shall endeavor to do the best for all parties. Letter from Mr. Woddell today and Mr. Mills writes almost daily. Mr. M. and Mrs. L. seem disposed to do what is right, that is they are (or rather he is) clever. I shall I hope by the 20th Dec. wind up all my business at Greenwreath not as Nan says forever, but during a lifetime. I am troubled and worried, do not expect to hear from me often, but will meet you at home Christmas.

Your Son,
Geo. A. Sparrow

At Cousin Picketts
January 28th 1871

Dear Mother,

I have not come up to contract in writing to you but you know the mail only leaves here once every week and the last week I missed the mail boy. To day it is raining very hard and has been bad weather. I have been here ever since I came in the county and cannot get away. They look upon me as one of the family and will not adhere to my staying any where else. Day before yesterday I spent at Cousin Sarah Manns. Eliza Sparrow was there and I spent a very agreeable day, in fact I must say that I have never met such clever people, nor have I enjoyed myself as much in <u>two</u> <u>years</u>. I feel cheerful and almost happy in fact I feel like myself once more. A great deal of this feeling I attribute to the fact that I have <u>drank</u> <u>no</u> <u>liquor</u> since I came here. Cousin Pickett is President of a Temperance Society here and I had intended joining it to day but the weather will prevent our going but I will join next week. I have not disposed of my horse yet, but can do so at any time for a good price, a great many having died here they are in demand. Dear Mother I feel more like a man now, and were it not for my <u>disgraceful</u> conduct in Washington would feel in better spirits than I have in many a long month. The community at large will not so easily forget that, but you and the girls <u>can</u> let the past be the past. It was not me but whiskey that disgraced you all so shamefully. Henceforth I shall endeavor to give you all no more trouble in that line. I am almost certain of getting into some employment here for the year and in fact have almost completed a bargain to rent a 2 horse crop team and all furnished. If I cannot you need not expect me to return to Washington this year <u>at</u> <u>least</u>. I will go to Norfolk or some other city to seek employment and if I can succeed on being a <u>sober</u> <u>man</u> this year then will I go home not before. Liza, Emiline and all the family send love. Em says tell Jennie she will write next week. Tell all the little children and Ivey that they must not forget "buddie" but think of him and pray for him often, and the day <u>may come</u> when instead of being ashamed of him they will feel proud of him. <u>Especialy</u> <u>remember</u> me to Jno and Mary McDonald. Their kindness to me I shall <u>never</u> forget and I desire that Cousin John especially should know that I appreciate it and am not ungrateful. If I myself am ever in a situation to return it, <u>you</u> will never forget it I am certain. I have never before known or properly appreciated my real friends. "Tis a bad tide that never turns." Should any letters come for me send them in care P. P. Spencer, Lake Landing. I have visited a good many of the young ladies here and find them very clever. Here at least my evil deeds do not stare me in the face. Love to all and let Father hear from me. Write soon.

> Your Aff. Son
> Geo. A. Sparrow

––––––––––

> Raleigh, N.C.
> Febry. 9ᵗʰ 1871

Dear Johnnie –

The Capitol bell is ringing for the legislature to assemble, but before going I concluded to write you a short letter. I want to write to your mother during the day if I can catch a chance to do so. The legislature meets at ten & the impeachment court sits at eleven O'clock in the Senate Chamber. I rarely go into the House of Representatives now, as I have to be with the managers & counsel in another room in the Capitol to examine witnesses & prepare the case for trial. Yesterday the court sat from eleven until five O'clock.

Gov. William Alexander Graham
Courtesy of the North Carolina Office of Archives and History
Raleigh, North Carolina

Governor Graham,[198] (by whom I sit) made a great speech about two & a half hours long. After he had concluded he handed me a little newspaper package saying, "Major here is a present for you." I told him I should send it home to the girls for a place in their album. It was the enclosed photograph which is a very fine one, & worth preservation. All the proceedings of the impeachment trial are taken down in shorthand by stenographers, & written out every night & printed the next morning. There are three of them now, & will be more here on Thursday next. The chief, Mr. Underhill is a very clever & intelligent gentleman from N. York & about sixty years old I suppose. The other two are young men. They all came to my room to see me last Sunday night, & I got Mr. Underhill to write in short hand the names of all the family, with his own name. The other two wrote theirs. It will do for a scrap book. The first time I make a speech, they are going to save it for me as

---

[198] William Alexander Graham (9/15/1804 – 8/11/1875) was born in Lincoln County and served as Governor of North Carolina 1845–1849. Education was a priority in his administration and a school for the deaf and dumb opened in Raleigh in 1845. Beth G. Crabtree. *North Carolina Governors 1585-1975*, North Carolina Division of Archives and History, 1974. p. 84.

taken down, & I will send it home to some of you. The other scrap of paper shows how they shorten letters – instead of <u>seven</u> marks to make an <u>M</u> they make one curved mark. The other marks below, looking like scratches, are "May it please the court." "Mr. Chief Justice & Senators," etc. One of the stenographers, Mr. Farbridge, writes a different system from Mr. Underhill, & neither can read what the other writes.

I was glad to receive your letter, and as it is your first to me, shall preserve it. I believe I have the first letters written to me by all the children. You must learn to write a good hand, and to spell & punctuate correctly. Mr. Latterthwaite & I took tea at Judge Fowles last night. Since I have been writing Mr. Tucker has been in to ask me to dine with him at 3 today. Judge Warren, & Messrs. Custer & Latterthwaite are to dine there. It is doubtful whether the Judge & I can go. I am proud to know that you are a good boy, attentive to your mother and sisters, and I trust & believe that you will learn no bad habits, such as drinking, chewing & swearing. I hope Ivey will be a good boy too, and as you are the larger, you must set him a good example. Tell "Sis Jennie" that I wrote for the cards for the Sunday School, & they will be sent to Mr. Dalton by Saturday's mail or sooner. I must close. Give my love to your mother & sisters & all friends & Ivey.

Affectionately
Your Father
T. Sparrow

P.S. As this letter will be so bulky, will enclose the photographs in your Mothers letter.[199]

---

[199] Thomas Sparrow Papers, #1878, Southern Historical Collection, The Wilson Library, University of North Carolina, Chapel Hill, North Carolina.

Major Thomas Sparrow.

From the Confederate Reveille, Memorial Edition
Published by The Pamlico Chapter of the
Daughters of the Confederacy
Washington, N. C, May 10, 1898

Governor William Woods Holden
Courtesy of the North Carolina Office of Archives and History
Raleigh, North Carolina

William Woods Holden (11/24/1818 – 3/01/1892) was the 38th and 40th Governor of North Carolina in 1865 and from 1868 to 1871 and was leader of the state's Republican Party during Reconstruction.

The trial for the impeachment of North Carolina Governor William Woods Holden began December 14, 1870. The main charges against Holden had to do with the rough treatment and arrests of North Carolina citizens by state militia officer Colonel George W. Kirk during the enforcement of Radical Reconstruction civil rights legislation. On December 15, 1870, Major Tom Sparrow appeared before the Senate and made eight specific charges of impeachment against Governor Holden. Holden was found guilty of six charges and was convicted and removed from office.[200]

---

[200] Edgar E. Folk and Bynum Shaw, *W.W. Holden: A Political Biography,* John F. Blair, publisher, Winston Salem, N.C. 1982, pp. 224-234.

Impeachment Trial
William Woods Holden

Following is the report made by Thomas Sparrow, Manager of the Prosecution for the House, for the Impeachment Trial of Governor William W. Holden:

House of Representatives
Wednesday, December 14, 1870

House called to order at the usual hour.

Prayer by Rev. Dr. Mason of the city.

Journal of yesterday read and approved.

Mr. Sparrow from the Judiciary Committee, submitted the following report in regard to impeachment:

The Judiciary Committee, to whom was referred, on the 9th of December, the following resolution, namely:

"Resolved. That William W. Holden, Governor of North Carolina, be impeached of high crimes and misdemeanors in office," have considered the same, and submit the following report:

That William W. Holden, Governor of North Carolina, unmindful of his oath of office, did, in July last, organize, arm and equip a military force, not recognized by, and in subversion of the Constitution of the State of North Carolina, which military force, so unlawfully organized, was not kept under subordination to and governed by the civil power, but was, by the order of the said William W. Holden, Governor as aforesaid, made paramount to, and subversive of the civil authority.

That the said William W. Holden, Governor as aforesaid, did, in the months of July and August last, without lawful warrant and authority, and in defiance and subversion of the Constitution, arrest and imprison many of the peaceable and law abiding citizens of the State, depriving them of their liberties and privileges, and certain of said citizens, so unlawfully arrested and imprisoned, did cause to be subjected to cruel and unusual punishment.

That the said William W. Holden, Governor as aforesaid, denied to citizens, unlawfully restrained of their liberty by his authority, all remedy to inquire into the lawfulness thereof, and in defiance of the Constitution, the Laws, and the Process of the Courts, he suspended the privileges of the writ of habeas corpus, claiming that he was governed by a "supreme law," whereby he could deny the privileges of the said writ when, in his opinion, the safety of the State required it.

In view of the matters herein set forth, contained in public documents, and the records of the Public Departments and the Courts, the undersigned, members of the Committees, who are a majority thereof, are of the opinion, that William W. Holden, Governor of the State of North Carolina, be impeached of high crimes and misdemeanors. They therefore recommend to the House, the adoption of the accompanying resolution.

	T. SPARROW,
C. W. BROADFOOT	R. P. WARING
LEE M. McAFEE	JAMES G. SCOTT
S. A. ASHE	W. P. WELCH
JOHN D. STANFORD	DAVID SETTLE
GEO. H. GREGORY	F. N. STRUDWICK
HENRY T. JORDAN	C.M.T. McCAWLEY
JOHN W. DUNHAN	J. D. JOHNSTON

Resolved. That William W. Holden, Governor of the State of North Carolina, be impeached of high crimes and misdemeanors in office.[201]

---

[201] *The Sentinel,* Thursday, December 15, 1870, Thomas Sparrow Papers, #1878, Southern Historical Collection, The Wilson Library, University of North Carolina, Chapel Hill, North Carolina.

Dear Father

I arrived here day before yesterday from Hyde where I have been since I left, expect to leave for there again some time this week. I have made an arrangement with Selby to cultivate a 3 horse crop on his farm this year. He is to furnish the team and feed and all the farming implements and the seed and will advance me pork and corn for the hands. He also gives me a nice little arrangement for living that is his Office right near the house and Mrs. Selby boards me at $8 per mo. The arrangement is not one that promises much money, but has its advantages the principal of which are that I am with <u>nice people</u> and in a <u>splendid</u> neighborhood. My tripp to Hyde was on the whole productive of more pleasure than I have experienced in several years. I found the people kind, hospitable, and lovely not withstanding a succession of bad crops has made them all comparatively poor. At Cousin Picketts they could not have been more kind. I saw a good deal of Cousin Sarah, Eliza, Lonzo, and Uncle Stephen. I staid one night with Mr Joe Mann near Fairfield where you and Col Carter staid and found him to be a <u>very clever</u> gentelman indeed. Staid one night and day also with Jacob Carter. I read last night aloud to all the family your speech upon impeachment and have to offer you the sincere congratulations of all the family and myself upon your <u>perfect success</u>. Even Johnnie listened with rapt attention. It is on everybodys mouth and everyone wants to read it. The northern papers notice it a good deal and some of them contained an account and description of your character and person. Already, dear as you are to the people of Beaufort and adjoining counties your action in the Legislature will render you still dearer to <u>them</u> and place you in a position before the people at large to be envied by all. Should the trial result in the successful impeachment of W. W. Holden "long after the granite walls of the Capitol shall have crumbled into dust" will the memory of the man who did so much for them be dear to the grateful people of the "Old North State," and in future it shall be my pride so to conduct myself as to no longer prove a thorn in your side but to add one small debt of gratitude to the already over flowing cup presented to you by a grateful people. I have <u>drunk no liquor</u> since I went to Hyde and have connected myself with the Friends of Temperance in which order I hold an office. I have never before "<u>since the war</u>" felt as I do now. The old saying says "Tis a bad tide that never turns." I stopped on my way from Hyde one night at Mr Reddicks at Pantego. He as well as most of my friends in Hyde advise me to study Law. I have been thinking of it myself and have finaly "<u>determined</u>" to do so. I am in hopes to make enough this year by economy and my own labor to support me while reading, and I expect to read some nights this summer. These are my plans. What do you think of them? And do they meet with your approval? If so give me your advice and say what books I can best read by myself. I will be glad to hear from you as often as you can spare the time to write. My Post Office will be at Lake Landing. I will take your speech and some late papers down with me. All the family are well and join me in love to you. Jennie says she will write you next week.

I am Very Sincerely
Your Son
Geo. A. Sparrow

––––––––––

Lake Landing, N.C.
March 2 1871

My Dear Father,

Your letter dated February 16th was received and afforded me more real pleasure than I have in a long time experienced. You mentioned having sent at the same time a bundle of papers, they never came to hand appropriated, no doubt by that nest of radicals in the office at Washington. The weather here now is beautiful and promises a good crop year. I have been at work nearly two weeks, this week plowing. The first day used me up pretty badly, but I am getting used to it so that I don't mind it much, tis not such labor as I prefer or expect to spend my life at, but with a good year, a certain way of making a living. Down here it is almost impossible to find out what is going on in the outside world and when we hear at all, it is long after it has become old every where else. As you say, this is one serious objection to the county, but I shall have very little time during the next five months to devote to reading being generally <u>tired</u> enough at night to retire early and sleep without lacking. I shall take your advice however and devote what spare time I have to reading trying to keep myself from becoming rusty. Last Sunday I took Mrs. Goslet up to Soule Church about nine miles from here, took dinner at her Fathers, Mr. Murray's, and spent the remainder of the day there enjoying myself vastly. They are nice people especially the <u>widow</u>. Staid Saturday night at Cousin Picketts. A good many people have asked me would you be down at court. I have told them I presumed not but that Mr. Sheppard your partner would. I am very comfortable here. Mrs. Selby feeds <u>high</u> and my quarters are as comfortable as they could well be. I consider board very cheap @ Eight Dollars per month. Dr. Selby is about now in New Bern. I have just finished a letter home and as it is growing late I must stop. Will try and write you once a week.

Affectionately Your Son
George

Lake Landing, N.C.
March 18th 1871

Dear Father

I received a short letter from you mail before last and per yester-days mail (Friday) two bundles papers cont'g two Sentinels and two N. Y. papers. I have just written a letter to Mother. I find that I have less time now for writing than I ever had before. Generaly when I quit work at night, I feel so tired that I am most all-ways ready for the bed. I sent the folks at home by this mail a speech I delivered at the Celebration of the Anniversary of our Temperance Council in Middle Creek Church some time ago. I had been requested by the members to do so and as I want to accustom myself to "facing an audience" thought this would be a good opportunity but was hurriedly prepared and written with a sore hand and I expect you will find some trouble in reading it - We had lectures the same night from three ministers and one or two other gentelman and mine was pronounced by almost everybody as the best. The church was full and I expected to be embarrassed but was not, only for a few minutes. The weather has been very nice for some time and I have been at the Plow hand by over two weeks and now quite an expert at the business. The Dr. and Mrs. Selby are very clever. Dr. spends most of his evenings in one room and I enjoy his company. Mrs. Selby too most always has some young ladies with her, has 3 now. So my time passes very agreeably when not at work. Cousin Sarah and Mr. Mann are very clever. I am there some part of most every Sunday. Tho every body in the county that I visit are very cordial indeed. From what I can learn your partner Mr. Sheppard made at Swan Market this Court quite a favorable impression. I am writing in haste to be on time for the mail and must close. Write as often as you can.

Your Aff. Son,
Geo. A. Sparrow

Copy

Dear George,

After to day I shall rent another office and leave this with its books to you.

I have lost all hope of you. God alone can rescue you and you have cast him off. Your Mother and I will pray for you.

Sue and her two blessed boys will sooner or later have to return to her friends and theirs and allow us to care for them. What will become of you God alone knows. I dare not express our fears. May He help you.

Affectionately Your Father

T. Sparrow

Geo. A. Sparrow
Washington

––––––––––

Washington, N.C.

April 18th 1878

My Dear Father

Your note was handed me last night on my return home. I appreciate that as well as the motives which prompted the writing it. It needs no written reply. The answer must be in acts, deeds, not in words. There were however one or two things in it which I feel constrained to answer as well on your behalf as on my own. You say that you propose after yesterday renting an office and giving me charge of the present one with its books. This must not be, and so far as I am concerned shall not be. If it is necessary for either one of us to leave, I am the one not you. It is your office and your books. It should never be said that my father an old and honored member of an honorable profession and who has been to his son a father among ten thousand has had to surrender his rights and his means of subsistence because he could not stay in an office with that son. Sooner than such should be the case. I would give up <u>law</u> and earn my bread by daily labor. Again, while it might be a misled conclusion it would at the same time do me <u>irreparable injury</u>, so much so that it would become necessary for me to leave Washington. I may be weak and have other faults but it cannot be said that I lack gratitude or a proper love and respect for my parents. I love you both and fully appreciate all the efforts you are now making on my behalf and I believe God will answer your prayers. Again, you say you have no <u>hope</u>. I have and a very strong one not only that I shall be a temperate man but that God will also in his own wise providence and at his own time bring me back into his fold. The devil has been making a stronger fight over me than he ever did any other man I reckon. He prompted me to tell Mr. Smith that I had never been converted. <u>This is not true</u> and I knew it at the time. There has never been a moment, not only during my calmer thinking moments, but even in the midst of excuses, wounded by all the chosen agents of the devil that I have not <u>felt</u> this to be true. I have been taught that Hope lasted while life did. It is a star whose brilliance may be dimmed by circumstance, but one that never sets forever until a sinner leaves this world and passes into the great unknown. I have not "cast off God" nor will I believe that He has cast me off.

"While the lamp holds out to burn

The vilest sinner may return."[202]

---

[202] Isaac Watts, *Hymns and Spiritual Songs, Book I*, Hymn 88, "Life Is the Time to Serve the Lord." Isaac Watts (July 27, 1674 – November 25, 1748) was an English theologian and hymn writer who is known as the "Father of English Hymnody." Watts wrote over 600 hymns and many of them continue to be used by Christians to worship and praise the same Savior Watts loved and served. Source: Hymnlyrics.org and Christianhistorytimeline. com March 11, 2010.

I must say in conclusion that already one part of your prayer has been answered. From this day I refuse entirely liquor of any and every kind. I feel that my resolution this time will be kept. There seems to be in me a something that tells me this. I shall not go to the office to day as I am not physically well enough. Getting wet yesterday on my cold has made that worse but I think has done me good other ways. You will at least go to the office to day will you not? In the mean time I would be glad of any suggestions you may make that aid me in carrying out my resolution and bringing about the other end which we all so much desire. With best love and feeling for you, Mother and all of you.

> I remain
> Affect. Your Son
> Geo. A.

Washington N.C.

January 11th 1881

Dear Father

I left here on Thursday morning last with Mr. Jacobs for Jordans Creek and did not return until Sunday evening. Was sorry to learn upon my arrival that you did not get to Raleigh in time to take the Speakers seat as George Brown assured me you would have received it. While down the country I was over at Makleys in Hyde County (Friday and Saturday). He is very much out with what he calls the "ring" about S. Martin and very desirous of getting some bill through the Legislature which will enable a party to a civil suit to remove it from one County to another. Says that he has several important suits in that County and if he can get them here he will employ us in all his businesses. His idea is to pass a law providing that either party may move a case, provided they will give a bond to pay all the additional expense incurred by the removal. In this view of the case I can see no very great objection to a bill as the opposite party would not or could not incur any additional expense. Please see some of the lawyers in the Legislature with you and get their ideas as to the practicability of the measure and if practicable prepare a bill and push it through. Again he desires to get a bill for the protection of and in the interest of the farmers regarding the merchants and all persons purchasing any cotton, either in the seed, in the lint, or baled to keep a book of the name of the party selling cotton, the amount and the date of purchase, and providing that farmers shall have the right when application to examine this book, and making it a misdemeanor either to fail to keep the book or to show it to farmers. All the farmers I have talked to both in this County and in Hyde are in favor of it. And if it were written "An Act to protect farmers in the Cultivation of Cotton" it would go through like a breeze. Makley said he had talked with Respess about it and he was in favor of it. He (Makley) agreed to pay me 25$ himself and to get some of the farmers to pay me if I would get it through. I am too busy this afternoon to draw the bill, but will do so tomorrow and forward it to you. Soon after you left two letters came from Mr. Jacobs to you. In one he States that your draft would be July and in the other that it had not yet been received. While I was writing this letter Gordon came in with the draft which the fool in Baltimore had returned saying he had no means to collect it. I showed Gordon the letter and told him to forward it to Mr. J – putting him all right. His merchant must have been an ass and not sense enough to know how to collect a draft which the dunce was anxious and waiting to pay it. I have had a great deal of trouble and vexation over the Jacobs matter and have been working hard to protect his interest. His son William left here yesterday to see the old man expecting to get back Saturday. I shall go down there again Friday. All well here and doing well except Mother who has a slight sore throat. Will try and write you at least once a week and keep you posted.

Affectionately Your Son

George A. Sparrow

––––––––––

Dear Father

Enclose you will find the bills I wrote you about a day or so ago. Since writing I have talked with George Rodman about them and he thinks them both good bills and ought to be passed. Do all you can to get them through it will be money for us. If the Legislature should pass the bill providing for Criminal Courts and make districts <u>look out for your interest.</u>

All well.

Affectionately,

George

––––––––––

Washington N.C.

January 21st 1881

Dear Father

After drawing the two bills enclosed in reference to fees, I have been instructed by parties to draw and send the others. They seem to me to commend themselves to every one at once as good measure. The bill as relations to oysters I drew at the request of a man (Mr. Foster) from Dare County, who expects to send up a petition to back it if necessary. You can hand it to the Representative from that County and can consult with him. Mr. Wisnall died night before last and is to be buried today at 11 o'clock. Hiram Petty was in my office yesterday and requested me to say to you that in the Prohibition movement if you could take a position <u>in favor</u> of it that would not compromise you politically he would like for you to do so — He is very much in favor of it. He also requested me to ask you to see what could be done towards abolishing the Specific Tax on Merchants upon the ground that it is unconstitutional. The Constitution says taxes shall be uniform and ad valorem.

All well.

Affectionately Your Son
George A. Sparrow

GEO. A. SPARROW,

ATTORNEY,

WASHINGTON, N. C., FEB. 8TH, 1886.

Mr. _____

DEAR SIR:

On the first of March, I shall move my office from my present location to the one formerly occupied by Mr. E. S. Simmons, on Market Street, and opposite the new Postoffice, where I shall at all times be glad to see not only my clients and those who desire to consult me professionally, but also my friends, who will find the latch-string out and a vacant chair, together with a cordial welcome. Recognizing my obligations to the people of the county especially, I desire at all times to bear it in mind.

Thanking you for your past patronage and good wishes and hoping that I may merit a continuance of them in the future,

I remain, yours very truly,

GEO. A. SPARROW,
Attorney

Chapter 8

Country Preacher

Only after George's father realized he could do no more and turned George over to God did a change come about. His prayers and those of his family and friends were answered. God spoke to him and he followed the path of the apostle Paul: "But this one thing I do, forgetting those things which are behind, and reaching forth unto those things which are before, I press toward the mark for the prize of the high calling of God in Christ Jesus."[203]

George Attmore Sparrow

---

[203] Philippians 3: 13-14 (KJV).

George A. Sparrow studied theology, passed the exam, and was licensed to preach the Gospel of our Lord Jesus Christ by the Presbytery of Albemarle at its Session on February 13th 1890 in the City of Raleigh, North Carolina in the First Presbyterian Church during the ministry of Rev. John S. Watkins, D.D (1878 –1892).

Trial sermon preached from Matthew 7:22 & 23. "Many will say unto me in that day, Lord, Lord, have we not prophesied in thy name? and in thy name have cast out devils? and in thy name done many wonderful works? And then will I profess unto them, I never knew you; depart from me."

Licensed at night after sermon and in presence of a very large congregation.[204]

First Presbyterian Church
Raleigh, North Carolina[205]

---

[204] From Rev. George A. Sparrow's *Book of Illustrations.*
[205] *History of the First Presbyterian Church, Raleigh, North Carolina 1816-1991.* Commercial Printing Co., Raleigh, N.C. p. 17.

Macon County Field, North Carolina

On the 12th day of June AD 1890 I arrived at Franklin, NC in Macon Co. with my family after a journey of 500 miles and took charge of what is known in the Presbytery of Mecklenburg as the Macon Co. Field. I had been written to previously by the Committee of Home Missions and instructed to visit the field which I did and concluded to accept the charge. Presbytery paying me 250$, Asheville Church 150$, and Morrison & Franklin Churches 125 each making 650$. The field consists of Morrison Church a nice country church 6 miles from Franklin – Franklin Church in the town, preaching at Dillsboro and other missionary points. Remained in this field from June 1890 until Aug. 16th 1891 when I accepted a call to the church at Rutherfordton in Rutherford County for ¾ of the time. Salary from that church 500$. In connection with this church I also preached at Sandy Plains Church in Polk County, a new one just built – this church paying 125$ toward salary and the Presbytery of Mecklenburg 100$ more.

Ordination

Took place at Dillsboro, N.C. in the Western N.C. R. R. 50 miles west of Asheville and in Jackson County on the 5th November AD 1890. Present W. S. P. Bryan 1st Church Asheville, Rev. W. I. Erdman Asheville, Rev. R. S. Brown Waynesville and Elders Scruggs from Bryson City Church and Slagle from Franklin Church. There was also present Rev. Walsen (Dutch Reformed) from Long Island who preached the Ordination Sermon.

The Presbytery of Mecklenburg at its Fall Session held in Hendersonville, N.C. could not ordain me because the letter of dismissal had not been received. An order was therefore made adjourning to meet at Dillsboro as above and proceed to ordain me – and also to look into the question of organizing a church. At the night Session of the Presbytery seven or eight persons came forward and gave their names as charter members for a church. A proposition was also made looking to the erection of a church building.

Presbytery appointed Rev. Brown and Rev. Sparrow and Elders Slagle and Scruggs a Commission to organize a church.[206]

On February 7, 1891 during the time Rev. Sparrow was serving these congregations, twins were born in Franklin, North Carolina, George Attmore Sparrow, Jr. and Hubert McCord Sparrow. Hubert McCord Sparrow died in infancy.

---

[206] Rev. George A. Sparrow's *Book of Illustrations.*

Franklin Presbyterian Church

The Presbyterian church in Franklin was the first church in Macon County, N.C. Considering the shortage of educated men willing to relocate into this new frontier of western North Carolina, it was difficult to organize a new church in the early years. Finally in 1833 families in the area desiring to follow the Presbyterian expression of Christianity were sufficient in numbers to convince the Presbytery to accept a plea for the organization of a church in Macon County.

The place of worship for those early years is unknown but in 1854 records show it was reorganized with seven charter members and a sum of $1,300 set aside for the construction of a church building. The twelve-inch walls were made of red clay bricks formed in Macon County by Joab Moore and his slaves on the banks of the Little Tennessee River. Window panes survive today as the original hand blown glass with large cast iron weights as counter balance inside the walls for raising and lowering the windows. The bell is thought to have traveled by oxcart to Franklin from its original point of Charleston, S. C. The old bell is still rung today to "make a joyful noise" and call believers to Sunday worship. The structure was built for the budgeted amount and is the oldest surviving brick building in Macon County.[207]

Sandy Plains Presbyterian Church
Tryon, North Carolina

Dedication

On Sunday 14 August 1892 the church at Sandy Plains in Polk Co. N.C. was solemnly dedicated & set apart to the worship of God.

See notice from Presbyterian:

"Sandy Plains Church: - On Friday before third Sabbath in August, Rev. C. M. Payne, D. D., of Concord, assisting the pastor,

---

[207] *First Presbyterian Church History*, Franklin, North Carolina.

Rev. G. A. Sparrow, of Rutherfordton, a meeting was begun at Sandy Plains, in Polk county. The Doctor's preaching was of such an earnest, instructive feeling and eloquent nature that it was apparent from the first. The people were deeply moved and the Spirit of God was with us. There were ten professions – seven of these were received into the church, three others will be at the next regular appointment, while many others were deeply concerned and asked prayer for their conversion. On Sunday, the 3rd, the house (which is a new one and a credit to the little handful that built it, being one of the most convenient, comfortable and best arranged country churches that we know of) was filled to its utmost capacity. Chairs from the wagons, benches, everything being brought into use. At the beginning of the morning service there were three infants baptized, then followed the dedication sermon preached by Rev. G. A. Sparrow from Psalm 17:4: "One thing have I desired of the Lord, that will I seek after; that I may dwell in the house of the Lord all the days of my life; to behold the beauty of the Lord, and to enquire in his temple." Then the church was reported complete, out of debt and ready for dedication. The building committee turned the keys over to the pastor, and then to the session with some appropriate remarks, the congregation singing the long metre doxology standing, as a token of their appreciation and acceptance. Then the church was solemnly dedicated and set apart to the service of the Almighty God. Rev. Dr. Payne offering the dedicatory prayer.

In the afternoon service was again held when the communion of the Lord's Supper was administered. It was a big day in our little country church and will long be remembered both in its results and its effects upon the hearts of the people. On Thursday night en route for home Dr. Payne preached in the church at Rutherfordton. As there is but the one church in Polk county, the good results of the meeting can hardly be estimated. PRESBYTER. "

Results of the meeting were: 1st Dedication of the new church, four infant Baptisms, administration of the Lord's Supper, ten (10) professions of faith & seven additions to the Church – three others to be received. Entry made Aug. 1892.　　G.A.S.[208]

──────────

Sandy Plains Presbyterian Church in Polk County, North Carolina was organized in 1858 although there had been preaching there before with Rev. Jessie Rankin holding service under a brush arbor. The first church (a small log structure) was built about 1861.[209]

Constructed   1877 – 1883

Rutherfordton Presbyterian Church

Was installed at Rutherfordton by order of Mecklenburg Presbytery on the Friday night before the 4th Sabbath of October AD 1891. Rev. R. Z. Johnson of Lincolnton, and C. W. Robinson of Gastonia officiating.

──────────

[208] Rev. George A. Sparrow's *Book of Illustrations*.
[209] Sandy Plains Presbyterian, Earliest Church in Polk County.

Rutherfordton was a village of 450 people. Among them was a small group of twenty zealous Presbyterians who sought to strengthen their religious principles. With emotional and physical enthusiasm, aspirations and continuity of spirit, they petitioned the Presbytery to organize a church. The Presbytery granted the request on April 3, 1834. Rev. John Sillman was directed to the area to assist in the church's early stages. Dr. R. H. Morrison, who was renowned for being the first president of Davidson College, and Rev. Daniel Lindley, D. D. organized the church in 1834.

The church worked hard through disappointments and successful challenges. The Rev. Thomas Davis described the church in 1851 with the following words: "8 members; no elder, gloomy prospect for continued existence." However, in 1859 Rev. Nathan Shotwell began a 15-year tenure. His sermons were one to three hours in length.

Rev. George A. Sparrow served as pastor at Rutherfordton through December 6, 1893.[210]

––––––––––

The following is an excerpt from Rev. Sparrow's *Book of Illustrations*:

On the night of March 16, 1893 while sitting in my study at work I heard violent screams which at first I thought were in the house, but upon going to the door discovered that flames were coming from the loft of the home of Mrs. Thos. Dixon about a square away. I hurried up there & found the entire house in flames, crowds gathered around and a party of men bringing Mrs. Dixon over the hill in a blanket. I could not see her face, but saw that her arms which she was holding over her head were terribly burned. I also learned that the two youngest children Thos. Fritz and the baby were in the house. Human aid was useless and they were consumed. Mrs. Dixon was carried to the home

[210] *Rutherfordton Presbyterian Church, Rutherfordton, N.C. 175th Anniversary* April 3, 1834 – April 3, 2009.

of Mrs. Matt Miller adjoining the Pres. Church and laid upon a bed. When it was discovered she was terribly burned, all her clothing entirely gone by the flames. When I entered the room she turned to me and said "Mr. Sparrow I'm burned to death." I replied, "No Mrs. Dixon, I hope not." She then said I want you to tell me about my poor little children. I know you will not deceive me. I went out and the physician not thinking it best to tell her about the children did not go back. Her husband who was in Shelby was telegraphed and reached her about 2 o'clk and was with her until death ended her sufferings at 7-1/2 o'clk in the morning. His grief was something terrible to see – deprived of home and everything in it (a beautiful one), wife and two children in a few short hours by the cruel flames. They were members of my church and she one of the most active and useful members I had. Almost the stay of the church, the last work she did in the afternoon only reaching home about two hours before the fire was to go around to the members and solicit subscriptions for a festive occasion which was to have been held at her home on Wednesday evening for the benefit of the church.

The facts as nearly as can be ascertained are as follows. Mrs. D. had dismissed the servants for the night, locked up the house and gone in the bedroom to undress and put to bed the children. The little boy Tom Fritz was ready for bed. His mother turned to do something setting the lamp a glass one on the table. The baby who was on the floor near it caught the end of the cover and pulled it over. The lamp breaking or exploding and the burning oil covering the floor. His mother picked him up, threw him on the bed, then seized a pillow, threw it on the flames and attempted to stomp out the fire. This set her afire and soon she was enveloped in a sheet of flames. Feeling she was burning up she ran thru the passage on to the front porch and screamed at the top of her voice. Then running back she fell in a heap in the middle of the burning room. About this time a colored man who was passing by ran in pulled her out and by the time he got back the room could not be entered. Sallie the oldest and only child left made her way out the back of the house and was saved.

Mrs. Dixon was taken from here to Charlotte & with the remains (what was received of her two little children) buried. I was to have gone & burial there[211] but unfortunately got to the train too late and was left. Thus ended the saddest and most condescending desperation of Providence it has ever been my lot to be associated with. The only comfort amid all the gloom and horror is that <u>she</u> was prepared and with her little ones went to dwell in a mansion secure from fire and all earthly dangers and where there is no more suffering.

Resolutions by Rutherfordton Church at the dissolution of the
Pastoral Relation Rev. G. A. Sparrow

Resolved. Existing circumstances <u>not</u> being their origin as this church deemed it necessary that our beloved Pastor Rev. Geo A. Sparrow do accept service in another field that deploring the necessity we do hereby accept his resignation as Pastor with great reluctance. We do most earnestly commend him to the love and care of the churches to which he may be called with our love and best wishes for his spiritual welfare and temporal prosperity. We transfer to them our beloved Pastor and his family of whom we were proud, to them a great gain, to us a great loss. May God's richest blessings attend him and his family is the earnest praying of a congregation which he has so faithfully so ably and so pleasantly served.   L. P. Erwin ,Elder Moderator

----

[211] Mrs. J. P. Dixon Age 32, Child G. F. Dixon Age 3, Baby John Dixon Age 1, Buried Elmwood Cemetery, Charlotte, N.C. Source: Charlotte-Mecklenburg Library, Carolina Room, Charlotte North Carolina.

Rutherfordton Baptist Church

Meeting commenced by Rev. C. B. Justice some time the latter part of March continued about two weeks. He was assisted by Pres. Pastor Rev. Sparrow who preached when requested and by Bud Hoyle M E Pastor. Good meeting. Much interest. Conversions about 25 or there about. Of the number professing conversion five young men – Thos. Sparrow,[212] James Carson, Henry Carson, Frank Dixon, Clarence Young. These united with the Presbyterian Church in Rutherfordton on Sunday the 9th April 1893. Three were also accessing to the Methodist and to the Baptist Church.

---

[212] Oldest son of Rev. George A. Sparrow.

Union Church Gaston Co. NC

Began a Protracted meeting in this Church on Saturday before the 3rd Sabbath in Sept. Preached twice Saturday & twice Sunday and received by Sunday night 6 accessions – 3 by letter & 3 on Profession. Monday rained had no regular services. Tuesday morning it rained. Tuesday night Rev. McAllister of Bethel Church S. C. preached and also Wednesday morning. Wed. night preached myself, and up to this time had received 19 into the Church, 16 on Prof., 3 by letter.

During the whole meeting 23 were received into the church on profession of Faith and seven by letter.

———————

Gaston County Field

On the 6th December 1893 I left Rutherfordton and took charge of Union & Olney Churches in Gaston County having accepted their call at Salary of 850.00 & the manse and all fire wood free. Preached the 1st Sermons at both churches on the 1st Sabbath in December 1893. One church is located about four miles from Gastonia and the other about seven. The manse, school house i.e. being at Union 7 miles from Gastonia in a very thickly settled neighborhood.

Was installed at Union for both churches (the officers & some of the members of Olney being present) & the church basically in a congregational meeting authorized this, i.e. the Commission consisting of Rev. Frank D. Hunt, Rev. Wharton then of Steel Creek, and Elder G. R. Hanna of Charlotte. Wharton could not be present and the work was done by Hunt & Hanna. The two churches numbered when I accepted the call about 300 members.[213]

---

[213] Rev. George A. Sparrow's *Book of Illustrations.*

Olney Presbyterian church was formed from a part of the Bethel Presbyterian church, York County, S. C. Bethel was organized in 1763. The existing records of Olney extend no further back than 1833 but authorities believe a much earlier date with preaching services held there prior to 1793. First Presbyterian Church in Gastonia is a daughter of Olney and has on its membership rolls today the descendants of the early members of the Olney congregation.[214]

––––––––––

Protracted & other meetings held

Began a meeting in the Shelby Pres. Church Rev. W. P. McCorkle Pastor on Thursday before the 3rd Sabbath in April 1893 and continued until Thursday night before the forth Sabbath April. Three decisions to the church.

G. A.S.

––––––––––

Rev. Sparrow preached at Glenn school house once a month for many years. On the second Sunday of every month Rev. Sparrow preached at Crowder's Creek school house.

---

[214] *Olney Presbyterian Church 1793-1968, Her 175th Year. History of Olney Presbyterian Church* by Rev. G. A. Sparrow.

Gaston County

On Sat. 21ˢᵗ April 1897, a son of Mr. Jno. Hannah, both the father and son being members of Olney Church, was killed at the Coffin Factory in Gastonia by becoming entangled in a shaft. He was terribly mutilated. Was a good boy about 16 years of age. He was buried in the cemetery at that Place on Tuesday following the service being conducted in the Presbyterian Church by myself.

"For what is your life."[215]

Union Presbyterian Church, Gaston County, North Carolina

---

[215] Rev. George A. Sparrow's *Book of Illustrations.*

The Union "meeting house" originally started in a brush arbor which had planks for seats. Summer preaching was conducted in the arbor prior to the first building being constructed.

A log meeting house was constructed on the current church site in 1843. At this time Presbyterians and Baptists worshipped here together. Four acres of land were donated for church use and the deed was recorded in 1845. Union Independent Presbyterian Church was organized on November 9, 1850. From this name Union demonstrates the harmony, union and cooperation of Christians in the community. In 1870 a frame church was completed. The Baptists later built Sandy Plains Baptist Church and in 1876 gave a quit claim deed to Union.

Rev. George A. Sparrow came in 1893 and brought great social reforms to the community and strengthened the work of the Church. The congregation more than doubled in size during his ministry. By now Union had a new Session building, a new manse, new land and a new preacher; but it still needed one additional blessing: a new church building to replace the old frame structure. Rev. Sparrow persuaded the congregation to build a brick structure that would draw people into a spirit of worship to God. Construction began September 17, 1906 with the first service held on June 16, 1907. Dedication was held August 19-23, 1910 after all loans had been paid.[216] Numerous sons and daughters of Union have contributed and supported their country throughout periods of peace and of war. A total of 65 members saw active duty during the Civil War. Twenty-one Civil War soldiers are buried in Union cemetery.[217]

---

[216] *Union Presbyterian Church 140th Anniversary Directory 1990* and Union Presbyterian Church, January, 2000.
[217] Union Presbyterian Church "Military Service."

The (old) Union Presbyterian Manse and the Sparrow Family.
Rev. George Sparrow and Susan
George, Jr. (13); Evans (7); Libby (10) Annie (22) Minnie (17)

During Rev. Sparrow's tenure at Union and Olney two children were born in the manse – Elizabeth Bonner Sparrow was born January 23, 1894, and Evans Crabtree Sparrow was born April 7, 1896.

As Mrs. Sparrow relates in her *Ideal Scrap Book*, the Union community proved to be a great place to raise their children:

> There was always some fun event going on in either the church or school house which was right across the road from Union Church. The school house was used as a community center which consisted of four rooms, an audience room, and stage.
>
> Box parties were held at the school house. The ladies filled their boxes with delicious eats, highly decorated them, and they were auctioned off to the highest bidder. One time the money made was used for a new basketball for the girls and what was left was to be the beginning of a sum for lights for the school house. There was a program in the school every two or three weeks consisting of

songs and recitations.

Revivals were often held at Union and Olney with folks coming from different denominations.

The Christian Endeavor Society was the name of the young people's group. Other organizations were: The Camp Fire Girls and Junior Aid Society (object improvement of church property). The Christian Endeavor Society held an annual ice cream festival and also sponsored oyster suppers.

Probably the most enjoyable and memorable times were the large picnics held at the church. Members and friends came from all around and there were always big tables of country ham, fried chicken, potato salad, deviled eggs, pies and cakes of all kinds, and tubs of tea and lemonade. In the afternoons the boys played baseball on the school grounds.

Hay rides, swim parties, watermelon feasts, possum dinners with "sweet taters" and all day visits were among the social activities in the community. The annual fair at the Union school house with all the exhibits and midway shows were lots of fun.

While living at Union three of the Sparrow children married local people. Thomas Sparrow married Katherine (Kate) Lavinia Wilson, Sylvester Brown Sparrow married Mattie Robinson, and Annie Foreman Sparrow married Robert B. Riddle.

On April 19, 1908 Rev. Sparrow lost his beloved wife Susan Brown Sparrow. This was a sad time for the family and community. She had been a loving wife and mother and dedicated Christian.

Two years later while attending a conference at Flora MacDonald College, Red Springs, North Carolina, a funny prank happened that would lead to Rev. Sparrow's second marriage. A group of mischievous girls swiped his hat and hid it in Miss Ewing's room. Elizabeth Bryan Ewing was head of the Art Department at Flora MacDonald College. When Miss Ewing found it, she boxed it up and sent it back to him by mail. That was the incident that started their romance and later marriage!

Art Room
Flora MacDonald College

Mrs. George Attmore Sparrow (Elizabeth) was Society Editor of the Daily Gazette for a number of years. The following are interesting events written by her during this time, taken from her *Ideal Scrap Book*:

——————

On Sunday a service for the enforcement of law and order was held in the church. The pastor, Rev. G. A. Sparrow, preached on that subject and that of the wonderful history – making record of the beginning of National prohibition.[218] A collection was taken up for the cause and a committee appointed. The history was also given of this section of the county 26 years ago, and the difference between now and then.

——————

I am keeping a gardening book and in it jotting down all sorts of nature records both of plants and temperature. On December 8, 1917, the temperature began to drop, on December 10th, the thermometer registered 15 degrees, was the same on the 11th, and very cold for a

[218] On May 26, 1908, by a referendum vote of 62 percent to 38 percent, North Carolina became the first southern state to enact statewide prohibition of alcoholic beverages. The temperance movement of the antebellum period expressed the concern of many North Carolinians about the social consequences of what was perceived as the wide-spread abuse of wine, beer and liquor, but the prohibition law of 1908 was the product of a more focused and organized movement which grew in the years following the Civil War. Increasingly after 1865, opposition to the traffic in liquor became a crusade against the saloon which was depicted as a source of evil and corruption. In 1908 the General Assembly called for a referendum on prohibition which, after an active campaign, the dry forces won. The manufacture and sale of alcoholic beverages in North Carolina thus ended eleven years before the Eighteenth Amendment to the United States Constitution brought prohibition to the entire country. Harry McKown, "May 1908 – Statewide Prohibition, (www.lib.unc.edu/ncc/ref/nchistory/may2006/index. html)" *This Month in North Carolina History,* May 2006. Provided by UNC Libraries / North Carolina Collection.

week. December 12th was 10 degrees. It snowed on the 11th, and we had several snows by January 11th. On January 11th, at night, we had one of those rare thunder storms that occur in the winter, a perfect tornado sweeping through the country, lightning flashing and wind roaring. We got up during the night and dressed, not knowing whether the roof might go off at any moment, but afraid to have light or fire. A great deal of damage was done elsewhere by the storm. January 22nd the ground, trees, bushes, and roofs covered with sleety snow, everything looks like fairyland. There were only five sunny days in January. Nine snows in a little over a month. February 3rd, the sun has forgotten how to shine. February 9th, a little milder, cars are beginning to go by oftener, many days not a car passed. February 28th, beginning to plant things in the garden. April 28th, strawberries ripe. This is a record of the Winter of 1917-18 at Union.

Following the end of World War I[219] a big celebration was given on Thanksgiving Day in honor of Union's returned soldiers and sailors. The flag had twenty-seven stars, and none of them were golden.[220] There was a large picnic dinner and in the evening the young ladies of the church gave the soldier and sailor boys a beautiful party in the school house. Decorations, games, contests and lovely refreshments delighted the hearts of those boys and made them realize they were all home to stay.

---

[219] Armistice Day, November 11, commemorates the day when World War I officially ended in 1918.
[220] A Gold Star would indicate killed in action.

It is an interesting fact to note that at last the weary farm horses and mules have a day of rest on Sunday. Now hardly a horse or mule goes to church. Almost every family at Union has a car and there are many new ones in the number.

––––––––––

Tuesday morning we laid to rest in the cemetery here one of the most notable women of this section during the days of the Civil War, Mrs. Miriam E. Howell, (November 22, 1829 – July 5, 1920) aged 91 years. During the war Mrs. Howell was left at home with the family to provide for, all of the men of the family having gone to the front. She was a very resourceful woman and she owned a loom. Cloth was hard to get and very expensive and although she could not weave very much at a time herself, she organized a weaving business and took in cotton and wool to be woven, then she got neighbors to come to her house and weave for her, paying them two yards for weaving a bolt. Many a neighbor was glad to give her time and work for the two yards of cloth and the people who sent wool or cotton to be woven paid Mrs. Howell for the bolt woven. Many a soldier wore home spun from her loom, and many a family was clothed in this way.

Such women should be honored by all, for they did a wonderful work, both for others and in taking care of their own families. They were women, but nevertheless true soldiers of the Confederacy.

Woodrow Wilson Fund

The Woodrow Wilson Foundation Committee of the Union section is composed of Messrs. Harvey Ratchford, George Wilson, Joseph Patrick and George Patrick. These were appointed Sunday and started with the first man giving $5.00. This is a splendid work, the furthering of anything that will keep alive the idea of perpetual peace, and prevention of all wars, and to name it in honor of the one who worked so hard for a League of Peace is a beautiful tribute.

––––––––––

A "Bundle Day" was held each year where bundles of clothes were brought and piled high in front of the pulpit. These were sent to Eastern countries, Bible lands, the Armenians and other countries to clothe the destitute. This was an answer to Josephus Daniels[221] call for help, and to the Governor's proclamation on the subject.

---

[221] Josephus Daniels (5/18/1862 – 1/15/1948) born in Washington, N.C. was a newspaper editor and publisher who was appointed by President Woodrow Wilson to serve as Secretary of the Nary during World War I. He was a close friend and supporter of President Franklin Roosevelt. A devout Methodist and a teetotaler, he is perhaps most famous in the Navy for having banned alcoholic beverages from ships. During World War I, Daniels created the Naval Consulting Board to encourage inventions that would be helpful to the Navy. He was concerned that the U.S. was unprepared for new conditions of warfare and needed new technology. Sources: Howard E. Covington and Marion A. Ellis, *The North Carolina Century: Tar Heels Who Made a Difference, 1900-2000*, 2002; Lloyd N. Scott, Naval Consulting Board of the United States, Government Printing Office, Washington, DC, 1920, pp. 286-288.

Election Day was a big day at Union school house. Grannie Ratchford, aged 96, cast the first vote placed in the ballot box. Voting was in one room of the school house and by nine o'clock there were so many cars out in the grove that it seemed like a party was going on. All day long they came and went, in some families three generations of men and women casting their ballots.[222]

––––––––––

The school is moving on finely. A number of debates have been held. One of these was on "Women Suffrage," another, "Resolved, That the Negro Had Been Worse Treated Than the Indian," and the last, "That Wilson is a Greater Man Than Washington Was." Mighty subjects to handle, but right valiantly have they been tackled. These boys who can tackle a football, basketball, or baseball, aren't going to stop at a little thing like a debate.

––––––––––

Union, October 10

Union is always interested in the Orthopedic Hospital[223] and was glad

––––––––––

[222] Constitutional Amendment XIX. "The right of citizens of the United States to vote shall not be denied or abridged by the United States or by any State on account of sex." Passed by Congress June 4, 1919. Ratified August 18, 1920.

[223] The North Carolina Orthopedic Hospital was a State institution for crippled children, 1921-1979. In 1909 Robert B. Babington of Gastonia read a newspaper account of how a crippled child was turned away from an orphanage and noted North Carolina had no facility for the care of handicapped children. Babington began pressing the idea of a state-funded institution to provide such care. His efforts finally met with success in 1917 when the General Assembly appropriated $20,000 for the construction of an orthopedic hospital provided that an equal amount in matching funds was raised locally. Selected as the first president of the institution's board of trustees, Babington led the successful fund drive. Oscar L. Miller was founding surgeon. Doctors Michael Hoke, Oscar L. Miller, and William Roberts, in succession, were the principal surgeons through 1966. Source: North Carolina Office of Archives & History – Department of Cultural Resources, North Carolina Highway Historical Marker Program: ID:O-78, Marker : North Carolina Orthopedic Hospital. December 16, 2010.

Joy W. Sparrow

to answer Mr. Babington's request for hens. The result of this was hens have been sent, and more will follow. This movement was started by Miss Mary Nolen and the Ladies Aid Society and the hens were collected and taken to the hospital by Mr. George Ratchford and Miss Elizabeth Huffstetler. If all the hens lay that have been given to the hospital, these children will have eggs enough to live on all winter.

Thanksgiving, 1921

On Thanksgiving morning there were services in the church by the pastor, Rev. G. A. Sparrow, who told the beautiful old story of the first Thanksgiving, and also gave an interesting account of the trip of the Puritans across the ocean, of their trials in England and Holland preceding it, and then again of that landing on Massachusetts soil only 120, and of the women's first wash day, after seven weeks of life on the ship; and the fifty graves that were there after the terrible cold of the New England winter. And yet after all that, in the next November they founded what is the custom that has grown to be the only national annual Thanksgiving Day of any nation in the world.

Union, November 29, 1921

Barium Springs Orphanage is very much richer by the collections taken up in the Union Church on Thanksgiving Day and the Sunday following. A goodly amount was raised.

There are two old ladies who used to live in the neighborhood, although they did not belong to the Union Church, and on Thanksgiving Day they too were remembered, and a box of fruit and other things was sent to them, to the County Home, where they now live.

Olney Presbyterian Church
Gastonia, N.C.

Rev. George A. Sparrow holds the distinction of having the longest pastorate of any Olney Minister (1893-1921). Before entering the ministry, Rev. Sparrow was a Confederate Army soldier and lawyer. It is recorded that 17 Revolutionary War soldiers and 45 Civil War soldiers are buried in the Olney church cemetery.

The records show Olney grew steadily in numbers and in spirituality during his pastorate. He preached at Olney on the second and fourth Sundays, morning and evening. On the second Sunday at 3 p.m., he preached at Glenn Schoolhouse which was "a mission and preaching point" of Olney Church. The school was located about three miles south of Olney near Pleasant Ridge and later was part of the Crowders Creek area.

Rev. Sparrow compiled a history of Olney Presbyterian Church in 1902 that was issued in a small booklet form by the Ladies Aid Society of the Church. A favorite expression of Mr. Sparrow, wrote Mrs. C. P. Robinson, Church Historian, was: "The Lord willing, there will be services here at this church on such and such a day."[224]

During Rev. Sparrow's pastorate at Union Presbyterian and Olney Presbyterian churches, Gastonia, North Carolina, his second wife Elizabeth Bryan Ewing Sparrow of Washington City, D. C., researched and recorded church history. Following are highlights of those interesting years and other stories passed down:

Now begins the story of the longest pastorate Union ever had, that of Rev. George A. Sparrow who lived among his people 28 years and 9 months and was laid to rest among many of them, back of the church, and near his beloved study.

Rev. George A. Sparrow was the son of a distinguished Confederate officer, Major Thomas Sparrow, who did much to help the South, as he was in charge of the coast and river defenses of Wilmington in blockade times. After the war was over, his father settled down to law, and it was fitting that the son should also be a lawyer. Young as he was, he became Prosecuting Attorney, but the young man became interested in religious work and left his law for the church. He had inherited a talent for speaking from his father and had been trained in the courts. This was a wonderful help to him. He often said if a man could not get his idea to his people in 20 minutes he could not get it to them at all, so his sermons were hardly ever more than 20 minutes long. Law had taught him to condense.

Rev. Sparrow was called to Union and Olney as pastor beginning December 3, 1893. At that time there were several large distilleries near

---

[224] Robert L. Hallman, *A History of Olney Presbyterian Church 200 Years,* Gaston Graphics, Inc., Gastonia, N.C. 1993.

the churches and much drinking. Rev. Sparrow and some of the most important men of the church decided to stop this. The result of their work was a law passed in the Legislature to have no distillery within 3 miles of a church or school, so the distilleries were broken up. The owners of these became some of our foremost cotton mill men, and strange to say Rev. Sparrow's great friends, some of them and their families joining his church. Union and Olney both prospered, the churches grew larger and there were large Sunday schools.

The Session was stricter in those earlier days. We find men suspended from church privileges for intoxication and swearing; one for purloining some cotton which really did not belong to him; several persons accused of fornication; and one young woman of the sin of dancing. Most of these were required to make a humble promise of reform and were forgiven.

The original log church was erected about 1843. The story is told that the old church had become so open that you could sit in the middle and throw your hat through the holes between the logs at any side. Money was collected and a frame church was built about 1859.

On August 6, 1884 a general Thanksgiving service was held to thank the Almighty for the good health and splendid crops and to give of their goods an offering "to beautify and repair His house." This seems to have been an all-day meeting. Often there were large summer outdoor singing schools. Seats were planks laid on sections of sawed logs which were split up for firewood later. Mr. John Riddle and a number of others were leaders of these schools, using the old American Tune Book. There is a story told of how the Leader looked down and saw a snake poking his head up at his feet. Knowing how the women would scream and the singers stampede, he brought his heavy foot down on the snake's head and with it squirming in the leaves went on leading the hymn.

During Rev. Sparrow's pastorate, talk began of a new church building. Rev. Sparrow was eager for it, and it was decided on. This third sanctuary was built in 1910, a church of brick with a handsome square tower, almost English in type. This Presbyterian Church would be an ornament to many a town.

The men of the church gave their time, a basement was dug for a furnace, and the men did all of the hauling with their teams free of charge, and quick, and the consequence was that Union has a church as handsome as any country church in the state, with every dollar paid. The dedication took place at a great meeting held August 19-23, 1910.

Union and Olney were part of the Mecklenburg Presbytery which stretched over such a great space with so many churches that the ministers found it hard to get over it and to all of the meetings. So, it was planned to cut the Presbytery into two parts, making the smaller one Kings Mountain Presbytery.

Dr. & Mrs. George Reese Patrick and Family
Courtesy of Debbie Patrick

In July, 1912, Dr. George R. Patrick passed away, after only several hours of illness. For years he had been an Elder at Union and lived near by. He was the beloved country doctor, night or day, in winter's cold or summer's heat, he never failed to visit his patients, and he and his pastor often went together, beloved friends.

Rev. Sparrow loved the special occasions of the church – Thanksgiving Day, Christmas, Easter, Mother's Day, May 10th, and other special times. One time on Mother's Day there was a mother's sermon, and cars full of flowers. The flowers were put in water all around the circular pulpit platform, and after the sermon, the Sunday School pupils took them to the cemetery and decorated every mother's grave on the grounds. The newer part of the cemetery is laid off beautifully, but no grave of a woman was neglected for fear that some mother might have been left without a bunch of flowers.

Joy W. Sparrow

In the Ladies' Parlor of the church hangs framed the service flag of the World War. On it are 24 stars and 3 silver ones. Union sent 27 young men into the war, 3 however were returned on account of some health question. One was a surgeon, the others privates or officers of several degrees.

During Rev. Sparrow's long pastorate, there were perhaps three outstanding events – the breaking up of much of the drinking of the neighborhood, the building of the handsome brick church, and the organization of Kings Mountain" Presbytery, of which he was a charter member and ardent advocate.

In 1920, with a good many mills having been built around Olney, Union and Olney decided to separate. In 1921 Rev. Sparrow was called by Union to serve full time. Olney was also to have a full time pastor.

Union was very prosperous; having services twice on each Sunday built the church up greatly. The Men's Bible Class, the Women's Bible Class and all of the rest of the Sunday School doubled, and their pastor was very happy, with his little home, his beautiful garden and flowers, and his devoted congregation but he was not to be left to them long, for the winged messenger was on the way.

On July 25th 1922 on a little visit to Montreat, he took a short walk, talking of how beautiful the view was, and returning, sitting in his chair with a smile on his face, he passed into the great beyond. They laid him to rest just back of the church, near his study, and among the friends who had passed on before.

Elizabeth Bryan Ewing Sparrow

Concord Cabarrus County

Preached one week in this church which is Rev. C. M. Payne D.D.[225] including 2nd Sabbath in June when the Sacrament of the Lord's Supper was administered. Preaching twice a day morning & Evening. The congregation was large and attentive and all seemed much interested and revived but <u>no visible results.</u> [226]

First Presbyterian Church, Concord, North Carolina
(Third Building, Cabarrus Avenue, Erected 1874)
Drawing by William Todd Aldridge

---

[225] Rev. Charles M. Payne (Rev. Sparrow's brother-in-law, married to his sister Maggie) served First Presbyterian Church, Concord during 1884 – 1894.
[226] Rev. George A. Sparrow's *Book of Illustrations.*

First Presbyterian Church
Concord, North Carolina

Through trials and tribulations a group of mostly Scotch-Irish first met in a dusty gin house and later in the summer months moved outside under a grove of live oaks. This was to be the first Presbyterian church in the small town of Concord, N.C.

In 1884 Rev. Charles Montgomery Payne was called to Concord. Rev. Payne seemingly possessed great energy, vision and intelligence. Not only did he attend medical school at Washington University where he earned a Doctor of Medicine degree, he then entered Union Seminary in Virginia. Later he served as a lieutenant in the Confederate Army, excelling in organization. (Mrs. R. S. Harris).

At the end of his ten-year stay in Concord, Payne resigned to take a post in Washington, N.C.[227]

Rev. Charles M. Payne

Margaret Justice Sparrow Payne
With 2 of their 3 children

---

[227] Leslie B. Rindoks, *The Psalm Singers of Concord Town, A History of First Presbyterian Church 1804-2004,* Publisher Lorimer Press, Davidson, North Carolina, 2004.

Bethel Presbyterian Church
York County, South Carolina

In 1764, just fourteen years after the first significant movement into this area of York County, South Carolina, Bethel Presbyterian Church was organized. There is no record of the building of the first and second houses of worship at Bethel but the third was built sometime between 1801 and 1811. The fourth which is the building that stands today was erected in 1873.[228]

During the Revolution, Bethel and other Presbyterian churches became noted as centers of opposition to British rule. This reputation is reported to have moved the British Major Ferguson to say, "I will spend one night in Bethel Church and leave it in ashes by day light." Ferguson, of course, was subsequently killed and the British defeated in the battle of Kings Mountain before the Major was able to fulfill his threat. [229]

---

[228] Bethel's History, www.bethelpresbyterian.org.
[229] 1987 Directory of Bethel Presbyterian Church, Clover, S. C.

During the years 1920 – 1922, Mrs. Elizabeth Bryan Ewing Sparrow was social writer for the local Daily Gazette. From the scrapbook of her many articles, on July 28, 1920 she wrote: "On Sunday a party of Gaston county historians went on a tour of old churches... . . . They drove to Olney, where they went into the cemetery and church and took photographs and notes. They then drove to Bethel, in South Carolina. This is another historic church; it is said that after the Battle of Kings Mountain, many of the wounded were carried to Bethel church and nursed by the splendid women of the Revolutionary times. This must be true, because there are many Revolutionary soldiers buried in the beautiful old cemetery. It has been noted that the women of Bethel fed and cared for many soldiers wounded in the Revolutionary War Battle of Kings Mountain."

Bethel is the mother church of Olney Presbyterian Church which was formed about 1788. Rev. Sparrow points out in his History of Olney: "Presbyterians were in the forefront of that battle and knowing that, we need not wonder why it is that Kings Mountain is surrounded by Presbyterian Churches, and that many of the lineal descendants of men who fought that battle are found as officers and members in those churches. It is history repeating itself, that whenever men have been most imbued with a true spirit of civil and religious liberty that Presbyterianism grows and thrives. . ."[230] In addition to Olney, Union, Allison Creek, Beth Shiloh, New Hope, Bowling Green, Scherer Memorial and Clover Presbyterian churches have stemmed from Bethel.

A total of 49 Revolutionary War and 46 Civil War soldiers are buried in the Bethel Presbyterian Church cemetery.[231]

---

[230] *Olney Presbyterian Church 1793-1968*, Published in 1968.
[231] Helen K. Grant, Historian, Bethel Presbyterian Church.

New Hope Presbyterian Church
Courtesy of
Hope Preserved: The Story of New Hope Presbyterian Church

New Hope Presbyterian Church was established in 1793 in Gaston County, North Carolina. Goshen Presbyterian Church, situated about seven miles northwest of New Hope, and Bethel Presbyterian Church, thirteen miles south in South Carolina, are the old mother churches out of which New Hope's first members came. Both churches still are very much alive and prosperous.[232]

In the *Ideal Scrap Book* on July 13, 1922, Mrs. Sparrow wrote: "On Saturday morning, Rev. G. A. Sparrow preached at New Hope church. It is always a pleasure for Mr. Sparrow to be at New Hope as that church and Union are close friends."

---

[232] History of New Hope Presbyterian, Gastonia, N.C., Published by the Women of New Hope Presbyterian Church.

1913 - 1966

First Presbyterian Church, Belmont, N.C.

The First Presbyterian Church of Belmont was organized in November, 1890 with twenty-eight charter members. It is a daughter of Goshen Church, North Belmont, N.C. which was organized in 1764.[233]

Rev. Mr. Sparrow's Sermons Greatly Enjoyed

Rev. G. A. Sparrow, of Union, preached two splendid sermons to crowded congregations at the Belmont Presbyterian church Sunday. His subject Sunday morning was "Heaven: Where and What It Is: Who Will Go There: How They Will Get There." The evening subject was "Hope, the Anchor of the Soul." His visit to Belmont was very helpful as well as very entertaining and greatly enjoyed by the Presbyterian congregation.

Mr. Sparrow has the distinction of holding probably the longest Presbyterian pastorate in the State, having been at Union 28 years.[234]

---

[233] *A History of First Presbyterian Church, Belmont, North Carolina 1890-1990.*
[234] *The Daily Gazette*, October 23, 1921.

Obituary

Rev. George Attmore Sparrow

July 14, 1845 – July 24, 1922

When the Church lost Rev. George A. Sparrow it lost one of the shining lights among the elder ministers.

Mr. Sparrow was born on the seashore at Beaufort, N.C. where his father had a summer home. His early days were spent with his grandfathers, Thomas Sparrow and John Blackwell in New Bern and his parents who had moved to Washington, N.C. His father was Major Thomas Sparrow, a fearsome soldier of the Confederacy, who had charge of the coast and city defenses of Wilmington during the Civil War. His mother Annie Blackwell was the daughter of John Blackwell of New Bern. Mr. Sparrow's great grandmother was a sister of Cyrus Field who laid the Atlantic cable.

Following in his father's footsteps, Mr. Sparrow studied law and became a very successful lawyer being born with a talent for oratory. He rose to be Solicitor serving for eight years and was a shining light in the profession.

He became very much interested in the work of the YMCA and with great enthusiasm became president of one of the largest chapters in the state.

His success in Law only helped to prepare him for his calling by God into the ministry. The man who could sway a jury by his eloquence was to leave all earthly preferment for the pulpit and preach the gospel. He studied theology, stood his examinations and was licensed to preach. By this time he had married Miss Susan Selby Brown of Washington, North Carolina. His first pastorate was in Franklin, N.C. in the mountains of the western part of the state, serving there for over a year. They then moved to Rutherfordton and from there to accept the call of two churches near Gastonia, N.C., Union Presbyterian Church and Olney Presbyterian. After serving both for 27 years, he gave up Olney and devoted his entire time to Union. Rev. Sparrow's pastorate was the second longest in the state lacking only three months of being 29 years. He seemed to never grow old and his vigorous preaching was wonderful. During these years his wife Susan died and she was laid to rest in the Union Presbyterian cemetery. His children grew up and went out to find paths of their own. Later he married Elizabeth Bryan Ewing of Washington City, D. C. who survives him.

Rev. Sparrow and his wife were spending a week in Montreat at the beautiful Chapman Home. He told his wife he felt so well and suggested they take a short stroll to the next cottage although his doctor had cautioned him that he had heart trouble. Upon returning to the Chapman Home in the glory of a beautiful sunset as he sat in a great arm chair, he closed his eyes and fell asleep only to awake in the heavenly city he had preached of only a few short days before.

Veranda at the Chapman Home, Montreat, N.C.
Courtesy of Montreat College Library

A handsome, brick Union Presbyterian Church with a square tower was built just a few years ago, replacing the old church constructed of wood. There is perhaps no more prosperous country church in the state. The congregations were large and the Sunday School had doubled in the last year. There was a large Men's Bible Class, a large Women's Bible Class, a Mission Study Class, Christian Endeavor and Junior Endeavor Societies. Communion was served during his last service prior to leaving for Montreat.

A country preacher he chose to be. He gave up many calls to large Southern cities, and several years ago, one week he had three calls, but he always said no and did not even tell his people. Such was the modesty of the man. He said he intended to live and die with them, and that he felt that the young people of his church were his own boys and girls, that he had helped to raise them, and they were all helping him, leading in prayer and helping in all the church society work.

It was a rare thing for him to come out of the pulpit, after one of his short, vigorous sermons, that the people did not gather around him and tell him they loved to hear him preach. His friends were never sparing in their commendations and this made him love them more, for love begets love.

Rev. Sparrow loved the ocean and would often quote
Crossing the Bar **by Alfred Lord Tennyson:**

Sunset and evening star,
And one clear call for me!
And may there be no moaning of the bar,
When I put out to sea.

But such a tide as moving seems asleep,
Too full for sound and foam,
When that which drew from out the boundless deep
Turns again home.

Twilight and evening bell,
And after that the dark!
And may there be no sadness of farewell,
When I embark;

For though from out our bourne of Time and Place
The flood may bear me far,
I hope to see my Pilot face to face
When I have crossed the bar.

His life had rounded out to the close. The life of George Attmore Sparrow was that of self-sacrifice, but a happy life — a man of God gone home to peace.

Robert Rainey

Blackwell Mansion, Astoria, New York
Courtesy of Greater Astoria Historical Society

Colonel Jacob Blackwell, the grandfather of Annie Blackwell Sparrow, wife of Thomas Sparrow, was the ancestor who assisted in establishing American Independence. He served as a member of the Provincial Congress 1775 – 1777. At the opening of the French and Indian War in 1754, he held a Captaincy in the Newtown militia and rose to the rank of Colonel. He was made chairman of the Committee appointed to select deputies to the "First Provincial Congress" and on May 22nd, 1775 was elected Deputy to the First Congress. On June 30th, 1776 he was elected to the Third Congress, and on July 9th was returned for the Fourth Congress. When the British overran Queens County, his large estate was seized and despoiled. With the persecution of the enemy becoming unbeatable he fled for protection to New Jersey. The British hacked the "Arrow of Confiscation" into his front door making it property of the Crown. This arrow marking still exists in the door and is in the possession of the Greater Astoria Historical

Society. Jacob Blackwell returned to this home and lived there through the British occupation and died there October 23rd, 1780.[235]

Governor Van Twiller was the first person to own Blackwell Island obtaining it from the Indians in 1637. Van Twiller lost it in 1652 when it passed into the ownership of a man named Flyn. In 1668 Captain John Manning, a British officer, bought it. He retired to the island after his sword was broken over his head at City Hall for his surrender of New York to the Dutch in 1673.

Robert Blackwell, who had married Manning's stepdaughter Mary, eventually took title to the property and held it until his death in 1717; the island bore his name until April 12, 1921!

The city of New York acquired the island July 19, 1828, and constructed charitable and corrective institutions. By 1921 the reputation of the workhouse and penitentiary on the island had attained such notoriety that the Board of Aldermen changed the name from Blackwell Island to Welfare Island.[236]

Welfare Island became Roosevelt Island in 1973 and is now a model planned community and thriving home to almost ten thousand people.[237]

---

[235] Source: Forgotten NY, "Behind the Gray Door," www.forgotten-ny.com/slices/Blackwell, 2008.

[236] Lou Gody, Editor-in-Chief; Chester D. Harvey and James Reed, Editors; *New York City Guide,* Federal Writers' Project, Random House, New York, 1939, p.423.

[237] Judith Berdy and the Roosevelt Island Historical Society, *Images of America Roosevelt Island,* Arcadia Publishing, 2003.

19th Century Map of Roosevelt (Blackwell Island).

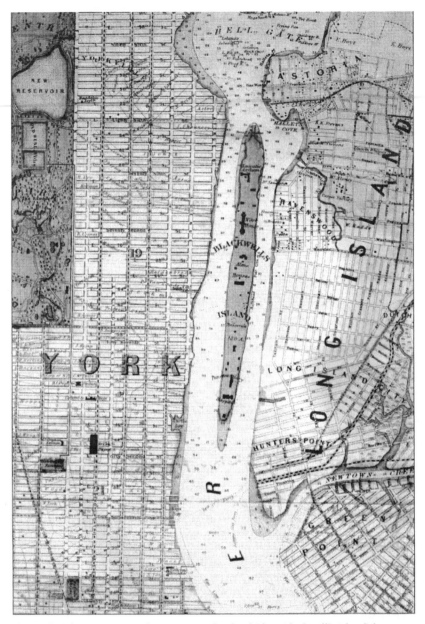

This mid-19th-century map shows Roosevelt Island (then Blackwell's Island) between Manhattan and Long Island in the east River. Two miles long and 800 feet wide, it runs parallel to Manhattan between 46th and 86th Streets. The locations of some early institutions—the penitentiary, the workhouse, the almshouse, and the asylum—are indicated.

Courtesy of Roosevelt Island Historical Society

Joy W. Sparrow

Thomas Sparrow
(10/02/1819 – 1/14/1884)
Major, Confederate State of
America

Annie Blackwell Sparrow
(1/02/1822 – 3/07/1901)
Wife of Thomas Sparrow
Married 4/24/1844

George Hubbard Brown

(5/03/1850 – 3/16/1926)
Brother-in-Law of George A.
Sparrow (Susan Brown Sparrow's brother). He was elected as
an Associate Justice of the Supreme Court of North Carolina
in 1904.

Laura Ellison Lewis Brown
(1/11/1850 – 3/09/1942)
George Attmore Sparrow's Sister-in-
Law. George Brown and Laura were
married on December 17, 1874. She
donated money for a library building in Washington, North Carolina. It is called the George H. and
Laura E. Brown Library.

Thomas Sparrow, Sr.
(8/31/1875 – 1/19/1955)
Oldest son of Rev. George Attmore
Sparrow and Susan Brown Sparrow,
married Katherine (Kate) Lavinia Wilson on November 17, 1897. Their children were Thomas Sparrow, Jr., Susan
Sparrow and Katherine Sparrow. They
were owners of Sparrow Dairy Farm in
Gaston County, North Carolina.

Evans Crabtree Sparrow
(4/7/1896 – 1968)
Youngest son of Rev. George Attmore
Sparrow and Susan Brown Sparrow.
Evans was a partner with Mr. Wil-
liam Blanton, Blanton and Sparrow,
wholesale grocers on College Street,
Charlotte, North Carolina.

George Attmore Sparrow, Jr.
(2/07/1891 – 7/24/1970)
Son of Rev. George Attmore Sparrow
and Susan Brown Sparrow. Served
in the Army during World War I.
He took his training at the Medi-
cal Officers Training Camp, Camp
Greenleaf, Ft. Oglethorpe, Georgia.
George was a junior partner in the
Law firm of Pharr, Bell, and Spar-
row in the Law Building, Charlotte,
North Carolina.

Dr. Thomas Delamar Sparrow
(9/11/1895 – 8/31/1971)
Son of John Blackwell Sparrow, nephew of
George A. Sparrow. Graduated from Davidson College in 1916, received his M.D.
degree from the University of Pennsylvania in 1920, and was one of the founders
of Charlotte Memorial Hospital. In 1965
he was the recipient of the Algernon Sid-
ney Sullivan Award from Davidson College and in 1966 they bestowed upon him
the honorary degree of Doctor of Laws.

Susan Selby Brown Sparrow
(12/12/1854 – 4/19/1908)
Wife of George Attmore Sparrow

Elizabeth Bonner Sparrow
(1/23/1894 – 7/01/1970)
daughter of George A. and Susan Brown
Sparrow. Graduated from Peace Institute
in 1912. Married Chesley Watkins, Sr.
They were the parents of Chesley Watkins, Jr., George Sparrow Watkins and
Susan Brown Watkins. Courtesy of Finch
Library, Peace College, Raleigh, N.C.

Annie Foreman Sparrow
(1/19/1882 – 2/12/1967)
Daughter of George A. and Susan
Brown Sparrow, married Robert
B. Riddle who was a farmer in
the Union Community and they
were the parents of three children:
Robert B. Riddle, Jr., Laura Riddle
Thompson and George W. Riddle.
Courtesy of Ann Riddle Plummer

Minnie Shepherd Sparrow,
(born 11/6/1887)
daughter of George A. and Susan Brown
Sparrow. Graduated from Peace Institute
and the University of North Carolina at
Chapel Hill. Married Clinton Walker
Keyes who graduated from Princeton
with a M.A. and PhD. He went to
France as a Lieutenant in World War I.

Dr. William T. Sparrow
(8/21/1825 – 7/17/1862)
Brother of Major Thomas Sparrow

Susan Brown Sparrow
and Thomas Sparrow, Jr.
Grandchildren of
Rev. George A. Sparrow and
Susan Selby Brown Sparrow

Pictures of Dr. Sparrow and wife Elizabeth are
Courtesy of Octagon House Restoration, Inc.
Hyde County, N.C.

Elizabeth Jennett Sparrow
Wife of William T. Sparrow

The Octagon House built for
Dr. William T. Sparrow and his wife
Elizabeth Jennett Sparrow is one of
only two antebellum dwellings known
to survive in North Carolina. It is a
unique Hyde County landmark.
Courtesy of Hyde County
Historical & Genealogical Society

Peace College,
Raleigh, North Carolina
Rev. George A. Sparrow served on
the Board of Visitors 1912 – 1915
and Board of Trustees 1916 – 1922

Thomas Sparrow (oldest son of Rev. George A. Sparrow)
and wife Katherine (Kate) Wilson Sparrow
with Grandchildren Mary Frances and Thomas Glenn Sparrow
and babies Jimmy Thompson and Bobby Suggs

Chesley Watkins, Sr., Elizabeth Sparrow Watkins,
George Sparrow Watkins, Clinton Walker Keys, 1940.

BIBLIOGRAPHY

MANUSCRIPT COLLECTIONS

Grimes-Bryan Collection #16, East Carolina Manuscript Collection, J. Y. Joyner Library, East Carolina University, Greenville, North Carolina.

The Papers of Jefferson Davis, Volume 7, the National Archives, RG109, Documents in the Official Records, Series 1, Volume 2.

Thomas Sparrow Papers, Collection No. 1, East Carolina Manuscript Collection, J. Y. Joyner Library, East Carolina University, Greenville, North Carolina.

Thomas Sparrow Papers, #1878, Southern Historical Collection, The Wilson Library, University of North Carolina at Chapel Hill, Chapel Hill, North Carolina.

VMI Archives and Records, Virginia Military Institute, Lexington, Virginia.

BOOKS, ARTICLES AND GOVERNMENT PUBLICATIONS

American Heritage College Dictionary, The, Third Edition, Houghton Mifflin Company, Boston, New York, 1993.

American Heritage Dictionary of the English Language, The, Fourth Edition, Houghton Mifflin Company, 2006.

Barrett, John Gilchrist, *The Civil War in North Carolina*, The University of North Carolina Press, Chapel Hill, North Carolina 1963.

Berdy Judith and the Roosevelt Island Historical Society, *Images of America Roosevelt Island*, Arcadia Publishing, Charleston, S. C. 2003.

Bridges, Hal, *Lee's Maverick General: Daniel Harvey Hill*, University of Nebraska Press, Lincoln, Nebraska, 1991.

Brown, Norman D., *Edward Stanly: Whiggery's Tarheel Conqueror*, University of Alabama Press, 1974.

Buist, Robert, *The Family Kitchen Gardener*, Orange Judd & Company, 245 Broadway, New York.

Cain, Angelique and Brandi Hymer, *Murder & Mayhem in Old Arcola*, Warria, Lexington, KY, 2000.

Carmichael, Peter, Senior Editor, Eberly Professor of Civil War Studies, West Virginia University, *Encyclopedia Virginia*, Virginia Foundation of the Humanities, Charlottesville, Virginia.

Cochran, Betty and C. A. Mann, *St. Peter's Episcopal Church*, Washington, North Carolina, 1822-1997.

Covington, Howard E. and Marion A. Ellis, *The North Carolina Century: Tar Heels Who Made a Difference, 1900-2000*, The University of North Carolina Press, Chapel Hill, North Carolina, 2002.

Crabtree, Beth G., *North Carolina Governors 1585-1975*, North Carolina Division of Archives and History, Raleigh, North Carolina 1974.

Dedmondt, Glenn, *The Flags of Civil War North Carolina*, Pelican Publishing Company, Inc., Gretna, Louisiana, 2003.

Directory of Bethel Presbyterian Church, Clover, S. C., 1987.

Dupuy, Trevor N., Curt Johnson and David L. Bongard, *The Harper Encyclopedia of Military Biography*, Harper Collins, New York, 1992.

Eicher, John H., and David J. Eicher, *Civil War High Commands*, Stanford University Press, Stanford, California, 2009.

Ellis, Edward S., A.M., *Library of American History*, Volume 4, The Jones Brothers Publishing Company, Cincinnati, Ohio,1918.

First Presbyterian Church History, Franklin, North Carolina.

Folk, Edgar E. and Bynum Shaw. , *W.W. Holden: A Political Biography*, John F. Blair, Publisher, Winston-Salem, North Carolina 1982.

Gody, Lou, Editor-in-Chief; Chester D. Harvey and James Reed, Editors; *New York City Guide*, Federal Writers' Project, Random House, New York, 1939.

Hallman, Robert L., *A History of Olney Presbyterian Church 200 Years*, Gaston Graphics, Inc., Gastonia, N.C. 1993.

History of the Arcola Presbyterian Church.

History of Douglas County, Illinois, Arcola Township. F. A. Battery & Co., Publisher, 1884.

History of First Presbyterian Church, Belmont, North Carolina 1890-1990.

History of the First Presbyterian Church, Raleigh, North Carolina 1816-1991. Commercial Printing Co., Raleigh, N.C. 1991.

History of the First Presbyterian Church, Washington, North Carolina, 1823-1973, Washington, North Carolina.

H*oly Bible, King James Version*.

Lloyd, Allen Alexander, *History of the Town of Hillsboro*, 1948-1949.

Loy, Ursula and Pauline Worthy, *Washington and the Pamlico*, Washington-Beaufort County Bicentennial Commission, Edwards & Broughton Co., Raleigh, North Carolina, 1976.

Manarin, Dr. Louis H., Compiler, *North Carolina Troops 1861 – 1865 A Roster,* Volume 1, Artillery, State Division of Archives and History, Raleigh, North Carolina, 1988.

Meyers, Jeffrey, *Edgar Allen Poe: His Life and Legacy*, New York City, Charles Scribner's Sons.

Minutes of the Synod of North Carolina for 1922.

North Carolina Department of Cultural Resources, North Carolina Office of Archives & History, 2008.

Olney Presbyterian Church 1793-1968, Her 175th Year.

Powell, William S., Editor, *Dictionary of North Carolina Biography*, Vol. 2 D-G, and 5 P-S, The University of North Carolina Press, Chapel Hill, N.C. 1994.

Public Laws of the State of North Carolina, Raleigh, Holden and Wilson, Printers to the State, 1859.

Randall, Ruth Painter, *Colonel Elmer Ellsworth: A Biography of Lincoln's Friend and First Hero of the Civil War*, Boston: Little Brown, 1960.

Reed, Col. C. Wingate, *Beaufort County, Two Centuries of Its History*, Edwards and Broughton Co., Raleigh, N.C. 1962.

Richter, William L., *The A to Z of the Civil War and Reconstruction*, The Scarecrow Press, Inc., Lanham, Toronto, Plymouth, UK, 2009.

Riker, James, *History of the Blackwell Family*, Annals of Newtown in Queen's County, New York.

Rindoks, Leslie B. *The Psalm Singers of Concord Town, A History of First Presbyterian Church 1804-2004,* Lorimer Press, Davidson, North Carolina 2004.

Robinson, Jr., William Morrison, *The Confederate Privateers*, Yale University Press, New Haven, Connecticut, 1928.

Rutherfordton Presbyterian Church, Rutherfordton, N.C. 175th Anniversary, April 3, 1834 – April 3, 2009.

Schmidt, Jay, *Fort Warren: New England's Most Historic Civil War Site*, Amherst, New Hampshire, Unified Business Technologies Press, 2003.

Scott, Lloyd N., *Tar Heels Who Made a Difference*, Naval Consulting Board of the United States, Government Printing Office, Washington, DC, 1920.

Shakespeare's *The Two Gentlemen of Verona*. Act 5, Scene 4.

Sifakis, Stewart, *Who Was Who In The Civil War*, America by Facts On File, Inc., New York, New York, 1988.

Smith, John Murphy, *The History of The First Presbyterian Church of New Bern, North Carolina 1886-1987*. Griffin & Tighman Printers, Inc., New Bern, North Carolina, 1988.

Sparrow, Elizabeth Bryan Ewing, *Ideal Scrap Book*. Union Presbyterian Church, Gastonia, North Carolina.

Sparrow, Rev. G. A., *History of Olney Presbyterian Church* by Rev. G. A. Sparrow.

Sparrow Rev. George A., *Book of Illustrations*, Union Presbyterian Church, Gastonia, North Carolina.

Sparrow, W. Keats, Article by, Professor, East Carolina University, *Dictionary of North Carolina Biography*, edited by William S. Powell, Volume 5 P-S, The University of North Carolina Press, Chapel Hill, N.C., 1994.

Thomas, Dean S., *Civil War Commanders*, Thomas Publications, Gettysburg, PA, 1988.

Thomas, John Payre, *The History of the South Carolina Military Academy*, Walker, Evans & Cogswell Co., Charleston, South Carolina, 1893.

Thompson, Waddy, *The First Book In United States History*, D. C. Heath and Company, Boston, Mass., 1929.

Tolbert, Noble J., Editor, *The Papers of John Willis Ellis, Volume Two 1860-1861*. Raleigh State Department of Archives and History, Raleigh, North Carolina, 1964.

Union Presbyterian Church 140th Anniversary Directory 1990, Gastonia, N.C.

Vass, Rev. L. C., A.M. *History of the Presbyterian Church in New Bern, N.C.* Whittet and Shepperson, Printers, Richmond, Virginia, 1886.

Wall, Joan, *Rutherfordton Presbyterian Church, Rutherfordton, North Carolina, 2009.*

Warner, Ezra, Jr., *Generals in Blue: Lives of the Union Commanders*, Baton Rouge: Louisiana State University Press, 1964.

Women of New Hope Presbyterian Church, *History of New Hope Presbyterian Church*, Gastonia, North Carolina, 1975.

NEWSPAPERS AND PERIODICALS

American Farmer, The, June, 1869, Worthington & Lewis, Baltimore, MD.

Central Illinois Gazette, October 26, 1859.

Daily Gazette, The, Gastonia, North Carolina, October 23, 1921.

Harper's Weekly, September 7, 1861.

Hyde County Historical and Genealogical Society, Volume XIX, Spring 1998, Number 1, Fairfield, N.C.

Ireland, Robert E., "The Tar Heel Citadel," *Civil War Times*, May 2001.

News Herald, The, Morganton, N.C. June 8, 1922.

Saturday Evening Post, The, August 19, 1843.

WEB SITES

Answers. www.answers.com

Beaufort County NCGenWeb Genealogy web site www.usgenweb.org

Bethel's History, www.bethelpresbyterian.org

Bioguide.congress.gov/
Biographical Directory of the United States Congress: /Burnside, Ambrose E.
Biographical Directory of the United States Congress: /Clingman, Thomas Lanier.
Biographical Directory of the United States Congress: /Davis, Jefferson.
Biographical Directory of the United States Congress: /Stanley, Edward.

Christian History Timeline website. Christianhistorytimeline.com

Christopher, Milbourne, "*45 Years A Wizard*," Magical Past-Times, sponsored by The Miracle Factory, Karr, Todd, Editor, Gary Hunt, Advisor Emeritus, On-Line Journal of Magic History, 2004 www. miraclefactory.net

Civil War Artillery, Artillery Glossary, 2011, www.jackmelton.com

Civil War Interactive, A Civil War Biography: Samuel Barron, www.civilwarinteractive.com/biosmain

Civil War Records, "Prisoner Exchange System." www.civilwarblue-grass.net

Dictionary of American Naval Fighting Ships. www.history.navy.mil/danfs/abbreviations.htm

Dictionary.com

dictionary.reverso.net/english-cobuild/secessionist

Encyclopedia Britannica Online, 2011, www.britannica.com

Forgotten NY, "Behind the Gray Door," www.forgotten-ny.com/slices/Blackwell, 2008

Hymnlyrics.org

Library of Congress – Chronicling America. www.chroniclingameri-ca.loc.gov/northcarolinapresbyterian

National Park Service, U.S. Department of the Interior, National Historical Park, CWSAC Battle Summaries., www.nps.gov/faqs.htm

North Carolina Civil War Image Portfolio, www.unc.edu

North Carolina Office of Archives & History – Department of Cultural Resources, North Carolina Highway Historical Marker Program: ID:O-78, Marker : North Carolina Orthopedic Hospital. December 16, 2010. www.ncmarkers.com

Spring, Manda, "Homeopathy Using the Deadly Nightshade Plant", Edited and Published by Maria Rippo on August 26, 2009. Home>Health>Alternative & Natural>Homeopathy.

thefreedictionary.com/secession

The Phrase Finder, Posted by Bruce Kahl on March 07, 2002, www.phrases.org

Thomas' Legion. General James Green Martin Biography, http://thomaslegion.net/martin.html

UNC Libraries/North Carolina Collection, This Month in North Carolina History, May 2006, (http://www.lib.unc.edu/ncc/ref/nchistory/may2006/index.html)

Webb, Kerry, The Civil War Circuit website, U. S. *Civil War Generals,* www.sunsite.utk.edu/civil-war/generals.html

Wikipedia. Categories: Camping equipment, Survival skills. 27 May 2010.

Joy W. Sparrow

INDEX

DD 4
DeLaguel, Captain 131
Delaware, Gunboat 243
Demill, Thomas A. 139, 140, 141, 142, 149
Dennison, Chaplain C.W. 114
Dillsboro, North Carolina 301
  Dillsboro Church 302
Dimick, Colonel 145, 148, 153
Dixon, Dr. 217
Dixon, Frank 310
Dixon, Mrs. Thomas 307, 309
Doane, Captain Daniel 87
Doctors Bill 11
Douglas County, Illinois 41
Downing, Steamer M. E. 92
Dudley, Dr. 83
Dunhan, John W. 286
Dupree, Mrs. 20

E

Eastin, Mr. 144
Elisha 168
Ellis, Governor John W. 73, 74, 75, 76
Ellison, Elisa 154
Ellison, H. E. 83, 180
Ellison, Mary 204, 224
Ellison, Mrs. H. E. 84, 224
Ellis, Steamer 93, 94, 95, 102
Ellsworth, Colonel Elmer E. 184
England 144, 264, 323
Erdman, Rev. W. I. 301
Erwin, L. P. 309
Everett, Edward 52, 53, 55
Ewing, Elizabeth Bryan 4
Ewing, Rev. Daniel B. 4

F

Fairfield, North Carolina 287
Falkland, North Carolina 275, 276, 278
Fanny, Steamer 114, 116, 117
Farbridge, Mr. 282
Fayetteville Arsenal 90
Fearing, Lieutenant 82
Federal Army 185, 232
Felthoune, Mr. 38, 56

G

Gallagher, Charles K. 80, 81, 102, 116, 123
Gallagher, M. A. 272
Gaston County, North Carolina 311, 313, 334
Gastonia, North Carolina 311, 312, 325
Geer, Mrs. Edwin 8, 18
Geer, Rev. Edwin 23, 35, 40, 120, 209
General Court Martial 163, 167
General Lawrence O'Bryan Branch 222
General Samuel Gibbs French 222
Gibbs, Mr. 44, 66
Gilliam, Captain 82, 83, 84, 85, 89, 92, 95, 100
Gilliam, Major 92, 98
Gilliam, Mrs. 84
Gilmartin, Neal 86
God 88, 90, 91, 122, 129, 144, 150, 154, 162, 168, 179, 183, 248, 254, 263, 264,
    265, 266, 291, 292, 299, 304, 305, 309, 314, 326, 336, 339
Goldsboro, N. C. 192, 193, 194, 205, 210, 212, 227, 228, 231
Gordon, Major William M. 188, 191, 192, 196, 201, 205, 207, 209, 215, 218, 224,
    226, 229
Gordon, Steamer 92
Goslet, Mrs. 289
Governors Island 126, 130
Graham, North Carolina 164, 189, 194, 197, 200, 205, 215, 216, 217, 218, 225,
    229
Great Britain 264
Greenville, North Carolina 153, 165, 178, 179, 191, 192, 240, 273, 276
Green Wreath, Pitt County, N C. 235, 236, 240, 241, 256, 262, 267, 269, 270, 271,
    272, 273, 274
Gregory, George H. 286
Griffin, R. & Co. 273
Grimes, General Bryan 199
Grimes, Lieutenant Bryan 102, 108, 109, 149
Grimes, Major Bryan 201
Grist, Fanny 84, 90, 208
Grist, Fred 212, 224
Guthrie, Mrs. 233
Gwynn, General 80, 82, 86

H

Hamlin, Hannibal 64
Hancock, Mattie 61
Hancock, Mr. 79
Hanks, B. J. 93
Hanks, Frank 12

Hanks, Mr. 10, 13, 84, 89, 197
Hanks, Mr. & Mrs. 164
Hanks, Private William H. 92
Hanks, Truman 88
Hanna, G. R. 311
Hardee, General William Joseph 80
Hardee's Tactics 81
Hardenburgh, Thomas 88
Harding, Captain 196
Harpers Ferry, Virginia 152, 182
Harriet Lane 104
Harris, Mrs. R. S. 331
Harrison, Mr. 163
Harvey, Ed 97, 191
Harvey, Jack 48
Harvey, Jim 51
Harvey, John 14
Harvey, Mr. 210, 233, 321
Harvey, William H. 112, 128
Harwick, Massachusetts 85
Hawkins, Colonel 113, 154
Henry, Dr. 41, 45, 48, 139, 189
Henry, John 62
Henry, Mr. 28, 32
Henry, Patrick 264
Hertford Light Infantry 82, 93, 100, 148
Hickock, Mr. 35, 39, 43, 44, 48, 56
Hill, Colonel 89
Hill, General Daniel Harvey 250
Hill, General James H. 171
Hillsboro Eagle Lodge 175
Hillsborough Military Academy 173, 174, 175, 188, 189, 194, 211, 212, 224, 225, 227, 228, 231
Hodges, Henry 212
Holden, Governor William Woods 284, 285, 286, 287
Holiday, General Thomas 3
Holmes, General Theophilus H. 191, 192, 222, 223
Hoskins, Rev. 153
House of Commons 195
House of Representatives 145, 280, 285
Howard, Captain 276
Howard, James 168
Howell, Miriam E. 320
Hoyle, Bud 310
Hoyt, Clara 83, 120
Hubbard, Captain George 3

Justice, Margaret Ann Blackwell 7, 18, 29, 30, 31, 65, 138, 153, 194, 205, 208, 212, 213, 214, 224, 225
Justice, Rev. C. B. 310

K

Keech, Jasper 240
Kendall, Misses 143
Kennedy's Artillery 73, 187
Kings Mountain Presbytery 327, 329
Kinston, North Carolina 188, 203, 232, 233
Kirk, Colonel George W. 284
Konlac, Miss 194

L

Lake Landing, North Carolina
  Hyde County, NC. 262, 280, 288, 290
Lamb, Captain John C. 92, 96, 98, 100, 146, 147, 150
Latham, Captain Alexander C. 233
Latham, Lieutenant 238
Latham, Mrs. 18
Latham, T. Gray 149
Latham, Thomas 137, 149, 151, 152, 154
Latterthwaite, Mr. 282
Leach, Mr. 13
League of Peace 321
Lee, General Robert E. 152, 219, 256
Letter from 139, 142
Letter from G. Potter, Jr. to Thomas Sparrow 138
Letter from James M. Blackwell to Thomas Sparrow 128
Letter from R. M. Blackwell to Thomas Sparrow 125
Letter from Thomas Sparrow to George Attmore Sparrow 291
Letter from Thomas Sparrow to Misses Kendall 143
Letter from Thomas Sparrow to R. M. Blackwell 127
Letter from Thomas Sparrow to Son Johnnie 280
Letter from W. E. Schenck to Rev. Thomas G. Wall 136
Letters from Annie Blackwell Sparrow 32, 137
Letters from George Attmore Sparrow to Mother Annie 187, 236, 279
Letters from George Attmore Sparrow to Sister 26, 197
Letters from George Attmore Sparrow to Thomas Sparrow 7, 8, 9, 10, 14, 17, 18, 19, 20, 28, 29, 30, 32, 33, 34, 36, 38, 39, 40, 42, 43, 44, 45, 46, 47, 48, 49, 51, 52, 55, 57, 58, 59, 61, 62, 63, 65, 67, 68, 176, 178, 180, 184, 190, 191, 193, 200, 204, 206, 208, 209, 210, 211, 212, 213, 216, 217, 224, 225, 227, 228, 229, 232, 234, 235, 236, 237, 238, 239, 240, 241, 267, 269, 270, 271, 272, 273, 274, 275, 276, 278, 287, 288, 290, 291, 293, 295
Letters from Thomas Sparrow to Governor John W. Ellis 74, 75

McCord, H. A. 2, 243, 256
McCord, Hubert 3
McCorkle, Rev. W. P. 312
McDonald, Jennett 88
McDonald, John 129, 280
McDonald, Mary 280
McKinnon, Charles 225
McMillan's Artillery 73
McMillan's Salt Works 238
McMillen, Colonel 243
Mecklenburg Presbytery 301, 302, 306, 327
Methodist Church, Washington, N. C. 15
Methodist Parsonage 167
Middle Creek Church 290
Miller, Colonel 277
Miller, Dr. Oscar L. 322
Miller, Mrs. Matt 308
Mills, Mr. Zophar 275
Minnesota 91, 103, 104, 105, 115, 121, 123
Minot 86, 89
Mitchell, Julia 200, 229
Mohamedism 162
Monticello 94, 95
Montreat, North Carolina 4, 329, 337, 338
Moore, Joab 304
Moore, Lieutenant 109
Morehead, Governor 150
Morganton, North Carolina 164, 206, 208, 213
Morris, Colonel 79, 80, 82
Morris Guards 93, 94, 98, 100, 102
Morrison Church 301
Morrison, Dr. R. H. 307
Mullium, James 86
Murdaugh, Lieutenant 97, 102, 108
Murfreesboro, Tennessee 165
Muse, Captain 92, 93, 95, 97, 112, 167

N

Nash, Mrs. 215
Nash School 189, 216
Nashville, Tennessee 165
Negro/Negroes 9, 83, 89, 94, 101, 118, 253, 254, 256, 257, 261, 262, 264, 322
Neuse River 217
New Bern, North Carolina 5, 21, 24, 45, 85, 86, 87, 88, 89, 122, 168, 170, 182,
    194, 205, 206, 208, 217, 227, 232, 243, 244, 251, 253, 274, 289, 336

Peebles, Major 278
Pegram, Colonel 131
Pender, W. D. 170
Perry, Tom 201
Petty, Hiram 295
Pew, Mrs. 9
Picketts, Cousin 279, 287, 289
Piridell, H. C. 58
Pitt Court 269
Plymouth, North Carolina 247
Polk, Cora Blackwell 14, 194, 197, 215, 225
Poole, Dr. 153
Pope, General John 165
Port Royal, South Carolina 237
Portsmouth, North Carolina 26, 27, 85, 89, 92, 97, 114, 194
Potter, Gilbert 138
Potts, Mary Pauline 197
Potts, Mr. 137, 272
Potts, Sergeant John R. 102, 125, 149, 151, 154, 234
Powell, HMA Cadet 179, 197
Primrose, Lieutenant 191, 192
Prohibition 295, 318
Provincial Congress 340

R

Raines, General 225
Raleigh, North Carolina 6, 81, 89, 97, 225, 226, 257, 280, 293, 300
Raleigh Register 63
Randall, John 267
Rankin, Rev. Jessie 306
Ratchford, George 323
Ratchford, Grannie 322
Ratchford, Mr. 321
Recollections of the Civil War 244
Reid, Captain Crawley 187, 188, 237, 238
Reid, Daniel 166
Revolutionary War 324, 333
Richardson, Miss 48, 149
Richmond, Virginia 192, 193, 198, 200, 205, 219, 256
Rich Mountain, Virginia 131
Riddle, John 326
Riddle, Robert B. 316
Roanoke Guarads 100
Roanoke, Virginia 149
Robbins, Sergeant Thomas H. 99, 100
Roberson, Colonel 232

Welfare Island 341
West, Dr. 90
Wharton, Rev. 311
Wheeler, Dr. 211
Whig Party 185
Whigs 170
Whitehurst, Lieutenant James J. 73, 99, 101, 108, 149, 151, 152, 225, 227
Whitehurst, Mr. 17
Whitehurst's Battery 73
Whiting, Major General 171
Wiley, Calvin H. 15, 17
Wilkes, Captain Charles 144
Willard, A. A. 201
Willard, James 167
Willis, William B. 99, 107, 108
Wilmington, North Carolina 163, 164, 165, 166, 171, 178, 189, 191, 194, 203,
    208, 211, 217, 218, 220, 224, 225, 229, 231, 255, 325, 336
Wilson, George 321
Wilson, Katherine Lavinia (Kate) 316
Wilson, Woodrow 321
Winslow, Steamer 97, 114
Wise, Lieutenant 97
Wiswall, Howard 149
W. & J. Bryce of New York 131
Woollard, Jacob 162
World War I 319, 329
Writings by Elizabeth Sparrow McCord 256
Wyman the Wizard 10

Y

Yankees 165, 167, 177, 189, 190, 191, 194, 200, 212, 217, 226, 238, 244, 248, 254,
    257
YMCA 336
York County, South Carolina 312, 332
Young, Clarence 310

Z

Zouaves 184

CPSIA information can be obtained at www.ICGtesting.com
Printed in the USA
LVOW110527020412

275638LV00007B/214/P